Leslie Fiedler

Leslie Fiedler

Kind of a Conversation

BRUCE JACKSON and
DIANE CHRISTIAN

Published by State University of New York Press, Albany

EU GPSR Authorised Representative:
Logos Europe, 9 rue Nicolas Poussin, 17000, La Rochelle, France
contact@logoseurope.eu

For information, contact State University of New York Press, Albany, NY
www.sunypress.edu

Library of Congress Cataloging-in-Publication Data

Names: Fiedler, Leslie A., interviewee. | Jackson, Bruce, 1936–, interviewer. |
    Christian, Diane, 1939–, interviewer.
Title: Leslie Fiedler : kind of a conversation / Bruce Jackson and Diane
    Christian.
Description: Albany : State University of New York Press, [2026]. | Includes
    bibliographical references and index
Identifiers: LCCN 2025035075 | ISBN 9798855805895 (pbk. : alk. paper) | ISBN
    9798855807226 (epub) | ISBN 9798855805901 (PDF)
Subjects: LCSH: Fiedler, Leslie A.—Interviews. | Critics—United States—Interviews. |
    Critics—United States—Biography. | LCGFT: Autobiographies.
Classification: LCC PS3556.I34 Z46 2026
LC record available at https://lccn.loc.gov/2025035075

Kublai domanda a Marco:—Quando ritornerai al Ponente, ripeterai alla tua gente gli stessi racconti che fai a me?—Io parlo parlo,—dice Marco,—ma chi m'ascolta ritiene solo le parole che aspetta.

—Italo Calvino, *Le città invisibili*, 1972

The story of your life is not your life; it's your story.

—John Barth, "Where Three Roads Meet," 2006

Contents

Acknowledgments

All photos by Bruce Jackson, except figure 11, which is by Diane Christian.

The original Hi8 video recordings of these nine conversations are archived in the Bruce Jackson and Diane Christian Collection, Library of Congress.

Our thanks to Leslie's longtime secretary, Joyce Troy, for the original transcription of the audio tracks. And to Ryan Bell, who compiled most of the biographical notes in "Personae" from public domain sources.

And especially to Richard Carlin, our friend and editor at SUNY Press, and to Diane Ganeles, Senior Production Editor at SUNY Press. The complex process of bringing this book to print—from initial evaluation of the manuscript through many stages of editing, tuning, tweaking, and design—has been consistently pleasant, fast, efficient, nuanced and smart. They've been splendid collaborators on this book.

Figure 1. Leslie, Sally, and Julia Jackson (Bruce's mother) at a party at UB Provost of Arts and Letters John Sullivan's house, 1974.

Introduction

Bruce Jackson: Encounters

Leslie Fiedler (1917–2003) was justly honored as one of the great American cultural critics. His writing is lucid, accessible, and informing. Leslie was taking smart looks at popular culture long before it became fashionable as a subject of academic study and analysis. His favorite books were probably *Huckleberry Finn* and *The Divine Comedy*, and he wrote wonderful essays about both. He also wrote about everything else. No matter what the subject, he never used jargon, which is why his work was and remains as useful and accessible to an ordinary reader interested in ideas about culture as it is to the various academic specialists who make careers doing such things.

His books—*An End to Innocence: Essays on Culture and Politics* (1955), *No! In Thunder: Essays on Myth and Literature* (1960), *Love and Death in the American Novel* (1960), *Freaks: Myths and Images of the Secret Self* (1978) among them—remain as current as when they were published.

Leslie was every bit as good a talker as he was a writer. My primary memory of Leslie Fiedler, covering most of the thirty-five years that we were colleagues and friends, is of Leslie talking and everyone else listening. He grew quieter the last two or three years of his life, when illness sapped some of his great energy. But before that, especially at dinners at his house or ours, Leslie would hold forth and the rest of us were happy to let him because he held forth so well. There were only three exceptions to that, one continuing, two of them singular.

The continuing exception was when Leslie's old friend Irving Sanes was at the table. Irv would tell long stories about our University at Buffalo colleagues Lionel Abel or Dwight Macdonald or other members of their shared literary past, and Leslie, as the rest of us, would sit in rapt attention. At some point I realized that Irv's stories were performances rather than simple narratives, and that what Leslie enjoyed, and the rest of us also, was hearing how Irv would deliver this or that narrative this time. It would not be uncommon for someone at the table to say, "Irv, tell the story about having dinner with Lionel," and Irv would tell about the time he and his wife, Mickey, had been invited for dinner with Lionel and his wife in their New York apartment and they sat down with Lionel and talked for a long time until one of them asked, "Lionel, where's Gloria?" and Lionel told them she was in the bedroom, dead. A pause; we'd all lean forward; Irv would say, "DEAD?" And then he'd mimic Lionel explaining that the New York medical examiner's office was on strike, so they weren't picking up bodies on weekends and since this was Saturday and she'd died Friday night, well, she was in the bedroom. Irv would pause again, take a bite of whatever was on his plate, then say, "So we had dinner."

When Irv performed his stories, Leslie leaned back in his chair and grinned happily, like a music teacher watching a favorite student play a piece they'd spent a lot of time getting right. The two singular exceptions were when the folksinger Pete Seeger and the civil rights attorney William Kunstler were visiting us. Bill and Pete were hugely energetic men of wide experience. I'd known Pete since 1963, and Diane and I had been friends with Bill since 1975. Leslie had great personal respect and admiration for both of them. Both were, like Leslie, great talkers. Leslie was quiet for Bill and Pete.

Even a good writer is like everyone else when it comes to personal stories: they tell certain ones again and again, varying this or that part to fit the company and mood and occasion, but maintaining whatever there is in the narrative core that makes the story worth keeping. They're more likely to tell polished stories in larger groups than smaller ones. An audience elicits more polished stories than does an interlocutor or two. Leslie was more likely to tell the stories we knew when we had dinners for eight or ten people at their house or ours than when it was just Leslie, Sally, Diane, and me sitting around a kitchen table.

After dinner in late March 1989 at Leslie and Sally's house, Diane and I had a long conversation about one of the stories Leslie had told (I no longer remember which). I said, as I had several times previously, "I wish I'd tape-recorded that dinner. I should tape-record these dinners."

"You won't," Diane said.

Figure 2. Leslie and Pete Seeger meeting for the first time at our house, 1992.

We both knew why. We'd discussed it in other personal situations several times before. Recording your life as it's going on subtracts you from the present. You do that and before it's even done happening, you're already archiving it. The present becomes the past fast enough as it is. Who has time for that; who wants that? Who wants to be out of the moment?

The present doesn't; history does. That night I wrote Leslie, saying that we loved the stories he told. I said that he was an important figure in twentieth-century American intellectual history and when he died most of those stories would die with him. Many dealt with things he'd written about. I asked if he would like to do a series of recordings in which we talked about some of the things we heard at those dinners over the years.

He responded immediately, saying he had attempted to write an autobiography but couldn't ever get it to work and that he'd be delighted to give this a try.

So, on nine occasions over the following five months in 1989—April 8, 22, and 30; May 7; June 10 and 27; July 18; and August 9 and 20—Leslie, Diane, and I met to talk on their patio or, if it was too hot or raining, in Leslie's study. (Sally was often there, though she rarely spoke once we started recording—usually only when the conversation turned to something she and Leslie had done together or when her life in Illinois came up.)

Those weren't conversations; they weren't interviews, either. We four knew one another too well for that. But they partook of both. They were, mostly, opportunities for Leslie to talk. There are generalizations here more at home in conversation than in print, things Leslie would justify or qualify in an article or book that he wouldn't in offhand remarks. Diane and I sometimes made comments or asked questions, but only rarely did we tell any stories of our own. Things he said suggested many, but we didn't say them; we knew many of the people he mentioned, but we rarely told our own parallel or contrary stories about them. That would have changed what was going on. Nor, with only a few exceptions, did we talk about the things that got the most talk-time when we were together in ordinary life: events of the day, situations at UB, the kids, gossip, health, politics, a book read, a movie seen . . . the kinds of things everybody who hangs out with anybody talks about.

The sessions were mostly focused on parts of Leslie's past: growing up, being Jewish, going to war, engaging the literary world, books that mattered back then and books that matter now. The structured situation—Leslie in a chair with a lavalier microphone around his neck, me operating a Sony camcorder, Diane and me sometimes asking questions that focused on a particular subject, Sally quietly sitting there, the whole thing beginning when I hit the record button and usually stopping when that day's 120-minute tape ran out—permitted Leslie to engage in a narrative mode in which he delighted. He could riff at will for an interested group who knew many of the nouns (so he didn't have to pause to identify the many people or places or scenes he was talking about). He did not have to suffer interruption.

Leslie & Us

Our lives intersected in many ways.

I was long aware of, but never until now paid much attention to, the fact that in addition to both of us being from working-class, nonpracticing, East Coast Jewish families (Leslie Newark, me Brooklyn), and both of us having spent our entire working career in universities (except for stints in the military—Leslie in the Navy and me in the Marines), we both shared a working style that set us off from many of our colleagues: we both wrote about encounters with primary objects rather than encountered primary objects through conceptual structures provided by others, and we both wrote in jargonless ordinary English, largely free of footnotes. Neither of us attended meetings of the Modern Language Association or submitted papers to its journal, *PMLA*. The bulk of our article writing appeared in places accessible to anybody; most of our books and articles are readable by anybody with an interest in the books' and articles' subjects.

And neither of us, I am certain, would be hired by the English Department from which Leslie retired and in which Diane and I still teach, nor would either of us have any interest in being hired by it now. The academic literary game now exists in much rarer air than the one we enjoyed.

Not only were we friends and colleagues in the same department (Leslie came to Buffalo in 1965; I came in 1967; Diane in 1970), but there were shared friends and acquaintances at different times, in different places. Leslie was nineteen years older than I, but the older we got, the less that age difference mattered. In Buffalo, as I noted, we had frequent dinners at one another's houses; we did birthdays; we did New Year's (usually at our house); and we did Fourth of July cookouts (usually at theirs).

He mentions "Dick Lewis": R. W. B. Lewis, who taught at Rutgers, then went to Yale, was a literary critic and Pulitzer Prize–winning author

Figure 3. Leslie celebrating his eighty-third birthday party at our house; Diane to his left, Sally behind him, Melissa Banta and Robert Creeley to the left, 2000.

Figure 4. A Fourth of July cookout at the Fiedlers'; UB colleagues William Sylvester (to Leslie's right) and Myles Slatin and Marcus Klein (to his right), 1997.

of a biography of Edith Wharton. My first encounter with Leslie was secondhand at Dick Lewis's house in Hamden, Connecticut, in late 1959. That led to a string of other interconnections.

Dick Lewis was my honors thesis advisor at Rutgers. In 1958, I was doing an obligatory year at Rutgers before going to law school. The law school dean required it because I'd just finished three years in engineering school and he thought I needed a year in the world of words. The two courses I took with Lewis—Modern European Novel and Twentieth-Century American Fiction—changed the course of my life. Dick knew as friends most of the writers we read in the first of those classes—Albert Camus, Alberto Moravia, André Malraux, Ignazio Silone—and told wonderful stories about them. I'd never before known anyone who knew the real people whose names were on book spines. Dick's book, *The Picaresque Saint*, came out during that year, and many of us got signed copies at his author's discount. I lost interest in law and headed into literary studies. He nominated me for a Woodrow Wilson fellowship.

I visited at his home in Hamden, Connecticut, when he was doing the nominating letter. During lunch, he got a phone call. He took it in another room. When he came back, he said, "You won't guess who that was or what he wanted. That was Leslie Fiedler. He's after the same thing you are. He's applying for a Guggenheim. He needs a letter of recommendation."

Leslie Fiedler was, to me, a then-major figure to readers of American and modern literature. His *An End to Innocence* and *No, In Thunder* were essential reading. We'd talked about them in Dick's American Fiction class the previous spring. "Why would anyone as famous as Leslie Fiedler need a letter of recommendation?" I said. "Everyone knows who he is."

"It's how things work," Dick said. "You'll get your turn." (I did. I still am writing those letters.)

When I got the Woodrow Wilson, Dick suggested I go to Indiana University for an MA in the School of Letters and a PhD in comparative literature. I would never have thought of attending a school in southern Indiana: I'm a Brooklyn Jew from Bed-Stuy. Indiana? I asked him why he made that suggestion. "Because they'll leave you alone." A few months later, he invited me to a dinner at the Princeton home of his uncle, Stringfellow Barr. The other guests were Horst Frenz, chairman of comparative literature at Indiana and his family. So Leslie's friend Dick Lewis not only inspired me to go into literature, but provided the financial means to do it, and sent me there on a first-name basis with my department chair.

During the first School of Letters summer seminar (1961), I became friends with the poet John Berryman; during the second (1962), with the poet and translator Robert Fitzgerald. Fiedler knew both of them from teaching in earlier years at the School of Letters and elsewhere. I would have the worst seminar I had in all of graduate school with Mark Spilka, who had been a student of Leslie's at the School of Letters (Spilka read aloud for most of each two-hour seminar from handwritten pages, never looking up); I would have the best class I had in all of graduate school with Jim Cox, also a student of Leslie's at the School of Letters. I would have many conversations with Bob Fitzgerald a few years later at Harvard, when he was there as Boylston Professor of Poetry and I as a Junior Fellow in the Society of Fellows. They all figure in our conversations with Leslie.

When Al Cook (who also figures in Leslie's narrative) was recruiting me to come to Buffalo, he listed his recent hires and said I wouldn't find literary company like that in any other US English Department. At first I was snooty: I had job offers from Penn, UCLA, and MIT. But Buffalo? Then I listened to him: he was right. Some of the names that drew me to Buffalo were poets Charles Olson, John Logan, and Robert Creeley; novelist John Barth; Shakespearian scholar C. L. Barber (whom I'd briefly

known at Indiana and who had been a Junior Fellow years before I was);
critic Lionel Abel—and Leslie Fiedler. I couldn't resist. (The Creeleys
would become Diane's and my closest friends in Buffalo.)

And, to bring the Dick Lewis story full circle, it was Leslie Fiedler
who nominated me for my 1971–1972 Guggenheim Fellowship.

I'm telling you all that because I think it factors into the kinds of
stories Leslie told and how he told them. He could, as he does in the April
22 recording, refer to the poet Robert Lowell simply as "Cal," because
he knew I knew Lowell from my Harvard years and that all of Lowell's
friends referred to him as "Cal," a nickname he got as a kid, a reference
to "Little Boots"—Caligula. (The phony friends of Lowell in those years,
John Berryman was fond of pointing out, referred to him as "Bob.") Leslie's knowledge that there were so many people, places, and institutions he
didn't have to pause to identify for Sally, Diane, or me eased and informed
the flow of his narratives.

These conversations also factored into our present. Leslie several
times here mentions a talk and article he was writing about Vietnam War
films. He saw film as our modern mythology, and those films as places
where our modern mythology and a current crisis intersected. Whatever

Figure 5. Leslie in his study a few weeks after the fire that destroyed his house,
1996.

he looked at, Leslie was always in the moment. He speculates in these pages about places he might publish that article. I published it: I was then editing *Journal of American Folklore*. I had done a special issue on folklore about the war in Vietnam. Some academic folklorists were enraged: "Why are you bringing politics into our academic world?" So I did a subsequent issue focusing on "American Myths: War Stories." Leslie's "Mythicizing the Unspeakable" was the lead article (*JAF* 103, no. 410 [October–December 1990]).

And then there was the 1911 Navy Colt .45 automatic, which he mentions carrying for Jack Brooks in Tientsin, China. It was a romantic handgun from my youth. I fired one on the range in Marine Corps bootcamp, but never subsequently: only officers had them, not grunts like me, who schlepped M-1 rifles. Leslie had it in his house on Morris Avenue in Buffalo. I was surprised when he told me that: I didn't know anyone then who had handguns in the house. Sally was always nervous about it. For Leslie, it was just a war souvenir, like the samurai sword he got at Iwo Jima.

For a month or so after the devastating fire in their house in 1995, Leslie and Sally stayed in our guest room. Leslie put two things in our basement walk-in safe: the samurai sword and Jack Brooks's Colt .45. When their house was repaired and they moved back, they took the sword but not the .45. I think they were both happy to be rid of it. It was never mentioned. It stayed in our safe until one day when a friend who was a National Parks police lieutenant was visiting. "Can you carry anywhere?" I asked him. "Yes," he said. "Do you need a permit?" "No." "Would you like a Navy 1911 Colt .45 in perfect condition?" He was delighted. He wrote me later that he and some other cop pals disassembled it for cleaning and lubrication before trying it out. "It still had Cosmoline in the barrel. It's never been fired!"

The Drug Bust

There is one other story that began, like the Dick Lewis story, before Diane or I met Leslie.

In May 1967, I was invited to brunch by Warren Bennis, a professor at MIT who was about to become head of the Social Sciences and Administration Faculty at University at Buffalo. Norman Zinberg, a Cambridge psychiatrist, with whom I'd been teaching at Harvard, thought we should meet because I was on my way to Buffalo as an assistant professor of

English. Saul Tauster, a poet and legal counsel to UB President Martin Myerson, was also at that brunch. During it, Saul got a call from Buffalo telling him that Leslie, then UB's most famous literary faculty member, had been arrested on a drug charge. It was all a setup and phony. I wrote about it in a *New Republic* article, "Blackballing the Fiedlers," and Leslie wrote about it in a book he doesn't mention here, *Being Busted* (1970). I would, not long after I came to Buffalo, testify as an expert witness on drugs in Leslie's appeal.

When Leslie's mortgage bank let him know they were calling in his mortgage because of the arrest, I asked Lawrence Pierce, chairman of the New York State Narcotics Addiction Control Commission (later a circuit judge on the US Court of Appeals for the Second Circuit), if he could lean on them saying this was inappropriate. Larry said, "I couldn't interfere in anything like that." There was a pause, then: "Let me see what I can do." A week later, the bank backed off and Leslie got to keep his mortgage.

Five years and an enormous number of dollars after the arrest, Fiedler's conviction was thrown out by the New York Court of Appeals, which ruled that Fiedler hadn't done anything illegal or been aware of anyone else doing anything illegal, hence there hadn't been any misdemeanor to plead guilty to. In essence, the court ruled that the whole procedure had been a sham.

In the article, I describe the attempt to drive Fiedler from his home and the withdrawal of his Fulbright invitation to Holland. There was more to come: Fiedler's appointment to an endowed chair at the university, scheduled for the following September, was rescinded when heirs of the family that had provided the funds complained to UB President Martin Meyerson about Fiedler's character. (Meyerson later used other university funds to provide Fiedler some of the support he had been promised when he'd left Montana.)

Joey Giambra, one of the detectives who had executed the search warrant on Fiedler's house that night, saw me in his Buffalo restaurant twenty years later. "You know Fiedler, right?" he asked. I said I did. "You want to do us both a favor?" I said I'd be happy to do that. He asked me when I was coming to the restaurant again. I told him. "Okay," he said, "I'll see you then." He turned up a few minutes after Diane and I got a table the next time we were there. He handed me a large envelope. "I've had this for twenty years," he said. "It's something we took that night, and

I took it out of the stuff they had at headquarters because I knew they were going to garbage personal things and I thought he'd want this back." I asked why he hadn't just given it back to Fiedler himself. "Me? One of the guys who busted him? He doesn't want anything to do with me. You give it to him. And don't tell him where you got it, okay?"

"Okay," I said.

"I never wanted to go in there," Joey said. "The whole thing was stupid from the beginning. We should have been out chasing bad guys and there we were, getting headlines for the captain." The envelope contained family photos: the Fiedler kids, small, smiling at the camera, playing with toys, the things kids do.

It was sad, this decent cop for twenty years trying to find a way to undo for Leslie Fiedler some of the damage he had unwillingly and unhappily helped inflict, never being able to just go up to Fiedler's house and say, "Here, this is yours, we fucked up, I never wanted any part of it."

When I gave Leslie the envelope I started explaining why I thought Joey had held on to it for so long and why he wanted to remain anonymous now. Leslie stopped me with a raised hand, the palm forward, like a Buddha. "I know why. Tell him it's okay. Tell him I said thank you."

So these conversations, literary and easy and casual, were grounded in a lot of history, a lot of shared knowledge, a lot of trust.

Protecting Buffalo's Jewish Floodgates

There is one final Leslie/Jewish/Buffalo story. Really final.

Sally called midafternoon on January 29, 2003. The first thing she said was, "I think Leslie's dead." She was, she told us, in the emergency room of Millard Fillmore Hospital.

Diane or I asked, "What are they telling you?"

"That he's dead."

And so he was. It was as gentle a passing as one could hope for. He'd been suffering from advanced Parkinson's for some time and had been pretty much housebound. That day, Sally told us later, they'd had lunch as usual. He'd had his usual bowl of strawberries. After that, he took his usual afternoon nap on a living room couch. He never woke.

Sally thought to have the funeral service in Temple Beth Zion, Buffalo's oldest and largest Reform temple. The thousand-seat sanctuary features gorgeous stained glass windows by Ben Shahn. It seemed the perfect place to bid farewell to the man who had been, until a day or two before, Buffalo's most famous living writer.

Things were moving along quite well, Sally told us, but then she got a call from the chief rabbi. He told her that Leslie could not be buried from the temple after all: he wasn't currently a paid-up member. She tried to argue. He told her that if it were up to him, they'd have the funeral, but the assistant rabbi insisted that permitting Leslie's funeral would cause problems.

"She says it will open the floodgates," the chief rabbi told Sally.

"To what?" she asked.

"To nonmembers wanting to have funerals here." He'd make the exception, he told Sally, but he couldn't deal with the assistant rabbi's opposition. He was very solicitous.

We told Sally we'd call a longtime friend of Leslie's and ours, Lauren Rachlin, a prominent Buffalo lawyer who was active in the city's Jewish affairs. He specialized in international trade law, but in the early 1970s he'd somehow become the house divorce lawyer for the University at Buffalo English Department. Among others, he'd done divorces for John Barth, Leslie, and me.

When he stopped laughing about the floodgates, Lauren said he'd intervene. He had been, he told us, president of the Beth Zion congregation until recently. He was certain he could bring the chief rabbi around.

He called a day or two later to tell us he'd gotten nowhere. "It's not him," Lauren said, "but he's terrified of her and won't go against her publicly. I told him that Leslie was the most important Jewish writer Buffalo ever had, that he had an international reputation, that being Jewish was one of his major themes. Nothing. *Bupkis.* A stone wall. She says he wasn't a paid-up member of the congregation and a funeral for him will open the floodgates."

"How about this," I said, "Diane and I will pay Leslie's dues in Beth Zion. A full year, retroactive. And he'll only need to make use of it for one afternoon."

That, Lauren said, seemed a reasonable solution. Reasonable it may have been; acceptable it was not. "No deal," he said in a call the next day. "She says they don't enroll dead members, retroactively or any other way. She said doing that would—"

"—open the floodgates."

I imagined an army of Buffalo's dead Jewish writers, advancing—like a mob in a George Romero movie—upon the Beth Zion sanctuary, nary a paid-up soul among them. Given enough time, I could be one of them.

So Leslie's funeral took place in the chapel of Forest Lawn Cemetery, about halfway between their house on Morris Avenue and ours on Rumsey Road, and perhaps a mile from Temple Beth Zion. His ashes remain in Forest Lawn's mausoleum, just about in the center of that triangulated space: their house, our house, and the house that wouldn't admit him if just to say a brief farewell.

I haven't a doubt that, as much as he disdained organized religion, Leslie would love this story, and that, were it possible, he'd tell it whenever he could and wherever it fit.

This Text

Leslie's longtime secretary Joyce Troy transcribed the tapes. Sometimes Diane and I made comments or asked questions that influenced what he said next; we kept those comments of ours in the transcripts. Leslie sometimes began a sentence with "And, so," when there was no connection for the "and" or the "so"; he sometimes said "actually" when there was no need for the adverb; he sometimes ended a sentence with "and so forth" when there were no other items left unsaid. These are the equivalent of beginning a sentence with "Um": a sound without meaning. They're sounds for the ear that in print are taken over by punctuation and typography: hyphens, periods, semicolons, new paragraphs. When those words did have content—when the "and" made connections not already implicit, the "actually" indicated something unusual really being done, and the "and so forth" pointed to further items not apparent—we left them in.

There are occasional lacunae. Sometimes we paused for a few minutes and picked up where we'd left off; sometimes we moved on to something else. Sometimes the recording was interrupted for a battery change and Leslie talked through it. Once, a squirrel grabbed one of Leslie's tomatoes off the vine and Leslie got up to chase it, dragging the video camera and tripod with him. We note brief pauses with *[beat]*, longer pauses with a line of asterisks. They suggest why the conversation might have pivoted or why a narrative was left unfinished.

Footnotes and academic jargon: Leslie, as I noted above, loathed both, as do I. He was better at avoiding both than I. He wanted what he wrote to be available to anyone. In his MLA Hubbell speech he says, "I am now routinely quoted in jargon-ridden, reader-unfriendly works I cannot bring myself to read, and am listed honorifically in the kind of footnotes and bibliographies I have always eschewed." In respect of that, there are no footnotes in what follows. The few times his use of a pronoun was so unclear we had to provide a proper noun, we did it by substituting the noun in bracketed roman text: "[Fred]." When we thought something needed a gloss for clarity but wanted to add it in our own voice, we inserted it in bracketed italicized text: *[Hoffman]*.

When we set about editing these transcripts, we first thought about organizing the material topically: Newark, Montana, being a Jew, the war, books, writers, Buffalo, and so forth. But then we read two books based on conversations that were organized simply by when things were said, Cameron Crowe's *Conversations with Wilder* (2001) and Michael Ondaatje's *The Conversations: Walter Murch and the Art of Editing Film* (2002). Both had a presence and energy rearranged conversations lack; both gave a sense of the dynamic flow of the encounters themselves. Structuring by encounter is less formal, less controlled, but finally, we decided, for this project far more useful. It gives a sense of the voice of the speaker in the moment rather than the organizing notions of the editors long after it. A few stories appear more than once; we kept some of those repetitions because Leslie was telling them differently, or using them in service of another point.

All four of us—Leslie, Sally, Diane, and I—knew you'd be there at the end to decide what it was all about.

Summing It Up—and Certifying It

Perhaps the best brief summary of Leslie's career was the speech he wrote when the MLA awarded him its 1994 Hubbell Medal for Lifetime Achievement. He didn't go to the award ceremony: he wasn't a member of the MLA and never had been. He asked our English Department colleague Victor Doyno to accept the award for him and to read his acceptance speech. He showed it to us before he gave it to Vic.

Leslie watched us as we read it; his face was expressionless. Not long after we began, Diane and I broke into laughter.

"Everything in that speech is true," I said, "but almost all of it is things they attacked you for in years past, but with the signs reversed."

Leslie grinned.

The speech ends, "Thank you, thank you very much." There are several ways you can utter that line. Vic Doyno was a very sincere guy; I'd known him since 1964: he was sincere the entire time I knew him. I'm sure he read Leslie's text very sincerely. His rendition of "Thank you, thank you very much" was surely sincere.

But there is a Jewish way of speaking where the intonation tells you that what is being said means exactly the opposite of what the words seem to be saying. It's an ironic tradition Leslie and I learned when we learned to speak. His generation could do it, as could mine (our children cannot, which is one of the things he ironically laments in these pages). Diane and I read it with that inverted intonation, which is why we broke into laughter, and which was how Leslie meant it. He knew most of the people hearing it in that MLA room wouldn't get the gag. They hadn't been getting his gags, or his points, for decades. Why should things be different now? Particularly with Vic reading them, in an intonation they understood and inhabited.

"This is superb," I said, when we quieted down. "Can we include it in the conversation book?"

"With my blessing," Leslie said, "with my blessing." No inverted tonality there. You'll find it after the final conversation.

We know of one thing that delighted Leslie far more than that 1994 MLA acknowledgment of what he'd been up to the past fifty years. It happened in December 2002, a month before he died, during an airing of an episode of *The Sopranos*. He talked about it in what was perhaps our last conversation.

At a family dinner, mob boss Tony Soprano's daughter, Meadow, brings up sexual desire in Herman Melville's *Billy Budd*, which had come up in her class at Columbia. Her mother, Carmella, response that "she"—this Leslie Fiedler—must be gay. Meadow, as our late friend Greg Dimitriadis wrote, "notes that 'he' is a famous literary critic—famous enough to have lectured at Columbia University."

For Leslie, being misgendered and misunderstood while being included in *The Sopranos* was better than any literary prize or any glowing review. He'd spent decades arguing that the boundaries between high culture and low culture, between art that matters and art that doesn't, were grounded in transitory choices, in fashion, but regardless of that fashion, all those cultural expressions, wherever you found them, addressed things that mattered. The MLA award was a grudging acknowledgment that he'd been right all along. For him, that episode of *The Sopranos* certified it.

Diane Christian: Leslie

Leslie was a colleague from my arrival at UB in September 1970 to his death in January 2003.

Sally, his wife since 1973, called me to the hospital where he lay dead at eighty-five, my age now, writing this.

Leslie makes a joke in one of these interviews that great women were born in 1939, meaning Sally and me, who were listening. Leslie got famous describing American themes of homoeroticism and misogyny. His genius limned those topics innovatively and well. I don't think he was misogynistic beyond inescapable male culture. He was known for tongue-kissing females, usually drunkenly and old-style-male, good-naturedly. Unlike many of his generation, (the infamous Harold Bloom comes to mind) he didn't to my knowledge exploit women students. I always had the protection of my history—having been a nun—and the fact that I married colleague Bruce Jackson the same year Leslie married

Figure 6. Leslie and Diane after Diane's commencement address for Buffalo Seminary, 1993.

Sally. Sally inherited Leslie's six children and brought two sons of her own. I inherited Bruce's three children, younger and far easier than Sally's lot. The symmetry, though, made for a certain closeness. I had done flowers for Leslie's daughter's wedding in 1972 and befriended Sally in various crises. Leslie wanted four more children to fill a Jewish tribal twelve, allowing Sally's sons addition to his three sons and three daughters. Sally demurred but Leslie often spoke of the desire however fantastical it might have been. He took a patriarchal stance which mixed his singular Jewishness with the usual male desire to leave children to the wives. He didn't write of his women and family issues, keeping in fact a guarded maybe kindly distance.

All this was going on while furious feminism flourished. I gave a conference talk in Sun Valley in 1977 where Leslie and Kate Millett were responders. I talked about Wonder Woman as female hero. Leslie loved it because he loved comics and Kate complained that I had to go to a comic to find a female hero. Leslie's tack was not to argue feminist complaint and not to engage it. Enough to point out deep misogyny. He was pretty enlightened actually, perhaps because he really respected female radicals from his youth (his first wife Margaret was one), as well as a few female editors and academics, but mostly women novelists like Harriet Beecher Stowe and Margaret Mitchell. Women have to work out

Figure 7. Leslie, Kate Millett, and Diane at Institute of the American West conference on "The American Hero," Sun Valley, 1977.

their own salvation, I think he might say. His was masculine, and linked to writing. "For me writing was power," he said. A kind of salvation too. He comments here: "I've grown up with this double feeling toward literature: it ought to be in the possession of people who know that it's a weapon to destroy all that's unendurable and tedious in life."

So his radical political views which his father worried would "ruin his career and be an endless series of shocks and surprises" didn't do him in. He made mental not corporeal war, as the similarly radical William Blake advised.

As you read our interviews here you see him over and over tracing his outsidership, first as a Jew, then as a political person, then as a literary rebel. His appraisals are brilliant and succinct and his energy is generous.

He was generous also as a teacher. Not just by being engaged and serious and entertaining, but also by being willing to abide ignorance, to patiently instruct. When he speaks of his teachers being dumb, it's not with scorn but acceptance. I often asked him to serve as second reader for dissertations I directed, both for his mastery and for the power of his name for the students. He never refused. My favorite memory was

Figure 8. Leslie and Allen Ginsberg during "Fiedlerfest," University at Buffalo Center for the Arts, 1994.

when he and Bob Creeley were second readers for a woman who clung to a belabored psychological interpretation of Coleridge's "Christabel." She was adamant that we allow her reading and we teachers three had terrific conversations about the poem disputing her.

We celebrated Leslie's eightieth birthday with "Fiedlerfest," two days of public talk and music and feasting. Leslie's choice of speakers was Allen Ginsberg, Camille Paglia, and Ishmael Reed, a perfect Fiedler trifecta. He'd never met Paglia but admired her writing on women and sex and her admiration of him. Ginsberg was a famous, queer, and Jewish poet whose father had run Leslie's high school poetry society in Newark. Reed, a renowned Black writer, had roots in Buffalo and UB. All were outsiders, mainline challengers, as Leslie thought himself, successful though he was. They represented his major interests: gender, eros, race, and Jewishness. His issues still mark the contentious quick of American sensibility.

Leslie ably navigated the academy to success on his own terms and maintained a cheeky rebellious persona, as his Hubbell Award speech illustrates. In a running conversation I had with him all those years about the Bible and gender issues, his answer to the question "What's the difference between male and female?" would be "Girls try to please their fathers and boys to upset their mothers." One of Leslie's charms was that he sought not arcane meanings but emotional truths. His writing, his power, reached to embrace outsiders and enlarge human compass, thereby "to destroy the unendurable and tedious in life."

More on Leslie

Leslie never got around to writing his autobiography, but he found various ways of skirting with it. Much of his fiction is autobiographical. *Being Busted*, his 1969 memoir about his 1967 drug arrest, focuses as much on his earlier years as it does on that bogus arrest and its consequences. In it, he tells some of the same stories he tells here.

Newark and being Jewish always loomed large in his imagination. He writes about both in *Being Busted* and he talks about them in his conversations with us and with Mark Royden Winchell, who interviewed him in 1988 for his biography, *"Too Good to Be True": The Life and Work of Leslie Fiedler* (2002). Winchell relied heavily on an unedited transcript of our conversations with Leslie for some sections of that book.

Winchell's book is a biography, but one that focuses most on events linked to Leslie's writing and to Winchell's discussions of the writing itself. He pays scant attention, for example, to Leslie's experiences in World War II. For that, you have to look at the letters in Samuele Pardini, ed., *Writing Home: Selected World War II Letters of Leslie A. Fiedler* (2024).

In his introduction, Pardini says Leslie and Margaret wrote one another almost every day while Leslie was overseas. Margaret seems to have kept all of Leslie's letters, but only 423 survived the December 14, 1995, fire in Leslie's house. Pardini's book includes all or part of 149 of them. (He says nothing about the whereabouts of Margaret's letters to Leslie, if any of those in fact survive.)

Only a few of Leslie's letters in the collection respond in detail to anything Margaret had written or might be doing. Leslie often writes that he hasn't gotten mail from her for days, then writes that several arrived at once. Irregularity of mail is not surprising during wartime; Leslie's minimal specific response to the contents of Margaret's letters is. That may be a function of Pardini's selection and editing, but we don't think so.

Many, particularly the longest, seem to be him using Margaret as an ear. Some feel like aide-mémoire, a writer getting the granular details of the day or an event down for potential use later. Books and authors are as much a presence in those letters as the physical world he then inhabited.

That fits what we know of Leslie. He never, so far as we know, kept a diary. He needed ears. He says in his conversations with us that most of his articles were spoken before they were written. He once told us that just about all of his articles resulted from an occasion or an invitation: a conference, a symposium, a lecture. Most of the writing derived from that. It may be that he sometimes he had a book in mind early on, so the talks were a way to get there, but that's not our sense of the way he worked. He had interests, he talked about them, some coalesced into a book—sometimes a book with a real or ostensible focus, sometimes simply a collection of pieces. Perhaps that's why he didn't write more fiction.

Little of what appears in the wartime letters to Margaret overlap the things he had to say about the war decades later. You'll find, for example, no mention in the letters of Jack Brooks and the Colt .45, nor of the party with fifty of his closest friends yelling, "Let's make the big love baby." You won't find the naked Marines rubbing one another down. The story he told us of the Japanese man he may have helped to his death in Tientsin is very different in *Writing Home*. By the time he told it to us, it was brief and crystallized; in his October 10, 1945, letter to Margaret, it is several pages of detailed notes on and reflections about the day. Of all the letters, it is perhaps the one that could most stand as a publishable story on its own. But it's not the story he later chose to tell, or even, probably, remember.

All of this goes to the two mottoes about the stories we tell beginning this book—one from Italo Calvino, the other from our friend and quondam colleague John Barth.

Figure 9. Leslie in our kitchen on his eighty-third birthday, 2000.

1

April 8, 1989

You can start me off.

Bruce: I would like to ask you in these sessions about particularly literary things that interest you and how you got into it, and what you've been doing since you've been doing it. Things like living in Newark, how a nice Jewish boy from Newark decided to do literature, how you got to Montana; what it was like being in Montana, how you got to Buffalo, and some things like the Shachtmanites that nobody else around here except you and Irv Sanes seems to know about anymore.

I've been thinking about those people because when I was in New York I ran into a woman who I have bumped into twice recently from the old Trotskyite days and was actually there in Mexico when he was assassinated. She was married at that point to a leading Trotskyite, who was one of those Trotskyites who got sent to jail under the Smith Act. Some of those things have been revived in my head.

She knew the kid who killed him. I met him once actually.

Bruce: You met Trotsky?

No, the assassin, who hung around Trotskyite circles and was a boyfriend of a young woman who was very close to Trotsky. He had worked his way in that way.

Diane: Was it his own idea?

He was working for the Russians. He had been sent to do it. The Mexicans put him in jail. I don't know what happened to him, whether or not he ever got out.

I had met him at in a party in New York. He had attached himself to some very unattractive woman, and he was a rather charming fellow.

Diane: How old was he?

He must have been twenty or twenty-five years old at that time. It's the age that everybody was at that time. That's what Gertrude Stein says: "That was the year everybody was twenty-seven."

Bruce: Our son Michael is twenty-seven this year.

Ai yi yi. My oldest grandchild is twenty-two.

Bruce: Ai yi yi, indeed. That's more of an ai yi yi.

Diane: Seth?

Seth. I'm getting hungry for great-grandchildren. If it were a girl there'd be a better shot.

Bruce: They can each do it equally well.

Yes, but the girls produce the children. It was arranged that way.

Bruce: Do you want to talk about Newark today?

Yes.

Bruce: Did you grow up in Weequahic or some other part?

I'm a real honest-to-god Newarker. Not only was I born in Newark. My father was born in Newark. I grew up in the part of Newark which I suppose is the Weequahic district, but it was kind of the crummy, lower petit bourgeois part. I went to school at Southside High School. The only other distinguished graduate of Southside High School I know is Ed Koch. It was in those days an extraordinary school. God only knows what happened in that school, but when we were sophomores in Geometry class our whole class was put in detention for two weeks because we were passing from hand to hand under our desks—second year high school students, right?—e. e. cummings's translation of Louis Aragon's poem "Red Front."

It was a school in which we had a literary revival. *Transition* was our standard reading matter in that class. I don't know exactly why it happened, but just a year or two before us there were a bunch of people who somehow were in touch with the literary scene. I suppose through New York. But I never got to New York. For twenty years I hardly ever got out of Newark, and that ten mile trip to New York seemed to me absolutely impassable. The only times I went to New York from Newark is when I went to work as a boy in a shoe store and I used to be sent to New York occasionally to carry packages of hose and shoes back and forth on the tube train.

My first traumatic experience in New York: I was in front of the Empire State Building, which had just been put up. A strong wind came down the street and my goddamn boxes of hose scattered all over Fifth Avenue. I went scrambling.

But somehow in this particular high school in Newark there were a bunch of kids—maybe fifteen, twenty, twenty-five kids—who discovered simultaneously the Revolution and avant-garde literature. The only doubts I had in my mind as to whether literature would be my career or not was, I was torn between my political aspirations and my literary aspirations. Some of the more serious Communists I knew said it was betraying the Revolution to waste your time in the frivolous pursuit of literature. You should concentrate on changing the world. I think I simultaneously read my first copy of *Transition* when I was thirteen and met my first Communist when I was thirteen. By the time I was fourteen, I had already been converted both to modernism and literature, and to the Revolution.

The group of people who grew up there, we thought of ourselves as being a chosen kind of elite who despised the rest of our fellow students. I've kept my contacts with the core group of those people. When it was the fiftieth anniversary of my graduation from high school, which was 1984, we all got together. The guy who introduced me to Communism is now a stockbroker in Dallas. One of the other people, who started out as a writer, then collapsed as a writer and came to work for the State Department and then was one of the original twelve or thirteen people who were in that first series of negotiations with the Vietnamese when they were trying to settle the war. He's now retired from several large corporations and lives in a fancy apartment in New York. Another one has been a producer of television shows and a writer of television. They've all got rich, and we've all got to a point where we can't talk about politics anymore. All we can talk about is the past. We talk about Newark.

I never lost my touch with Newark at all, because, as you probably know, my mother, though she theoretically moved outside of Newark, only went as far as Irvington, where if she walked a half a block she was back in Newark again. She could look right down Springfield Avenue and see those burned-out stores where the riots occurred. She actually was born in New York City, but my father was born in Newark and lived in Newark all his life long. At one point there was a conference on urban affairs held in the Newark branch of Rutgers, where people came from all over the world to talk about life in the city. But the only two people there from Newark were me and LeRoi Jones. I can't call him any other name except LeRoi Jones. And in the audience both our mothers were sitting: his mother and my mother.

So Newark is a real place for me. Essentially it was a very exciting place and I learned lots of things in Newark. I hated it. I felt really imprisoned and trapped. I guess that's one of the reasons why I wander so restlessly about the world ever since. You asked why I went to Montana. Well, any place outside of Newark was okay.

It's only later that I discovered that's why everybody went to Montana to begin with. Not because they wanted to go *to* someplace, but because they wanted to get the hell *out* of someplace else. That's the whole basic motif of the western movement in the United States.

Bruce: The movement from.

The movement *from*: right. It worked out fine. I didn't know exactly what I was going to, but you couldn't have imagined anything that was more non-Newark, anti-Newark, than Missoula, Montana.

Bruce: Was your Newark Jewish?

Yeah. The Newark I lived in was Jewish. The grade school I went to, we must have been ninety-five percent Jewish. When the Jewish holidays came, all the students disappeared, and even the few loners in the class who weren't Jewish stayed out too, including a boy whose name was Christos Christopholos. I thought it was really great for him to stay home on Yom Kippur. He was a Greek boy who was in our class.

I lived in a situation which in some ways, I'm not sure what it explains in my life, but it's important for me: we were absolutely an almost entirely Jewish student body and not a single one of our teachers was Jewish. They were all suburban Gentile ladies. They were from the WASP world. And they sort of discovered me, those ladies, and they tried to teach me to talk right so I could mingle unnoticed with the great Gentile multitudes.

One thing which began to happen to me in school—and I have mixed feelings about it—is they took my mother tongue away from me, my *mamaloschen*, the language of the streets which I spoke with the kids, which was a language which was full of Yiddish words. None of us could speak Yiddish, but we knew how to say *schmuck*, at least, and *mumser*, and so forth. Our inflections were Jewish and some of our pronunciations, but I was brainwashed out of it so finally I have ended up speaking no recognizable dialect, just general American, right? It was odd.

They thought of themselves as missionaries, I think, those teachers who were rescuing us for the high life. But we went much further than they did, so that they were shocked and horrified. The first teacher I ever had who thought I was a writer hoped that I would someday be able to write very successful detective stories. Instead I was dreaming of the Revolution of the Word and becoming James Joyce.

I had a double experience as a kid. Because before I went to school in Newark my father had lived for a while—he was a pharmacist and had a drugstore—in East Orange, New Jersey, where I went to the school where not only all the teachers not Jewish, but every other kid in the school except me and my brother were Gentiles. It was the bad old days before anybody ever worried about separation of church and state, so we had "chapels," assemblies, chapels once a week where the Bible was read. We all said the Lord's Prayer, which I pretended to say, really mouthing obscenities, because I felt somehow I was betraying something.

That was the school in which the only kind of religious division—nobody really realized I was a Jew for a long time—but sometimes during recess time or after school when we played in the playground, the kids would divide up against each other, with the Protestants over on one side of the playground and the Catholics on the other.

One marvelous occasion when they thought all hell was going to break loose, they wanted to make sure everybody was on the right side and they asked me which I was, Protestant or Catholic, and I said Jewish and the ecumenical movement was invented and they all joined together and all chased me all the way home screaming, "You killed our Christ."

This disturbed my father so much that he moved back to Newark. He sold his business in East Orange, and we left. I was in kindergarten through the first three grades of school in that school.

That third grade was also the great turning point in my life because I had a teacher who dearly loved me and was pleased with everything I did, but I could never please myself. I performed well enough to please her but I could never live up to my own expectations, which were beyond anything. And I would burst into tears when I did something not as well as I thought I should. One day she took me aside and said, "Leslie, don't cry. You're going to be a great man." And I believed her. I honestly believed her. I didn't know what a great man was exactly. But I honest-to-god believed her. Her name was Miss Wessel, who I will never forget. What a lovely lady. So then we moved back to Newark and then I was in schools all the way through high school where the students were all Jewish. High school was maybe eighty percent Jewish.

In some ways after I got to Newark I began to believe there were only two kinds of people in the world: Blacks and Jews. Because when I was in junior high school I went to school in the third ward of Newark, which is the core of the Black ghetto in Newark, where most of the kids in the junior high school—it was just the ninth grade in that school—were White and/or Jewish, and all the kids in the primary grades and in the neighborhood were Black. It was there that I learned about race relations in America, because if you were Black or White, you didn't walk down the street alone; you walked in a pack. Both ways, we were a pack.

My deepest visceral reaction to memories of Newark is of despair and disgust, but when I think about it I realize I learned lots of things in Newark. There were two institutions, if you can call them that, in Newark which really educated me more when I was a kid than the schools I went to. One was the Newark Public Library, which is one of the great public libraries of the world. It is one of the largest open-stacked public libraries. The one in downtown Newark. It's absolutely marvelous. There's quite a good museum next to it, too, as a matter of fact. There, you were absolutely free to wander, and I would wander through and at age fourteen I pulled Marcel Proust out of the wall, first in English; and then when I was fifteen I tried to learn enough French to read *À la recherche du temps perdu* in French.

But I was getting educated in another way because I worked on Saturdays from the time I was thirteen. On lunch hours I would go across from the shoe store in which I worked to Military Park, which is the heart of Newark, where all the hobos and bums would hang out, and I would sit and listen to the stories they told and learned kind of street smarts from them. We used to be entertained everyday by the most literate among all the hobos, who was a guy called "Frenchie" who would sit and read aloud chapter after chapter of Jack London's *The Iron Heel* to the rest of the bums in the park. But you know, that was the first time somebody made a homosexual pass at me. Guys would tell me that when they combed their hair that morning, their scalp began to fall out because they had reached that stage of syphilitic decay. So I learned about life in Military Park.

The setting was so marvelous because that park is called Military Park because it's dominated by a huge Gutzon Borglum statue called *Wars of America*. It also was a place where itinerant preachers would turn up and also Communist speakers. I also learned what it's like to heckle. By the time I was thirteen or fourteen—fourteen, it was—I was also trying out talking on street corners myself.

Diane: What did you talk about?

I talked about how Roosevelt was a Fascist, FDR was a Fascist and was protecting the capitalist system in America. I also would stand in front of people I didn't approve of. I learned how to heckle and I learned how to confront hecklers. In some ways my style is street-corner style. In Newark, the audiences I spoke to were basically White audiences, but when I went off to graduate school, my first jump outside of Newark was Madison, Wisconsin, which annoyed me in some ways and I would always flee to Chicago. In Chicago I used to speak on the southside in Washington Park and I would talk to all-Black audiences. I learned this exchange: you would say something, and they say, "Now you're preachin', brother." And I'd say something else, and they'd say, "Go right on preachin.'" I learned that back and forth thing.

Also in Newark, the other thing I tried doing: we got very interested in theater. That was mixed up with our politics. We learned the Stanislavski method. Later, it got shortened to "Method" acting. We studied the theory of the thing and we had a small group that put on plays.

We learned how to cry. We learned how to laugh. We also learned the same thing that I learned on the soap boxes on street corners, that the motion has to go back and forth from the stage to the audience, from the audience to the stage. For a long time I was tempted away from my chosen career as a writer/poet, as I thought of myself in those days. I thought of becoming an actor. Really for a long time I kept acting. I used to do amateur acting all through my early years in Montana. And even after I was here in Buffalo I acted a little. I once did the narration for Lukas Foss's *Oedipus Rex*, the Stravinsky thing. I acted in a play of Al Cook's once; the most miserable play that was ever written on the face of the earth. I can't even remember what it was called. All I remember is that we actors would say, "Can't speak this line," and the director would say, "Strike it out." It was half as long when we produced it as when we started rehearsing the thing.

I used to go into New York and was associated with a group called the Theater for Ideas, in which I once appeared in a—it was not a full performance, it was kind of a stage reading of—*Faust*, in which I played Faust and John Simon played Mephistopheles. This was typecasting all the way.

Bruce: This was when?

This was in the sixties. Sixty-five maybe. Irene Worth showed up one night and sat in the audience and watched me and I almost fainted with bliss and joy.

But then I decided I'm stuck in this single part of the professor, so I've been acting that way ever since.

Diane: How did you get into that role to start with? Did you decide to be a professor?

It sort of happened by accident. The one thing I had in life was Gutenberg skills. I was good at reading and writing and I just kept on going to school. I never really planned to go on, but it turned out to be the thing to do.

Finally when I graduated from high school, it looked for a while as if I wouldn't be able to do it. Then it suddenly became the desirable goal for me. It was the pit of the Depression when I graduated from high school in 1934. I had got a small scholarship to NYU. I came home one day and my mother and father sat me down for a family meeting and said, "We can't afford for you to go to school. You have to go to work for a while. Even with the scholarship we can't do it." There I was, a great overgrown boy of sixteen, tears streaming down my face; and I swore I'd go there and stay there, and I haven't got out ever since. Six months later I was able to work it out.

Diane: Did you go to NYU?

Yes. I went to a strange part of NYU. It doesn't exist anymore. It's New York University Heights. It's up in the Bronx. It was kind of a nice campus; it had a stadium on it where they had concerts in the summertime. It was a very strange school. It was very small. It's one of the few schools in New York that has an honest-to-god campus, and there were just two campuses, an arts college with fifteen hundred students and an engineering college with fifteen hundred students.

And once again, I was in the same old ethnic trap. The arts college consisted ninety percent of Jewish people, eighty percent of whom were intent on being doctors. Half of those made it. And the engineering school was ninety-nine percent goy. In those days Jews couldn't make it in engineering at all.

Diane: Did they try?

They were discouraged from doing it because they knew it was very difficult, if not impossible to get jobs. There was a kind of closed-door policy against Jews.

We were a very politically active campus. That was where I became a Trotskyist. At NYU Uptown. I was already beginning to have doubts that I had never officially become a member of the Communist Party. There was a character, a very strange character, who was the kind of guy who could arrange to get you a passport if you wanted to go to Spain to fight. I always thought he was a fellow student. Later I have gone through the lists of people who were in school, and I can't find his name anyplace. I think he was a goddamned agent who was there the whole time. This may be romantic fantasy on my part. He said, "Don't attempt to judge us until you join." So I actually joined the Young Communist League group on the campus. One of our people did go to Spain and was killed.

Diane: Did you think of going?

Yes, I thought of going for a long time, back and forth, yes and no; finally hated myself because I didn't go.

Bruce: Felt guilty?

Guilty as hell. So I went around doing senseless committee activities, to me, raising money for this thing I didn't dare to go to. I was scared to go.

I had been a member of the Young Communist League for only six months when I decided it was absolutely intolerable. That's when I dropped out and became a Trotskyist.

Diane: Why was it intolerable?

I began to find more and more things that I objected to. I became aware of all the things which are now official knowledge to everybody about what Stalinism really meant, which in some ways was known to people in the movement. They said, "It's the price you pay." But I thought the price was too big to pay, so I became a Trotskyist.

Then I really ran into something: all my closest friends ceased talking to me. They were all Stalinists. Only one of the Stalinists I knew, a guy called Arthur Zeiger, still remains my friend. He's been my friend to this very day. He and I collaborated on a book once, an anthology which was put together.

It was as if I had become a nonperson at that point. It was like taking a new personality. When I joined the Communist movement I took one name, which oddly enough before I had ever met any of the people who had actually owned the name, was "John Simon." That was my name as a Communist. I thought "Simple Simon." It was a joke on myself: I thought, "What's an anonymous first name? 'Simple Simon.'" Since then, I have come to know three or four John Simons. When I became a Trotskyist I called myself Dexter Fellows; he was the PR man for Barnum and Bailey Circus in those days.

Al Eisner, one of my closest friends from my high school days, on the other hand, made up for it. When he became a member of the Young Communist League at Harvard, he took the name of Leslie Fiedler. I actually have a program someplace in my files in which he acted a part in *Waiting for Lefty* under the name of "Leslie Fiedler." I figure my biographers will be very confused.

Bruce: All those HUAC files. They will be very confused.

He died at age twenty-three.

Diane: How?

Cancer.

In some ways the most important figure of my life was Al Eisner.

Diane: How was he the most important figure?

I'll tell you why. I envied him a lot. He did all the things I wanted to do first. He was the first person I ever knew who got published. Al Eisner got published when he was fourteen. He used to write for *Field and Stream* and *Our Weekly Messenger* and so forth. He could mock any style and then he went off to Harvard, the school we dreamed about going to but never thought we could really make it. When he was there, he was a roommate of Lenny Bernstein, who actually has a piece of music dedicated to him. And he went off to Hollywood as a junior script writer at age twenty-one. And, at age twenty-two, he began to develop a kind of cancer which galloped through his whole body. Started in his balls, went to his brain.

His death for me is like all those deaths you read about, Edward King and so forth. It blew my mind: it was me who was dying. The first poem I ever had published was written to him. And the first story I ever had printed was really about his life and death.

The reason he went to Harvard was because when he was fifteen our Latin teacher, who was fiftyish at the time, I guess, fell in love with him, quit her job, set up an apartment, kept him, sponsored him, sent him off to school. Last time I saw her was a year or two after he died and she kept assuring me that he was haunting the apartment she had in the old Village and took me around to show me the places where he appeared. She was found dead about six months later. She had cut herself off from all her friends and nobody knew she was dead until the milkman smelled her rotting through the door.

This was Hattie, who taught me Virgil. Al and I were in the Virgil class together. Virgil has funny feelings for me too. Al was a strange fellow. It gave me a taste of glory while he was with Hattie. I go to visit them and they'd take me to eat at restaurants I didn't dare enter; buy me cigars which in those days cost a buck, real Havanas.

Diane: Were they lovers?

I guess they were lovers. It's hard to tell. The first poem I ever published was a poem called "Oh, Al." A story called "The Fear of Innocence" was really a story of Al and Hattie and me all mixed up together, slightly fictionalized. Al was an Eagle Scout. He was extremely handsome. And though he was as Jewish as I was, he looked like a clean-cut American boy.

There were a lot of us who thought we were going to be writers. And some of us more or less made it. Some thought they would be actors. Nobody really made it as an actor, though the guy I was talking about before, one of my oldest friends, a guy called Eddie Jurist, later became a writer for television and a television producer. He invested his money wisely in parking lots and supermarkets and is doing all right. He remains a Stalinist to the bitter end. He went off to Michigan where he was a contemporary of Arthur Miller's.

Being a Communist is a funny thing because in some ways if you were in the official okay Stalinist movement, that was a way of social climbing as well as revolution. You could meet the kinds of rich people who gave parties that you had never seen before. And girls who honest-to-god went to Vassar and Sarah Lawrence and places like that.

Bruce: Nobody talks about that aspect of it.

It's an important part of it. It was social climbing.

Diane: Was it like religion also?

The first time I ever saw Vassar I went to some sort of huge Commie anti-Japanese demonstrations, which had a great erotic thrill as well as a class thrill for me, because the girls were tearing off their silk underpants and throwing them in the fires in protest against the Japanese silk trade.

Bruce: Higher! Higher!

It was a weird world. *[A bit of a silence, then:]*

Start me again.

Diane: How long were you a Trotskyite?

I was a Trotskyite through the last two years of college and my first two years as a graduate student at Madison. I worked one summer as the organizer of the local Young People's Socialist League, Fourth International, as it was called those days in Newark.

When I did some of my first teaching, I taught public speaking to trade union organizers and workers who fell into our clutches. Then, when I went to Madison, I organized the first Trotskyist movement in Madison, and I remained a Trotskyist right up to—certainly past the time when I was married. The first item of furniture that Margaret and I bought for ourselves (we were married in 1939) was a mimeograph machine so we could turn out leaflets and distribute them in front of the classes of professors, pointing out that they were social Fascists.

Bruce: A very romantic guy.

It was at that point that the great split came in the Trotskyist movement. I always kept drifting leftward. The Cannonites were closer to the old hardline Stalinist position; in terms of theory, they thought that the Soviet Union was still in some sense a Socialist state, though corrupted. The Shactmanites were far to the left and thought that the corruption in the Soviet Union went all the way back to Kronstadt and to Lenin himself. But, anyhow, I went with them; and even within the Shactmanite movement there were strong divisions, and I tended to the side which was led by, I was a Burnhamite, James Burnham, who later became an extreme conservative and right-wing political theorist and wrote a whole series of books.

I was on the same side as Dwight Macdonald, though Dwight Macdonald was thought of in the movement as an idiot. He was not highly articulate in a polemical situation. He would always go to small pieces and stutter. And the Old Man himself, as we always called Trotsky, had even said some very snide things about him. He didn't have a very high opinion of his brain power.

Diane: Did Macdonald know this? [Leslie doesn't respond.]

So I presumably went off on a honeymoon trip. My whole marriage was shot through with this, where we actually went to the convention where the Trotskyist movement split, held I think it was in Cleveland or someplace.

Diane: Margaret was the same as you?

Margaret was a Stalinist when I first knew her. I had won her over from the ranks of the Stalinists. We kept her in there for a while as a double agent. We were much into double agents in those days.

I got into a lot of trouble. The only way I could go to school was on—even when I was an undergrad—was on scholarship; and they took my scholarships away from me my fourth year for political reasons, not academic ones. But fortunately, I won a prize for excellence in Italian studies and two public speaking prizes, so I was able to afford my tuition bill.

Bruce: This was at NYU?

This was at NYU. And then, my files were so full of references to my politics that I wasn't accepted for a while; it seemed as though I wouldn't be accepted into any graduate school. NYU didn't accept me at all.

The most damaging letter came from my Italian professor. I was much into Italian those days. I was beginning a major ambitious translation of *The Divine Comedy*. I used to have long conversations with him. He was a man called Quinby, who was an American by birth, but an absolute confirmed Fascist, supporter of Mussolini. His wife, I think, was an Italian woman. It turned out the letter which really killed me in my files—somebody later showed it to me—was from him, which said, "Mr. Fiedler is a very brilliant student, but his politics are suspect and he will never be a scholar or a gentleman."

But fortunately, the University of Wisconsin was still full of what I love to call the Wisconsin idea of progressivism in those days.

Bruce: The LaFolletters?

Yeah.

When I was at the University of Wisconsin, I was a member of the Young Progressives. The family had all split up. Susan LaFollette became a Trotskyist. Young Bob was an old-fashioned progressive, and Phil LaFollette, one of the sons, actually became a right-winger; sort of a hard-core Fascist.

We went into the progressive movement, the Young Progressives, in order to fight it out and see if we could convert some people to Trotskyism. At any rate, they finally gave me enough of a scholarship so I could afford to go, which arrived at the very last minute. And I went tearing off.

That was the poorest time of my whole life. I lived on forty cents a day in those days. That was my food allowance. Every day: it was forty cents.

Diane: What could you get for forty cents?

A fine bowl of chili for twenty cents. All the crackers I could eat. I would go into the Wisconsin Student Union and pick up people's empty coffee cups—you could get refills free—and take them back. I would go to the teas that were given by the sorority girls and eat all the cookies in sight. You could get free buttermilk if you went to the ag school.

Diane: Were you married at that point?

That was the year before I was married, 1938 and '39. '40 was the year I was married, and Margaret had a little money.

Diane: Was she at Wisconsin, too? Is that where you met?

Yes. She was also at the University of Wisconsin.

When I was at Wisconsin, all kinds of fascinating people were there, including Norman O. Brown. But we never spoke to each other for two reasons: he was in Classics, I was in English; but worse, he was still a Stalinist and I was a Trotskyist.

Bruce: He remained a Stalinist after the Molotov-Ribbentrop thing?

Yeah. His politics are really strange. The last time I saw him, which was in Santa Cruz, three years ago, I discovered he's a strong supporter of Khomeini.

Diane: Oh, god!

We went for a peaceful walk in the woods and I got all this pro-Khomeini bullshit.

Diane: What's wrong?

I don't know; I refused to let him; I wouldn't listen. I wanted to have a peaceful conversation about being retired. I wanted to know what it's like to be retired, because at that time he was retired and I was approaching it. And he persuaded me not to retire. He said he had plans for finishing three books when he decided to retire and hadn't been able to write a single line since retirement. I really only got to know him after I got here and he was in Rochester still.

Diane: What did you think of him?

I admire him a great deal. He's full of wonderful ideas. If you think of him as a kind of poet, I think he's all right. He puts things together the way a poet puts them together. When he tries to think too hard, he gets into trouble. I remember once saying to him while we were disagreeing about something, "Our presumable grounds of disagreement are superficial. The main trouble between us is I'm a Jew and you're a pagan. I don't mean a Christian; then I could talk to you. But you're a pagan."

Diane: Is he?

Yeah. He really is. He really, really is. He thinks he's a Christian.

Diane: A fellow whose very close to him told me that he's really a puritan.

Oh, that he is, too! That's part of the pagan world.

Bruce: It doesn't account for any of it, though.

He is a very strange man. I know some wilder stories. He's a very complex and fascinating human being.

Ihab Hassan was his student once. They were at Wesleyan together. Hassan once discovered that Nobby was slipping off every afternoon mysteriously. And he thought finally there's going to be some nice, juicy sexual scandal in his life. One day he followed him very cautiously and discovered he was going to the Arthur Murray studios to learn how to dance.

[laughter and pause] Sally's met him.

Diane: What do you think of him?

Sally: I liked him.

It's impossible not to like him, in a way. He's got a classical Oedipal hangup. He had a kind of Mexican-Indian mother and a Scotch-Irish father.

Diane: What kind of wives?

He's had one wife all his life, who seems a very quiet, housewifely lady.

Diane: An Italian professor told me that he thought he stirred everyone up but he did nothing himself and he thought there was some sort of bad faith in this.

I don't think it's bad faith. I think it's quite clear in his own mind. It's his job to stir up and it's other people's job to be stirred. He does this in perfect good faith—with himself.

Bruce: Were people in your family political, Leslie?

My grandfather was political. My maternal grandfather, I'm talking about, who in some ways remains for me the ideal human being. He was, when he came to this country—I'll tell you a little bit about him so you'll understand him.

When he was thirteen years old he was apprenticed to a cabinet maker in the old country, and he ran away and he wandered through Europe. He came from Galicia and he finally got to Germany. He finally got to Hamburg. He finally earned enough money so he shipped out to America. In America he was all his life long a working man. He worked all over the country, including here in Buffalo, where he spent four years from, I think, 1904 to 1908. One of my aunts was born in Buffalo. My grandmother, who was a very tough lady, said my Aunt Matilda would never have been born if they had been in Newark, but she didn't know an abortionist here. Working-class ladies always had abortions, don't kid yourself.

My grandfather was a Socialist by the time he came to America and he remained a Socialist until FDR came along and his social-democratic ideas got fused into the New Deal. All his life long he was a leather worker. He worked in an industry which at that time wasn't unionized; but he was a secret union organizer all his life. There's a story attached to this, which tells you what I think of my grandfather and why.

Times got very bad and they were beginning to fire people in the plant he worked in, and one of his closest friends turned him in to the boss for being a secret unionizer. And he got fired. Some years later he came to this aunt I was telling you about, Aunt Matilda, and he said, "Tildy, I want you should take me some place." She drove and he didn't.

As she was driving she said, "We're driving in the direction of the house that Smitty lives in." Smitty was the guy who turned him in and got him fired. And my grandfather said, "Yes, we're going to go to see Smitty." And she said, "Why are we going to see Smitty?" "He's having bad luck and I know about a job for him." Aunt Matilda said, "But Smitty is the one who had you fired." My grandfather said, "Everybody is human." That's the way he was.

He was also the one who told me all the fairy tales before I ever read them in a book. An unbroken oral tradition, right? And he used to tell them to all the kids in the neighborhood. And like an idiot, I never took down his versions of them. They just slipped away; he had the best version of "The Princess on the Glass Hill" that I ever heard.

All his stories began the same way. He always—when he told them to me, at least—made them very male centered, boy centered. All his stories began, "Once there was a young man who got on a white horse and rode out into the world." He himself was more of a peasant and ran around with a bunch of kids who would jump on a local farmer's horse and ride and steal stuff from the orchards. He had a mark on his foot which he claimed came from a horse's hoof; I think it just happened to be shaped like that, but he had a great story about jumping on a blind horse who ran into a tree. I couldn't believe anything he said, but it was all done in very good humor.

He was the strongest human being I ever knew in my life, and the gentlest. We used to beg him to feel his muscles. He was little. Slight.

Diane: But strong?

Incredibly strong. And bullied all his life long by my grandmother, who was much smaller than he was, whom he could have broken in half with one hand. She bullied him. She was absolutely analphabetic, and he could read and write and spoke six or seven languages. He taught himself to read. He used to read aloud to my grandmother stories from the *Forverts [a Socialist Yiddish-language daily in Yiddish established in 1897]* which I realized years later were Isaac Bashevis Singer's. He knew a lot. He also told me the story of *The Merchant of Venice* the first time I ever heard it.

Bruce: He told it as a story?

Yes: he told it as a story. I thought it was about a bad Litvak *[Jews with roots in Lithuania]* who gave the Galitzianers *[Jews with roots in western Ukraine and southeastern Poland]* a hard time. He was political.

My father was political in his own way. He always claimed he was a sturdily independent voter who always ended up voting for the Democratic candidate.

Bruce: I know that pattern very well.

Even Al Smith. And he was extremely anti-Communist.

Talk about puritans. I grew up in a real puritan household. My father used to write letters to the newspaper about how the world is going to hell; it's now full of long-haired men and short-haired women who confuse liberty with license.

I remember 1927 very well. I remember the crowds on the streets when Sacco and Vanzetti died. I remember the excitement when Lindberg flew across the Atlantic. They were all in that same year.

Diane: How did your family feel about Sacco and Vanzetti?

I don't know how they felt about it. I can't remember what they said about it. All I remember is that there was a kind of hush over all of Newark, or at least the part of it that was visible to me. Our teachers talked about it a little bit.

Diane: And said what?

They said dangerous people were being executed.

But, in a way, the main sense I got was not anything angrily said, but that everybody was upset because it raised all the critical issues and that people were disturbed. They were disturbed.

I remember that year: that's a downer, that whole experience. That's it. And the upper of Lindberg flying.

Diane: Was your family at all religious?

My grandfather was quite anti-religious. Theoretically, anti-religious. But every once in a while he would take me when I was a little kid, when the high holidays came, to one of those store-front synagogues they set up. He would always say the same thing to me. "Not because I believe, but so you should remember."

The only religious member of my family was my paternal great-grandfather. I knew him slightly. That family came over pretty early on my father's side. I can remember an immense scene when he died. I must have been around eight or nine or ten years old. He was an extremely devout man, and a friend of his delivered a graveside sermon, and everybody screamed in Yiddish—which I didn't understand a word of—and everybody screamed and yelled and a couple of the women fainted, and so forth. When I got home I got somebody to explain to me that what he had said was, "This man suffered the worst indignity that can be visited on a human being. He saw his children die before him. He lived to a very old age and this is because in America they have abandoned their faith."

He was the last religious person.

Bruce: Were you bar mitzvahed?

Yes. Over my father's dead body. My father was a militant atheist. When I was a kid he used to give me these *Little Blue Books* of Haldeman-Julius. My father brought me up reading Robert Ingersol and Tom Payne, but when I got to be about twelve my mother for social reasons (though she was not really religious at all) thought I should be bar mitzvahed. So they turned me over to learn enough Hebrew to be bar mitzvahed. I went, but in those days I was rather cocky, and we would spend half of my lesson time with me trying to persuade the rabbi that the Jews were racist in their treatment of the Blacks and that religion was the opiate of the people. His response to which was always the same: "You read like a Cossack." And I did indeed read like a Cossack.

Diane: Was politics a transfer or a substitute for religious ideals?

I felt no attraction to it. It affected your whole life, so in some ways, it was. Later I felt terrible that I had missed an opportunity to learn Hebrew. In 1946 and 1947, when I was at Harvard I went to the Divinity School and studied Hebrew. I learned enough to make it into a class in exegesis of the Prophets. We spent one whole semester reading the god-damned fifty-third chapter of Isaiah with Robert Pfeiffer, who believed in nothing except grammar and syntax. But the class was fascinating because there were some believing Jews in it and some believing Christians as well.

I never went to a seder in my life until I gave one myself.

Bruce: How did you know what to do? Read a book?

I read a book. Look at us!

We organized this little, teeny-tiny religious community in Missoula, Montana, and we held kind of a community seder. On the faculty there must have been five or six Jews, and in town there were maybe five or six more, so that if anything serious was going on and you wanted to get a *minyan* together, it was touch and go every inch of the way. It was sort of riotous because most of the Jewish faculty members had *shiksas* for wives. One of my kids said to me once—maybe it was Jennie—she said, "Women are never Jewish, father, are they?"

My best friend on the faculty in Missoula was an old Eastern European Jew—his name was Joe Kramer—who had sort of a unique history in the United States. He was brought over by a society which was set up to settle the Jews on the land in the United States. Keep them from clustering in the big cities. He had never been in New York. He entered America through Galveston.

Bruce: I never heard of Jews coming in through Galveston.

I don't know how many there were—maybe hundreds. And Joe Kramer was one of them. He came in through Galveston.

He worked on farms. He actually judged pigs at one time or another in stock shows. He finally managed to get into an ag school and then into a graduate school and got a degree in botany. He used to teach one of the most popular courses in Montana, mostly to foresters: Forest Ecology.

He was an absolutely unreconstructed hard-core Stalinist. He bar mitzvahed Kurt, because he still remembered when he had gone to *cheder*. He said, "I am absolutely an orthodox Jew, except that I don't happen to believe in God."

The students loved Joe and he would always try to socialize the lesson. He would take them up on the side of the hill, and he would say, "You see, on this side where the wind blows, the grass doesn't grow. On the other side where the wind doesn't blow, the grass grows. Do you *blame* the grass because it can't grow on the side where the wind blows? Should you blame people in society?" He spoke with a comic East European accent, and the students would try to make him a westerner. They called him Smokey Joe. They gave him a nice, western nickname.

Diane: Did you argue with him about God?

We would argue until we were exhausted and then we would go to the local saloon and have ourselves a couple of beers. He considered it was his duty to make everybody suffer, so on registration day he would cruise through the room where we were registering and pick the youngest, freshest, most naïve-looking freshman instructor who was registering and walk up to him and say, "Tell me what course I should take to find out what is the good life and how I should lead it."

His kids, on the other hand, grew up ashamed of him because he didn't look like an American, he didn't talk like an American. He would always say, "They're status quo kids." One of them is a reporter. "Couldn't he go into a socially useful profession?" he would say.

Diane: Did he ever get in trouble for his politics?

I think he was held back from promotion for a while, but after a while he became such a fixture.

Montana is a very strange state. It's a state with no middle. It's got a strong left wing and a strong right wing. It's always kind of touch and go. There was a big cluster of Trotskyites, for instance, in Big Timber, Montana, one little, tiny town; and the miner's union was a Stalinist-controlled union for a long time. It was a Wobbly Union for a while, the Western Miner's Union. Then when they became the Mine, Mill and Smelters Workers Union, it passed into the control of the Communists. And the Anaconda Company had such a good contract with the Mine, Mill and Smelters Union that whenever the legislature would pass anti-Communist laws in the days of McCarthyism, the company would lean over their shoulders and say, "Don't appropriate any money to enforce this. We don't want to rock the boat. We've got a good contract." We used to call it the contradictions of capitalism.

They saved my life, the Mine, Mill and Smelters Workers Union. There was a point when I got into bad trouble at the university because I called on the president publicly to resign as president of the university. And he did what everybody tells you what is the most stupid thing in the world to do in any kind of a tight situation. He handed in his resignation and said to the State Board of Education in effect: "If you believe the faculty, fire me; if you believe me, fire the faculty, or those who are making the trouble." I was the leader of the faculty that was making the trouble. The board split on it and there was one vote that was hanging one way or another. A delegation from the university went to see the guy and said, "Vote to accept the president's resignation and save Fiedler." The guy who had some high office in the state said, "Why should I vote for Fiedler and not for the president?" And the spokesman for the university talked about the good of the university and the educational interest of the students, and he said, "Fuck the good of the university. That's like home and mother. Who's on your side?" He said, "I got a guy from the Mine, Mill and Smelters Workers Union here." He said, "You've got my vote!"

Bruce: Montana was also an early important center for feminism.

It's the home of Jeanette Rankin.

Bruce: We met her granddaughter there.

My [son] Eric was for a while Jeanette's secretary and companion. He at that point was about twenty and she was about ninety. The Rankins are a strange family. Her brother, Wellington Rankin, was the largest land-holder in the state of Montana. He had this immense ranch, which was about a quarter of the state. He was a really right-wing Republican, and she had a strange combination of right-wing politics and feminism.

You met Mackey Brown.

Bruce: Who's a real fan of yours.

Mackey's mother was her granddaughter. Mackey's mother was an early propagandist for Planned Parenthood. They are a very powerful family. Wellington Rankin, on the other hand, always boasted that when Gary Cooper was a kid, he had worked for him on his ranch. Wellington had taught Gary Cooper to box.

*Bruce: Did you read the [Carl] Bernstein book about his parents—*Loyalties?

No, I didn't.

Bruce: It's a nasty book, really a vile book. The parents are wonderful. And he doesn't understand what they didn't understand. He doesn't know that it's an ironical book.

That makes it fascinating.

Bruce: Some of the years and some of the politics are the same years that interest you.

Politics in Montana were very strange. You get the most marvelous internal journals of the Communist Party in a little Montana university library, because the librarian for many years was a Communist Party member. It was thanks to his membership in the Communist Party that I was able to walk through the stacks and come across of a copy of Henry Roth's *Call It Sleep*, which he had ordered. He had bought one of only a thousand copies that had been sold and had stocked it there.

Montana is a very political state. Everything is so naked and out in the open. When I first came there, a young, assistant professor of political science who had the office next to mine and was at that point a member of the Socialist Party was Mike Mansfield. Mike Mansfield could get all the votes in Montana, because on the one hand he was associated with and had been a trade union member. He grew up in the Miners Union. On the other hand, he had been a Marine. One thing he never voted for was gun control. You can be sure of that. It would have killed him in that state!

Diane: What year did you go to Montana?

1941.

Bruce: And then you went into the Navy?

I went there before the United States got into the War. I taught there for a year and a term, then went into the Navy.

When I got out I went for a little while to Harvard to be restored, redeemed, recuperated.

Diane: Did you like it?

Harvard? I loved it! It was a playground! We just played. I was in the ideal position. I wasn't a faculty member and I wasn't a student. I was doing postdoctoral study, so I took whatever courses I wanted, heard all the gossip on all sides, and everybody was very nice to me. I got to be sort of friendly with *[F. O.]* Matthiessen, who asked me to do a couple of his classes for him. He wanted me to talk about Jewish poets, Karl Shapiro and so forth. Harvard was changing in those days. It was the first time that families were on the campus. They set up those Quonset huts, temporary places, and there were kids swarming all over and you had this strange mixture of people who had gone through at the regular pace, plus people who had come back from the war. The place was full of all kinds of fascinating people.

In Matthiessen's class in modern poetry, the star of the class was the present Poet Laureate of the United States, Richard Wilbur, and an undergraduate sitting dumb in the back of the class was Bob Creeley. He didn't say a word, as far as I can remember, all year long. You know the crazy way they do at Harvard of putting graduates and undergraduates in the same class. It was great. I wanted to learn Hebrew; I took a course in Hebrew. I took Harry Wolfson's course in the *Physics* of Aristotle. I took whatever popped into my crazy head. It was, for a lot of people after the war, a chance to live a second adolescence.

Bruce: Harry Wolfson was one of the first Jews who had tenure at Harvard. Ben Botkin took me to meet him when he was an old man.

It was nice. Henry Popkin was there.

Bruce: I can't imagine a young Henry Popkin.

You don't have to remember a young Henry Popkin: he looked exactly the same at age twenty-two as he does now. Henry Popkin: he looked so weird. On the other hand, he was running a very good magazine in those days. I can't remember what it was called. He was the first person who ever published Dick Wilbur, as a matter of fact. Popkin was one of Harry Levin's favorite students. Nobody ever looked up anything in the graduate school, they just asked Henry, because Henry remembers everything. I don't know if you know this about him. I met him when the *Encyclopedia of the Theater* had come out, and he was in England, far from his own library. He was asked to review it, and he said, "I found twenty-two errors in it. Unfortunately, I couldn't reach my books, or I am sure I could have found as many more." But when he went to take his orals, he blew them; he froze. Nobody could believe it.

When I was ready to leave Harvard, I had offers of a job in Berkeley and in Santa Barbara. I decided to go back to Montana. In the first place I don't like to be hunched. I didn't want to get into an up-or-out situation right away. I figure, "I'm going to write at my own pace." In the second place, I had come to believe I had something to learn in Montana. And I did. It turned me into a populist.

Diane: Was Berkeley the same as it is now—trying to be Harvard?

Yes. It was even worse in those days.

Diane: When I turned down Berkeley it was right after I'd left the convent. I thought, "I know perfectly well how to do this world."

The head of the department was Willard Farnham. He was the one who came around to Harvard doing interviews. It was after that time that they fired Al Cook. They said he was a dilettante, oddly enough because he was studying Hebrew at the time, and they thought this was a frivolous thing to do.

Diane: They turned down a lot of good people, a lot of extraordinary people.

Harvard has an ancient and honorable record of firing a lot of good people, too.

Bruce: Which has been good for the rest of us.

Right!

The chairman in Montana, the head of the department, he was for life. He talked tough, he scared everybody to death. He never could bring himself to fire anybody in his life.

He was one of the reasons I went back. He was a marvelous man; his name was H. G. Merriam. He was one of the first batch of Rhodes Scholars from the United States. He was a great exponent of Western literature. He ran a magazine called *Frontier and Midland*. It was one of the first magazines to take Western literature seriously. He himself had come from Wyoming, and when he was at Oxford they apparently gave him a very hard time. They weren't used to Americans. They asked him questions about "What are things like in Wyoming?" and so forth. He was a kid who had grown up peddling papers in front of the Brown Hotel in Denver; made it the hard way. But he made that a damn good department, especially in writing. He was the guy who hired Richard Hugo. But he was a strange combination. He had only one requirement, and he influenced me in some ways. He said, "You come into this school, any course you teach is your course; you can do anything you want in it. But don't let me catch you ever sitting down when you teach." And he would walk around and peer through the windows to make sure you stood up! He didn't believe that anybody could teach properly sitting down. He lived to be ninety-two or ninety-three years old.

Diane: I felt funny when I first taught graduate seminars sitting down. My professors stood. At Hopkins, they never sat.

When I first taught in Italian universities, they were still in the old system, and the *bedello* would come in with you, take your coat off, and push the chair forward for you to sit down, and the class would stand at attention until you sat. The first time that happened to me I looked over my shoulder to see if there was an admiral in the room. I stood only for admirals and the grand God Jehovah; but all that's gone. The sixties destroyed that, even in the Italian universities. But they had other lovely things, like the academic quarter of an hour. Students really sat and waited.

It was from Montana that I went to Italy. It was 1951, I guess. It turned out to be for two years. I thought it was going to be for a year, and then I couldn't bear to leave. I went on a Fulbright; it was a strange and exciting thing. In the last years of Mussolini, the Italians had discovered American literature, which he frowned on, and so it was considered a revolutionary activity to be interested in American literature, and people turned to American books as underground books. It was the radical writers like *[Cesare]* Pavese and *[Elio]* Vittorini, who did the first translation of American books into Italian. But there were no courses in American literature given in any Italian universities at that point. So the lectures I gave at the University of Rome were really the first lectures given in the university on American literature. At this point there are now thirteen chairs in American literature in Italian universities; and three or four of them are held by old students of mine.

Bruce: You have an early article on Pavese.

Pavese had just died when I got there, but one of my first memories was wandering through the streets of Turin with a guy named Gabrielli Baldini, who had been a friend of his, drinking more and more grappa and weeping. "This is where *Moby Dick* was discovered for the Italians. From this window Pavese threw himself."

Pavese's suicide was in some ways triggered by Matthiessen's. He left the same note that Matthiessen left: "Ripeness is all."

Diane: That's it?

That's it. *[Not quite: the note Matthiessen left in the hotel room he jumped from read, "How much the state of the world has to do with my state of mind I do not know." The last words in Pavese's diary were "All this stinks. Not words. An action. I shall write no more."]*

I taught not only there, but at the University of Bologna and the University of Venice—Ca' Foscari University.

Diane: Did you teach in English?

I taught in English every place except at Bologna. They told me at Bologna nobody understood English. I did it in Italian. I had somebody help me with it. The guy who helped me with it is now the dean of all the professors of American literature in Italy, a magnificent fellow called Augustino Lombardo, who, because he's a Sicilian, he's a dead ringer for George Washington: a blond, blue-eyed Sicilian.

~

Bruce: Did I ever tell you about the night we were in Florence when the Communists won the election?

No.

Bruce: The Socialists won, but they are not in power yet. So they are driving up one side of the Arno blaring their horns; the policeman drives down the other side of the Arno chasing them. He has to chase them because they are not in power yet; he can't catch them because they will be in power soon. So every time they would go over one of the bridges, he would go over another to the side they'd left. We spent half an hour watching this: their cars carrying the red flag, and his blue light going up the other side of the river.

Communists and Socialists are sure in power now in Florence, entrenched forever. The last time I was in Florence, I was invited there by the Instituto Gramsci Tuscano, which is to say the Socialists and Communists, who had decided for reasons of their own, which soon became clear to me, that they were going to organize the convention to which they would invite people from all over the world to talk about Jewishness and anti-Semitism. And they were very scholarly discussions: Jews in the Middle Ages, Jews in Ancient Greece. God-only-knows-what. Jews in Egypt.

But in between were official party spokesmen, who got up over and over again and they made a speech with the same monotonous theme: "The gulag is not Auschwitz. The gulag is not Auschwitz." They had bad conscience. There are hardly any Jews in Italy. I kept saying to people, "This big interest in Jewishness and anti-Semitism: How many Jews are there in Italy?" Do you know? Thirty thousand. That's it. At the most there are probably only fifty thousand.

On the other hand, a considerable number of the leaders of the left-wing parties in Italy are and were Jewish. A considerable number of the leading industrialists of Italy are and were Jewish, including Olivetti. Quite a few leading Fascists were Jewish. I mean official members of the party. It's really weird. But of course they've been there forever. This is an old immigrant population there. They are fifteen-hundred-year-old families. Though there was some ghettoization of Jews, there were never any pogroms against Jews organized by Italians themselves in Italy. And the closer they were to the Vatican, the safer they were.

Diane: Why are there so few?

Just many never came.

2

April 22, 1989

Bruce: Do you want to talk about Abbie [Hoffman] today?

Yeah, we can talk about him today. And you want to talk also about
the New York intellectuals, my odd relationship with them?

Diane: Yes.

Okay.

*Bruce: Let's do Abbie first. You caught on to his probable suicide pretty
quickly.*

He was a classic manic-depressive. He dealt with himself by using
all kinds of drugs, and drugs and booze together. It seemed inevitable
that if he ever did it he would do it the way he did, with a combination
of pills and whisky. I only saw him two or three times in my life and I
never saw him any way except high. But *really* high.

The last time I saw him was kind of interesting. It was when there
were big demonstrations. It was 1970, I guess it must have been, or '71, big
demonstrations going on at Yale on behalf of the Black Panthers. Abbie and
Jerry *[Rubin]* had moved into Calhoun College, of which I am an associate
fellow. Dick Lewis called me up one day in an absolute panic. He said to me,
"I can't talk to those people. Nobody here can talk to those people. Come
up and interpret for us." So I flew up and I was the interpreter, a kind of
intermediary between the two. That was the third time I was tear-gassed.

Bruce: You were tear-gassed at Yale?

I was tear-gassed at Yale. The whole occasion was ridiculous. Because
all of Yale had gone crazy. When I first came in I went to one of the other
colleges—I can't remember which one—and Allen Ginsberg had a group
of students together in the courtyard of the college and they were all

chanting together, "Om, om, om . . ." And he saw me out of the corner of his eye and he went, "Om, om, *shalom* . . ." *[laughter]*.

The other time I spent some time with Hoffman—Bruce, you were present at it—was at the big party here.

Bruce: That was the first time I met him. It was also the first time I met Ginsberg.

Yeah. It was a strange occasion because everybody that was here, either just before that or shortly thereafter he got arrested. It was Abbie Hoffman, Jerry, and Tim Leary. I was there and John Sinclair was there. The one guy that didn't get arrested was Allen Ginsberg. Allen Ginsberg never got arrested. He has a certain amount of built-in caution. He always knows when to withdraw or not be present.

Bruce: He was in Chicago for a while, too. He preached at Chicago.

Either he's lucky or circumspect, and or both.

Figure 10. Leslie (standing, left), during the 1969 University at Buffalo conference on drug use; Allen Ginsberg and Timothy Leary, seated, at center right.

I remember Abbie and Jerry and Mike Levenson shooting pool here at my house. Jerry came down and said, "We've just discovered a proletarian poet from Buffalo." Who turned out to be Mike Levenson. He was a merchant seaman at the time. One of his many careers.

Bruce: An appropriate career. Because he was as close to the Ancient Mariner . . .

I guess we have to throw Mike in that, too. I guess he got arrested at one point or another, or a couple of points.

[pause, then]

Sort of a natural connection between that and the other thing there you wanted to talk about the other day: my strange relationship or non-relationship with the New York intellectuals.

The other time in my life when I served as an interpreter between two groups was at a very strange occasion. IT&T organized a huge conference which was held in Florida. The man in charge of it was an old, old friend of mine, whose name is Mel Tumin, who has been for many years now a professor of sociology at Princeton but was one of the original group of Trotskyites in Madison, Wisconsin. Mel organized the thing and he invited everybody to this. On the one hand he invited all of his old friends from the New York group of Jewish intellectuals. Sidney Hook was there, for instance, and Lionel Trilling was there. Then he decided, in addition to that, he ought to invite some people out of different areas of the world, who ordinarily didn't talk to each other. Among the people who came was Truman Capote. One of the strangest scenes at that whole occasion was Truman Capote dancing with Sally. Truman Capote, when he stood on tiptoe, reached up to her knees. Kate Millett was there, too. Kate Millett and Truman Capote were not talking to Trilling and Hook, and I was the go-between. I was the only one who could talk to both camps. I would carry messages back and forth. This was a strange occasion.

The local headlines—newspapers—were full of ironic headlines about Kate Millett and Truman Capote being there and various other people. Somebody was there from CORE. This was organized by the heart of the military industrial complex, so-called. They paid a lot of money and they fed us very good food.

This was the time I was taken off just a few miles down the road to do a show with Bill Buckley, who was also one of the participants of the thing.

Bruce: This is an incredible array of people.

It really was. They were also very proud of the fact that they had two Nobel Prize winners there: Gunnar Myrdal was there and Saul Bellow was there. The point of the whole thing was that this place, which was on the East Coast, north of most of the other fashionable places, had decided that they wanted to get a branch of the University of Florida set up. So the invited audience were people mostly from the various units of the University of Florida: administrators and faculty members, and so forth.

Bruce: All of whom must have been astonished.

It was kind of hilarious. This was the crazy occasion in which Buckley said to me, "I'll send a car to pick you up." And the car turned out to be driven by an off-duty narc, who when we came to the first place where he had to pay a toll on the highway said to me, "Listen, could you give this guy fifty cents? All I have with me are marked hundred-dollar bills."

This is my fate in life, communicating across what are usually impassable barriers where people don't talk to each other.

Let me talk about this in a kind of general way. Most of those people I hardly knew at all. For instance, when I was beginning to be published as a writer, the place where I was most usually published was the *Partisan Review*. I met Philip Rahv only twice in my life and at that point my communication skills broke down completely, because I found I couldn't talk to Philip Rahv. Philip Rahv's usual style was to say, "When I say thus and thus and thus and so, what do I mean?" And you were supposed to give the answer to that. Which meant that your part of the conversation was just the interpretation of his question. So I really never had any close relationship with him at all.

And then I made a terrible mistake. After I had been writing for them for several years and was thought of in general by people who didn't know much about it as being part of the group, I wrote an article about the *Partisan Review*, which was called "*Partisan Review*: Dodo or Phoenix?" and I came out leaning toward the Dodo side. I received the only letter I ever got from Philip Rahv himself, instead of one of his underlings. He said I was banned forever from the pages of the *Partisan Review*.

Bruce: That's one worth framing.

I think I still have it someplace. I never throw anything away.

The problem was that I never saw those people because I was most of the time in Montana and when I wasn't in Montana, then I was dashing off to Athens or Rome or Bologna or someplace. And the way they lived, they only spoke to each other and they all lived within ten or fifteen blocks of each other. I was learning to talk to other kinds of people. When I went out from the University of Montana, I would go to little, tiny villages and towns in Montana and talk to ladies' reading groups about books. It was the best education I ever got in my life. I learned to talk to ordinary people, a different language. One of the reasons why I stayed in Montana, finally, was I decided it was good for me not to meet anybody really for weeks and months, years at a time, who had not read the same books I had read, understood all the personal references and literary allusions I made, but lived in a completely different set of associations, and so forth. So I had poker-playing friends and friends with whom I would talk about the heating plant and people who taught me how to dig up a garden for the first time. It's a habit I picked up in Montana and it's stuck with me for the rest of my life.

So when I came there *[New York]*, and would go to an occasional party, I always felt like I was a foreigner, a stranger in a strange land. The only group of those people I was ever associated with, I knew in Chicago, not in New York and those were in the very earliest years before I had ever published anything very much at all, practically nothing.

When I was a grad student in Madison, at the University of Wisconsin, when I couldn't bear my fellow graduate students, I would flee to Chicago which was only 150 miles down the pike. I would hitchhike to Chicago and there was a group of people which consisted of Saul Bellow, Isaac Rosenfeld, Lionel Abel, and a guy around whom it all centered, who started out as the most promising writer of all, who actually published two novels and then gave up writing novels and moved into a completely new world. His name was Harold Kaplan; H. J. Kaplan, sometimes known as "Kappy." He wrote for years the "Paris Letter" for the *Partisan Review*. The last member of our group was a very strange guy. Kappy at that time was going to the University of Illinois, and he, like I, used to flee to Chicago. He would occasionally bring with him one of the most fascinating, mad human beings I've ever known in my life, whose name is Willmoore Kendall. Willmoore Kendall was the guru of the far right in those days. He was Buckley's teacher at Yale and gave him his political ideas. Kendall was finally so embarrassingly right wing that Yale bought up the rest of his contract and he went off and lived in Franco's Spain, where he really felt at peace.

We used to have these incredible shouting matches. You can imagine with Lionel there and imagine a right-wing Lionel. Even more right wing than Lionel would become in the years since.

Bruce: Was Lionel always like that?

Lionel was always like that; whatever he believed in, his lack of manners were the same. He never really believed in human beings; only in ideas. And words.

Some years after this whole thing broke up, one night about eleven or twelve o'clock, Willmoore Kendall—the phone rang and the voice on the other end said, "This is Willmoore Kendall; do you remember me?" He said, "I've been brought here to give a speech to YAF," Young Americans for Freedom. "I can't stand these pustular, stupid kids. I need somebody intelligent to talk to. Come to my hotel. But don't let anybody know who you are or that you're coming to see me." I went to see him and the first thing he said to me was, "What ever happened to all those bright, bright young men"—meaning Saul Bellow, Isaac Rosenfeld, Lionel Abel—"and all their dull, dull wives?" He was a ferocious misogynist.

Those were the people that I really knew, and some of those relationships I've kept up. Just last week, as a matter of fact, my phone rang in the middle of the night and a voice on the other end said, "This is Lionel." You could always recognize Lionel's voice, anyhow. He called to tell me that Kappy's wife had just died. So all those old memories came floating back in my head.

With Saul Bellow, I kept up a longtime relationship, which finally broke up completely. For many years I knew him and I visited him at the University of Minnesota when he was there. It was through Saul Bellow that I went to Princeton for the first time. I was in New York on one of my infrequent trips there and I met him and he said, "I'm going down to Princeton to see Mel Tumin. Do you want to come along?" I went along and we sat around and there I met Richard Blackmur for the first time and John Berryman. And with John Berryman and Richard Blackmur there, you can imagine that there was more drinking than eating and more eating than anything else except talking.

As Blackmur got drunker and drunker and drunker, all his misery came out and he began making first anti-Black remarks, then anti-Jewish remarks. Then anti-human remarks. But he and I remained good friends, oddly enough. Because Blackmur was the kind of anti-Semite who always had to have a Jew in residence, so he would always invite to one the position which he had open at Princeton. He was the chief force in deciding who gave the Christian Gauss lectures there, and he brought a person to help him with his creative writing students, who were always Jewish. It was always Saul Bellow, Philip Roth, real Jews.

Bruce: Real Jews.

Yeah: real Jews.

Saul and I drifted further and further apart. He began writing me letters saying things like, "We were never really friends, were we? Why the hell doesn't somebody tell you you're way out in left field?" And the last recorded remark that Saul Bellow has ever made to anybody about me was made to a common friend of ours who he had run into in Amsterdam. It was in the Rijksmuseum. The common friend said, "Leslie's in town; would you like to see him?" And Saul Bellow said, "Leslie Fiedler is the worst fucking thing that ever happened to American literature."

Bruce: Do you know what you did?

Yes, I know what I did to have deserved it. First of all, I developed certain ideas which ran contrary to his almost from the start, but people didn't recognize it at first. Saul resented everything that happened to the world from the moment that modernism had been invented. He was against "angst"; he was against "alienation." He wanted to believe that the old bourgeois humanist values were still alive and well.

That was bad, but even worse was the fact that although I was one of the first people who ever wrote reviews of his books, which assessed him for what he was worth, at his true worth, after a while I stopped reviewing him. He's a very paranoid fellow, and he sat there saying, "Leslie isn't reviewing my books. It means he hates me. Why does that bastard hate my books?"

We did meet him with his last wife. When we were younger and more foolish, he would usually bring me to see the woman he was about to marry and ask my advice, and I would always say things like, "If I saw her coming down the street, I would cross to the other side." And then he would marry her. But this time it was very polite. Sally was with me. This is his most recent.

But in the days when I knew him in Chicago, he had not yet published his first book and all of those bright, bright young men were all living on the money that their dull, dull wives made working at various kinds of jobs. And waiting for it all to happen. I felt a real connection to him because though I never knew him there, before he went back to Chicago again, he and Isaac had both been at the University of Wisconsin, where they were both close associates and friends and students of a very fascinating guy, who went right wing before any of them. His name was Eliseo Vivas. He was a Colombian or Venezuelan, I forget. He was from South America, and he always referred to Isaac and Saul by code names. So those were the people I did know and with whom in various ways I kept in touch.

But the people who were associated with the *Partisan Review* I hardly knew. Delmore Schwartz I only met at Harvard. He was there when I was there in '46, '47. He was doing some Briggs Copeland thing. *[A Harvard visiting lectureship for writers.]* At that point he couldn't be reached. He came to have dinner with us one night. He had published some of my poetry; a good deal of it—as a matter of fact—in those days. We had exchanged letters. When he came he was very drunk because he wasn't sure that we would have the proper drink for him—he was drinking nothing but gin at that point—he had a hip flask full of gin with him. He was the last man I ever saw carrying a hip flask in the modern world. It seemed like the 1920s.

All my early stuff was published in that little cluster of magazines which was associated with them. Not only *Partisan Review* but *Commentary* and *The New Leader*. And when it was started in England, *Encounter*, of which Irving Kristol and Stephen Spender were the editors. The back pages in *The New Leader* were presided over in those days by Isaac, and in some ways I remained a close friend with him.

I published a lot in *Encounter*. The one person out of that whole group of editors who actually became a close friend—we were very close indeed for a while, but now we are completely alienated from each other; in the past ten years we've exchanged two or three stiff letters—was Irving Kristol. He was the best editor I ever worked with in my life. When he queried me about something in one of my articles, it would usually turn out he had seen something which I had missed absolutely, and it would take me in the direction where I could do something better than I had done before. He was smart, smart, smart. But he was made to be an all-rightnik; even when he was a Trotskyist, he used to wear double-breasted suits. It was considered hilarious.

Diane: What's interesting is that Encounter *was a CIA-funded publication.*

There's no doubt that the CIA funded at least two of those journals. *The New Leader* was a social-democratic thing and was run by a marvelous man called Saul Levitas, who would say when I met him occasionally—his son is now the editor of *The New York Times Book Review*, Michael Levitas—Saul Levitas would meet me on the street and say *[in Yiddish accent]*, "You write something for me? I can't give you enough money, but at least enough to buy a baseball bat for one of your children." He was absolutely open about having CIA money. Stephen Spender always pretended that he didn't know that *Encounter* was being funded by the CIA.

In my funny way, I live in all worlds. The journal that exposed the CIA backing of *Encounter* was a magazine called *Ramparts*, of which I was a contributing editor. So I figured I was on both sides. It didn't bother me, as long as they printed what I wrote, I don't care who pays for it. But it was considered very bad form.

I knew Irving Howe a little. I knew him from the Trotskyist movement. But he disapproved of me from the very start.

Diane: Why?

Mostly because I had a sense of humor, something which he lacks entirely. Two things he lacks: the first thing I knew from the moment I met him, the second thing was pointed out by Randall Jarrell in an article many years ago which said, "The only trouble when Irving Howe writes about literature is the fact that Irving Howe hates literature. Politics failed him and he had to find some business he could go into."

The real problem was that our branch of the Trotskyists in Madison, Wisconsin, was always in trouble because we were too boho *[bohemian]* for them. I mean in some ways our lifestyle came more out of the leftover twenties than it did out of the thirties. The little house where most of us lived had two names, which showed the two sides of our heads. One of its names was the "State Street Soviets" and the other was the "Goat's Nest."

He never thought I took it seriously, and when I consider the fact that somehow I realized in back of all this that it was a little absurd for a group which, as we used to say in those days, could hold its conventions in a telephone booth to think of changing the world. It was really like being crazy, except you were crazy with twelve people instead of just one. You had a vision of reality which didn't correspond with anybody else's vision of reality.

There were many things which left me alienated from those people, not only the fact—which I was talking about earlier—that I had learned to talk another language in the hinterlands of America; and not only the fact that I somehow thought that this was all a great joke on the world, and the greatest joke of all would be if the revolution really worked—at which point I would go into immediate opposition. Trotsky had a very highfalutin name for that. He called it "the Permanent Revolution": as soon as there was a revolution, there had to be another one.

But I was also a proper academic, which none of them were. The funny part of it is, they all ended up teaching after a while, when everything collapsed under them. And none of them had gone through the regular PhD regime. Not a single one. Irving Howe not; even Alfred Kazin not. Certainly not Philip Rahv, who taught at Rutgers toward the end of his life. As a matter of fact, they were ferociously anti-academic. It was considered the worst thing in the world to be involved with the academy, the university (they never said "the university," they always said "the academy"). Because the tradition they came out of was a tradition of nonacademic intellectuals, and the only person they admired who was a proper professor was Richard Blackmur —

Diane: Who wasn't —

—who never went to college at all, much less got any graduate degrees.

Diane: Was he thought to be political?

He was, but he always described himself as "conservative/anarchist," which is as good a description as any. At least he wasn't a Stalinist, like his buddy Kenneth Burke.

Bruce: I didn't know Burke was a Stalinist.

Burke was a Stalinist and Malcolm Cowley was a Stalinist.

Malcolm Cowley is the man who kept me out of the Institute of Arts and Letters for many, many years. He never forgave me for the article which I wrote about the Rosenbergs.

Diane: Did Burke remain a Stalinist?

No, at the end of his life he was not. But Cowley always sort of kept the vestiges of it to the bitter end. Maybe it's a personality type. Somebody (a Stalinist) once said to me, "If I heard you reading a selection from the Old Testament, I would know you were a Trotskyist." Just style. Stalinists have a certain style. I can walk into a room and see who the old Stalinists were, though they may be twenty years away from their involvement.

And then, of course, the other thing which separated me from all those people and from the great tradition of American writers, is I was actually a member of the military forces.

Bruce: Did they all avoid it?

They all avoided that in one way or another; so did everybody else: Melville, Hawthorne, Henry James. Mark Twain was the only American writer who ever joined the military forces. He joined the Confederate side and he deserted after ten days when somebody fired a bullet and he realized you can die this way. Mark Twain has the very great distinction of having been a rebel and a deserter.

I remember when I wore my officer's naval uniform for the first time, I ended up at a party with Paul Goodman, whom I knew slightly, too, mostly because his closest friend was married to an old, old Newark friend, a woman I had known when I was a kid in high school. We had a rather passionate discussion at the time. It was a little embarrassing to me because I never knew exactly why I had joined. I volunteered. I had two kids.

Bruce: You could have avoided it.

Easily. But all of my students were disappearing, and I thought in my crazy way, "I'm not going to be cheated out of the experience of a whole generation I'm growing up in. I don't have to believe in war to be in it." I knew very well from the literature I read that after you're in it ten minutes nobody believes in anything but surviving and getting home, whatever the war, whatever side you're on, whatever the hell you're fighting for. So I went off and did it.

Saul didn't. He writes a book, *Dangling Man*, where he talks about waiting for the thing. Isaac spent the war as captain of a garbage barge on the Hudson River. None of the other people went.

Paul Goodman was a sad fellow, and I never knew him very well, but I kind of liked him for reasons which I never explained even to myself very well. But the last time I saw him, he had gone to a meeting of new-style anarchists, who weren't pacifists at all the way he was. He put his arm around my shoulder and he said, "They spit on me as I walked out of the room." I think Abbie ran into a little of that feeling too. Toward the end of his life the kids were going in completely different directions than which he was going. But it happened to him even earlier. He got up at a meeting—I can't remember the president of Yale—but he tried to lead the crowd in a chant of "Fuck president so and so." And instead, they shouted back, being in high spirits, "Fuck Abbie Hoffman." He was able then to take it as a joke. It was the super-joke.

I've never lived in New York in my life, as it happens. I went to school in New York, in the Bronx, to a part of NYU that was called "The Heights." It was a little, tiny arts college of fifteen hundred people. But I used to commute every day; two hours each goddamned way, back and forth by trolley car, tubes, subway. I used to cheat on the tubes. You had a little ticket they punched and you'd spread a newspaper on your lap and you'd get the part that was punched out and stick it back in and spread a little dirt over it and you could get three or four rides for the one price.

I lived once for thirty days in New York when I was sent to Advanced Naval Intelligence School. It's pronounced "anus" for the acronym.

I taught one summer at Columbia and they gave me a university apartment and I lived there. That was when I got to know Cal *[Robert]* Lowell. I was drifting around New York at that point. It must have been in the early sixties or late fifties; somewhere between '59 and '62. When I knew him he was in one of his up phases. I mean when he was not in the pit of despair, he glowed with a golden glow. He was one of the most beautiful human beings when he was in his good time.

I would always come into New York as a kind of a tourist and a stranger. As I think I said to you last time, it was in those years that I was slowly being turned into a populist underneath my Marxist skin. That really began to happen when I was in Madison. We had joined the Young Progressives. We thought we would penetrate them and win them over. Stalinists had moved in, the Trotskyists had moved in. The rest of us didn't care. We were mostly interested in having picnics and seeing who could drink the most beer. I remember having a contest one night with a Stalinist. We began screaming at each other, but as we drank more and more beer, we got more and more loving. He was a guy who had actually fought in Spain, and he used to tell me how he would take a sack full of hand grenades and go out and kill Trotskyists as well as Fascists or anarchists, all the enemies of the people, whoever wasn't on the right side. But he passed out first, and I carried him home on my back. So I figured that was one for the old man.

Lionel *[Abel]* was incredible, really. He could be one of the funniest human beings. I can remember some of the things he said. He was once talking about why Norman Podhoretz admired Norman Mailer so much, and he said, "He finally met an intellectual who was even dumber than he is."

I was the one who recommended to the committee that was making the choice for Norman Podhoretz to be the editor of *Commentary*. He is a good editor. I mean mechanically. He's very good at keeping a thing going and getting writers lined up, and whatever the hell it is an editor does. But when I meet those people I can hardly talk to them at all, though Lionel Trilling was always very nice to me, so as old followers of Trilling, they always feel they have to be at least passably polite.

Diane: Did you know Midge Decter?

I knew Midge Decter before she was associated with *Commentary*. I knew her before I knew Norman.

Diane: Did she change?

No. She's always the same. She was always ferocious. Her politics have changed a little bit. Nobody ever changes. Lionel is the same mad Lionel he always was and will be to the day of his death. But those people were proper intellectuals. Proper academics. They had a regular route they would take. They would pass out of Lionel Trilling's hands and they were sent to Downing College to work with F. R. Leavis. Steven Marcus was another one of those products.

Bruce: He taught at the School of Letters one summer, the same summer John Berryman was there. Berryman was trying to pick up a stonecutter's girlfriend one night and was about to get killed. I was the bartender in the bar. I told him he had to stop because these guys were going to beat him up. Finally, I just picked him up and I carried him out of the bar. Steven Marcus was following me out of the bar pounding on my back, saying, "Do you know who that man is? He's a famous poet!"

I did two spells in the School of Letters. It began as that strange alliance between the *Kenyon Review* and the *Partisan Review*. The first time I went there I was still pretty young. It was 1952, which makes me thirty-five. It was just after it moved to Indiana *[from Kenyon College]*. The faculty that year consisted of Kenneth Burke, John Crowe Ransom, Richard Blackmur, Randall Jarrell, Robert Fitzgerald, and me. Jarrell and Fitzgerald and I were known as "The Boys." We used to sneak off and swim in the quarries.

We had some distinguished students. The one who the students thought was their prize student was Hilton Kramer. He still owes me a paper from a course he took with me. Hilton Kramer also flunked his exam which we gave him. He came into this group which consisted of Blackmur and Burke and so forth, and thought he was going to be asked questions about the New Criticism and the first thing they did was toss him two lines of poetry which rhymed and happened to come from Shelley, and say, "Where does that come from." And he said, "heroic couplet." He was dead.

The second year I went there, William Empson taught. There was a famous story that he was supposed to give the—there were a series of evening lectures, and his lecture was announced as a lecture on "poetry and criticism." A nice general title. He probably said give it the most general title *[thinking]*, "I can talk about anything." He appeared dressed in a Chinese Communist uniform, drunk out of his skull, spilled his drink over his notes, teetered on the edge of the platform the whole time he was there, with people betting whether he would fall over or not, and delivered an impassioned attack on United States foreign policy in defense of the Maoist regime.

Diane: Did you ever hear him talk about religion?

I've heard him talk about everything. I used to go and talk with him during the time we were there that summer. I would walk into that miserable flat of his, which consisted of nothing but piled-up dishes which had spilled out over the floor, stuck together. He had a way of feeding himself by combining two cans of anything which he picked at random off the shelf. I walked in the first time and he said, "You know, you Americans believe we British are filthy. But I *am* filthy." We had great political discussions, but we would talk about lots of other things, too. He was great when he talked about something he knew about. He was a little naïve about politics. His wife was really intelligent about politics, and he got his ideas secondhand from her.

We had an impassioned discussion one night about the Maoist regime, which started at 7:30 or 8:00 in the evening and it got to be four in the morning and at that point Margaret was calling the police. She thought we had been in some terrible accident, and we were having a friendly discussion.

The man I truly admired in that whole group was John Crowe Ransom.

Bruce: He was Berryman's closest friend.

He was Randall's friend, too. Randall I liked on sight. We discovered we shared several strange tastes. We were both very fond of Kipling and fairy tales and so forth.

Ransom used to say, "Call me John." But I was never very able to call him anything but "Mr. Ransom." He seemed to come out of a different world which had ceased to exist before I was born. I would send stories to the *Kenyon Review* and he would say, "Where did you ever meet people like that?"

That school was a marvelous idea in the beginning. Two of the papers that were written for me while I was there were published immediately: one became the core of Mark Spilka's book on *[D. H.]* Lawrence. Jim Cox was one of my students. His first published article on the sad initiation of *Huckleberry Finn* was written as a paper for that course. He went to Dartmouth and is now retired. Another of my students who's retired before me.

Bruce: He gave a class on teaching that we were all required to take there. It was one of the best classes I had in graduate school.

He was a great teacher, known as "Gentleman Jim."

Bruce: He was wonderful. The worst course I had was given by Mark Spilka. He had this very tiny handwriting, like someone who wrote Greek. He would come in with this big sheaf of papers, all handwritten, which he would never look up from for a three-hour class. He just read. it was horrible.

You can imagine having a class full of Jim Coxes and Mark Spilkas. Most of those people are students who have now retired and fellow faculty members who are by and large dead. Even "The Boys." Fitzgerald is dead and Jarrell is dead. I did a little thing for a memorial volume for Jarrell, talking about our swimming in the quarries. He couldn't swim. He never learned. He would paddle around, holding on to a log.

I was uninvited to come back there because I wrote a story full of people who were identified. It was fiction, but it was based a little on what happened to me that summer. It was called "Pull Down Vanity." The only character who was done close to life was Blackmur. The main character I made by combining myself and Randall Jarrell in an absolutely improbable way.

He was a strange teacher. He taught at girls' schools, and one of the things he did was to stand in front of a class and read some lines of a favorite poem of his and look up at the class and say, "Isn't that dovey?" But he was smart. He wrote one of the best essays on Whitman anybody ever wrote. It's called "Walt Whitman: He Had His Nerve." That's his style.

I forgot one person. Francis Fergusson also taught with us.

Bruce: At the School of Letters? He was Dick Lewis's uncle.

Yes. If you know Dick Lewis even a little, you realize how improbable an encounter between him and Abbie Hoffman is. The only thing that saved Dick Lewis is the fact that he's married to a nice Jewish girl.

Bruce: Nancy? I never knew Nancy was Jewish.

Her father was Jewish. Dick descends from a long line of Episcopalian clergymen. Dick was a good friend in the days when we were in Princeton. Two masters of Calhoun College I knew both turned out to be in Princeton in those days: Dick Lewis on the one hand, and Charlie Davis. The idea that Charlie Davis became Master of Calhoun College . . . He kept that picture of Calhoun up over his desk all the time! His son was just in Buffalo; he gave a concert. He's a jazz pianist, Tony Davis. Marvelous.

Bruce: I was on my way to law school and had some courses with Dick Lewis and that's how I wound up going into literature. It was in between when I was in engineering school and starting law school.

Dick Lewis in those days was teaching at Rutgers. He always wanted to be in Princeton, but they wouldn't let him in. Princeton was miserable. He lived in Princeton. Princeton: all the good people either they never let in at all or they fired as quick as they could. Julian Moynihan was absolutely first-rate. O. B. Hardison. It was unclear whether he quit or they fired him, but they made life a little impossible. He was just brand-new. Most of the faculty was unendurable.

Diane: Did you know D. W. Robertson, the Shakespearian, at Princeton?

Not really: I ran into him once or twice. I knew Magoon in the days when I was at Harvard. He was a strange man. He was a real Nazi. He wore patent leather shoes when he went out in the evening. F. P. Magoon. Now the Harvard English Department is as bad as Princeton was at its worst.

Diane: Who was the great one at Harvard who said, "Who is competent to examine me?"

Bruce: George Lyman Kittredge.

Diane: Kittredge. Did you know him?

No, I didn't know him. But one of my oldest and best friends in the world, who just recently died, a guy called Seymour Betsky, who spent the whole last part of his life teaching in a Dutch university, the University of Utrecht, was Kittridge's last assistant.

Bruce: This whole relationship of you to that New York gang, it says something about what gangs are. Because from the outside, it looks like people like you were absolutely central to that crowd for all those many years.

I know it does. Even when I had just sent two articles or book reviews to the *Partisan Review*, there was an article attacking the *Partisan Review* which appeared in the *Hudson Review* or some place, listing me as one of the monstrous gang. But they never accepted me.

My closest relationship with that group was through a marvelous woman—I don't know what her official title was, but she was a woman of all work there. She did all the work. She did a lot of the reading. Her name was Catharine Carver; Katy Carver.

The best magazine editor I ever met was Irving Kristol; the best book editor I ever met was Katy Carver. Katy Carver was a woman who thought she was a writer when she started and was disappointed and never recovered from it. Her love life never worked out. She made one ill-fated relationship after another. The great love of her life was Ralph Manheim, the great translator of both French and German, who also is an old friend of mine. Katy could never make any kind of a permanent relationship with him. She finally went to England, where she worked for Oxford University Press, and took a job with them doing schoolbooks. All the while she was doing that she kept in touch with her boys; and whoever we did books with, she would read them. I was one. Saul Bellow was another. What's his name, the Henry James man, the guy who did the gigantic book on James? Oh, shit: anyway: it's an endless list.

I think one of her dreams was that when Saul Bellow got the Nobel Prize—which she never doubted for a moment that he would—that he'd send her enough money for a new dress and invite her to come and see it. But in his typical fashion he managed to pick a fight with her, too, and the thing blew up.

I recommended her for various PEN prizes which are given to editors, but she refuses and takes her name off the list. She was one person I could really talk to.

It was through Katy and Ralph Manheim, who lived summers out in East Hampton, which in those days you could still get crummy places, that I met Jackson Pollock, who it turned out was a great admirer of "Come Back to the Raft Ag'in, Huck Honey." It appealed to his Western soul. I had a chance to watch him work in the early fifties.

Diane: He died not long after that.

Yes.

I had an interesting experience recently. People who are doing a gigantic, monumental, really beautiful book on Jackson Pollock asked me to read the manuscript of it recently and help them put it together, knowing I have a special feeling for him.

The first time I laid eyes on one of his abstract paintings, I said "That's a Western painter. That's a Western landscape." Recently I went out to Montana and some group asked me to talk and I talked on two Western painters, Charlie Russell and Jackson Pollock. His early paintings actually had Western subjects: canoes going down river, Indians. But the palette remained the same.

Bruce: Leon Edel! [Remembering the name of the Henry James biographer a few minutes earlier: Henry James: A Biography, 5 volumes, 1953–1972.]

Leon Edel. He really milked it. Katy worked through all those books.

Katy was the one who worked with me the first time I ever tried to put a book together, *Love and Death in the American Novel.* She got me to cut two hundred pages out of the original manuscript. At one point

I knew I would either hate her for life or love her forever. It's love her forever that I do.

Diane: Did she really have a hand in all the Boys' books?

Oh, yes, she did. She was an active editor. She would query things, and you would have to fight to the death to save them. If you could convince her, fine. Much of this she did after hours. She had no other life, except her books. She always went home with a pile of manuscripts. I think somebody told me she's living in Italy now. By the time she was forty or forty-five, she decided she was going to be an old woman.

Bruce: Is the Pollack-Russell thing written or do you just talk it?

I just talked it; I never wrote it. I may try to put it together sometime. They have a special meaning for me, because they are the two painters I didn't buy when I could have afforded to, because I couldn't afford to even at the price. I could have bought a Charlie Russell for fifty bucks. I didn't have the fifty bucks. They were hanging in saloons where he traded them for drinks. The man who was in charge of art lectures in the course which I ran for many years in Montana, called Introduction to the Humanities, once said, "I consider it my duty to teach people that Rembrandt is good and Charlie Russell is bad."

We really thought we were Apostles to the Gentiles. Almost all of us came from the East or the Midwest.

Bruce: John Ford collected Russells. He used them to design some of his movies.

You can see it.

Bruce: He knew him as a young man.

There were lots of people who used to talk about Charlie Russell as a living memory when I first went to Montana. It was a long time ago, but he was gone already in '41 when I first went there.

Bruce: A lot of people came to Montana in living memory —

Nobody in Montana went back more than three generations. People would talk about their grandfathers and grandmothers, and they were pioneers. A lot of them from Virginia, like many Western states. They were refugees from the Civil War and they came into Montana. Montana had an anti-miscegenation law on its books for many years because of that.

There had been a Communist who was the head librarian in Montana just before I came there. We had the most improbable books. We had an internal theoretical organ of the Communist Party from those days, which was called *The Communist*, as well as huge piles of *The New*

Masses, and Henry Roth's *Call It Sleep,* which was on the shelf in the library in Montana where I discovered it.

The man who had the office next to mine in those days thought of himself as a Socialist. He was an assistant professor of political science, specializing in the Far East along with Mike Mansfield. Mansfield was known only as "Mike" to all the inhabitants and former inhabitants of the state of Montana. There's only one Mike Mansfield. He had been a miner and a member of the old Marines in China in the real old days, the "horse" Marines. So he could get votes from everybody: he had the union votes, he got the military—"we love our military"—vote; he was a Roman Catholic. Montana is a Catholic state. The senators almost have to be Catholics.

I suppose next to the Catholics and the Mormons, the Protestants come up a poor third. There had been a number of Jews in Missoula and throughout the state in the old, old days. A lot of Jews came out, the way that Goldwater's family came out, settlers, and so forth. But they used to say in Missoula: there were more Jews in the graveyard than there were on the streets. We could get a *minyan* together only if somebody had some visitors from back East.

A few Jews gradually began to come into the university. The local state organizer for the AF of L was a Jew. The best defense lawyer in town was a Jew. I once saw him get a guy acquitted. He used to invite me down for his cases. It was theater for him. The guy had pumped five bullets into the back of a man. With six witnesses, he got him acquitted, mostly by bringing the accused's three little girls to walk back and forth in front of the jury with their white smocks on and bows in their hair.

Bruce: I remember a bar in Missoula with wonderful portrait photos.

Eddie's Club. It had those photographs by Lee Nye. Lee Nye did the first picture of me that ever went on a book jacket. Bars were the best thing in Missoula.

Montana has always been full of writers. A guy I knew, who had a difficult book, after a while we began a relationship and we began to think of ourselves as old friends; he was Bud Guthrie, A. B. Guthrie. He came from Montana, lived for many years in Kentucky and moved back to Montana, and died there. He taught in the university during his life there.

Figure 11. Leslie giving one of the keynote talks at 1977 Institute of the American West conference on "The American Hero"; he is bracketed by Paul Krassner on the left and Bruce Jackson and Greil Marcus on the right.

3

April 30, 1989

I've just been involved sort of long-distance in a lawsuit. My lifelong publisher went bankrupt.

Bruce: Sol Stein?

Yes. Somebody wrote me a fan letter the other day asking for a signed picture, saying, "I have just read your latest book and enjoyed it very much." This is a book called *Fiedler on the Roof*, which Stein & Day was supposed to publish but never did. We never even signed a contract for it, but it had been announced in his publicity. And now I am wondering if his receivers bootlegged the book. I've never seen the book, I never saw galleys —

Sally: We're trying to track this guy who wrote the letter down.

My other theory is this guy was just lying, that he just got the thing out of *Books in Print*, where it is actually listed.

Sally: We called the people who have the rights to the book now, or would if Leslie had ever signed anything. They said, "Oh, we're out of stock, we're trying to figure out whether to do a reprint."

I'd submitted the book. It had been informally accepted. He had actually advertised it. But knowing what was coming up, I guess, he held off signing the contract so I would keep the rights.

Bruce: I can find out if a copyright exists for it in the Copyright Office.

The point is, I know that book does not physically exist at all. Meanwhile, I've sold the book to another publisher. With the same title, which I love. I like the publisher and I would like to deal with him; David Godine. Does that mean anything to you?

Diane: Yes. He's a good publisher.

Yeah. He makes pretty books and he's somebody I can talk to.
Diane: When did this happen? When did you get this letter?
Sally: A week ago.

The guy who wrote me apparently exists. He is listed—as having an unlisted number. The whole thing is really insane.

Bruce: I have had two books plagiarized. One was an anthology of nineteenth-century articles. I edited and annotated. It's not the sort of thing that anybody has in his head. This book was published by Quadrangle. It's the sort of book I ordinarily would have been sent to blurb or review. There are, as you know, certain books you automatically get. This had a differ-ent first article, a different last article, and one other article was different. Everything else was all stuff from my anthology. Then about two years later there was a criminology book. I'd done a book called A Thief's Primer. *It was based on interviews with a safecracker and a check-writer. I commented on the interviews and I got other people to comment on them. A few years later, guy out in California published a book about a professional thief who was a safecracker and a check-writer, which my guy was. The interviews were different, but it had exactly the same structure. You can't do anything. But guess what was the only book of that kind of criminology not listed in his bibliography?*

The thing was a lot of headaches long before that because nobody knew what was going to happen to my rights. Sol Stein had kept almost all of my books in print.

Bruce: You used to be with Beacon. Was he with Beacon when you first took up with him?

Sol was an advisory editor for Beacon. The first three books he published with Beacon were *[Richard Wright's] Notes of a Native Son, An End to Innocence,* and, for the first time in America, *[George Orwell's] Homage to Catalonia.* All in 1955.

Diane: Wow!

Bruce: Is he totally out now? Is he doing anything else?

The thing is now owned by something called BookCrafters, who apparently made his books and who are chief creditors.

Bruce: In Michigan?

In Michigan.

Bruce: We've used them. They printed our computer book.

They're playing with the notion of going into the publishing busi-ness, which drags the whole thing out.

Bruce: Who owns the rights to all your books? Did they go with that or do you have them personally?

I own the copyrights but he owned the publishing rights so they've got it. They got it; it's in their hands. Godine would also like to bring back into print three of my other books. I've written a formal letter to them, asking if the books are in print. If the books are not in print for six months, then the rights revert back to me. That's more or less standard.

Sol Stein went through the wringer on the whole thing. Apparently he got screwed in every possible way, which I don't understand fully. After a while he wasn't writing to me anymore, but he would call me up and in hushed tones, for fear that his staff or somebody else was listening, he'd tell me what was happening. He's writing a book about the whole thing.

Bruce: Who's going to publish it?

He'll sell it to someone. All his books are published by other people. He's published a lot of books.

Bruce: His novel The Magician *did very well.*

It was strange having him as a publisher, because after a while he began to think he was my mother. He would tell me what was good for me.

Bruce: I remember you saying that after The Magician *came out, he was giving you advice on writing fiction. You said, "Do you know what he SAID?"*

The only way *Love and Death in the American Novel* is in print now is in Penguin. It took Penguin—English Penguin—all these years to decide that this was a classic and about five years ago they put it in print.

Bruce: Is it in other languages?

It's in Japanese; it's in Italian; it's in German; it's in French; it's in Thai. It's in Thai!

Bruce: But not in America.

It's not available in America.

Diane: That's a nice blurb from George [for Fiedler's The Inadvertent Epic*].*

Steiner? When I delivered the Christian Gauss lectures, which were the beginning of this book, in Princeton in 1957, there was a wise-ass young kid in the back row, who asked embarrassing questions. It turned out to be George Steiner. He then talked his way into some position at the Institute *[for Advanced Study]* there. God only knows how.

Bruce: George is a great character.

He's a very strange character.

Bruce: I like George. He's perverse —

It's hard to like him, but you can do it.

Bruce: Did I tell you about when we visited him in England? As you know, he's got a withered right arm. The previous time I'd seen him, I'd stuck out my right hand to shake hands; he stuck out his left hand. So I took my right hand back and we shook with left hands. Before we went to visit him, Diane and I had stopped off at the Fitzwilliam and had bought a bunch of things, so we had packages. I said, "He shakes hands with his left hand," so we shifted all the packages to our right hands. He opens the door, looks at the packages, puts out his right hand.

His great enemy and oldest friend/enemy in the whole world is Al Alvarez. They were in Oxford together. Al claims Steiner has a perfectly good arm which he keeps strapped to his side and wears the other one for sympathy. Al tells marvelous stories about him. He tells about taking George home with him when they were fellow students together, and Al's mother kept walking around the table, looking at George and looking at him. She finally called Al out in the kitchen, "Al, I don't like that boy. He looks like he plays with himself." They've been swapping maliciousness for many generations.

George is hated in England by most people —

Diane: And in America, too.

—because at one point he was being paid more than anybody else in England because C. P. Snow had made this special sort of chair for him in the college he was in.

Diane: I thought he wasn't being paid by Cambridge.

He wasn't being paid by Cambridge. He was never a proper don at all, but he was a Fellow of the College. Snow set up some special chair in the college for him, not in the university. Churchill College, or whatever the hell it's called. Then he went to Geneva. One of his problems is he doesn't know where he belongs.

There's another famous story—which obviously I got through Al Alvarez—about him. George was once the chairman of a conference, which had some people speaking. It was done in English, but people had come from France and Germany, and so forth. Isaiah Berlin was the one representative from England. At the end of it George got up and he said, "One of our problems here is though we are all speaking English, it's not the native language of any of us. Your language is French; your language is German; I don't know whether my language is French, German, or English. And you, Sir Isaiah, I suppose your native language is Yiddish?" That's as far as the story goes. Silence and consternation.

Personally, he's always been very nice to me.

Bruce: I met him through a mutual friend at the Institute for Sex Research in Bloomington, a sociologist named John Gagnon. Then he turned up at Harvard while I was a Junior Fellow. That surprised me because Harry Levin and those guys were very snooty about people like George. And then, immediately the next semester, Harry had a visiting job in Cambridge. Things worked their way through my naïveté.

You began to learn how the academic world really works.

Diane: When Love and Death *first came out, did it cause a scandal?*

When it first came out, it did indeed cause a scandal. I mean, there were all kinds of problems with it. I seem to be dogged by bankruptcy all my life long. The first edition was published by a small fly-by-night publisher who went bankrupt on the day it was supposed to be published. The book was in print, but all the copies were locked away in a warehouse. But fortunately, somebody bought them out and it got circulated.

Most of the reviews of it ranged from condescending to scandalized. But for reasons which I don't understand, a review of it appeared on the front page of *The New York Times Book Review*, and it was done by Malcolm Cowley. Malcolm Cowley has never liked me all his life long, and he intended for this review to be as nasty as possible. But it turned out to be, as they say in the trade, "a selling review." That is to say, what he said about it, though it was not favorable, was intriguing to people who bought it and so the book began to sell. It's not been out of print from that day until this. It's been translated into many, many languages, printed several times in paperback in England and the United States; published in England; published over and over again. And when Stein & Day came into existence, he bought the rights for it and kept it in print continuously.

The only understanding review of the book which appeared when it came out was by Benjamin DeMott. It was a little condescending, too, but at least he understood what was happening in the book and what I was doing.

It's a book which had the same fate as all the rest of my books, almost all the rest of my books. It began by everybody saying what a miserable thing it was and then suddenly without anybody changing his mind in print ever, passed to a second stage where people began ripping it off without acknowledgment; and then the third stage where everybody suddenly decided it was a classic. So a classic it is. You know, it's in the John Kennedy Library, it's in the José Martí Library in Havana, Cuba.

It's become a standard book in American literature, without anybody, except Ben DeMott, who is the honorable exception, saying anything intelligent about it. Some of the English reviewers were better, though many of them took it to be an anti-American book. And those Englishmen who were pro-American said, "Fiedler is fouling his own nest." That's a direct quote from one of the reviews which appeared. So it's been a strange book with a strange fate.

I did a revised edition of it, but it's a strange kind of revised edition. I didn't change anything in it, I didn't add anything to it, but I cut it down, slimmed it down. It was too long to begin with. I told you last time that Catharine Carver had persuaded me to cut it down by a couple hundred pages, and I myself cut it down by nearly another hundred pages. I think it's better for being slimmer. I did a little rearranging. It's at least sixty-five or seventy pages slimmer. At least that.

Even before it came into existence as a book, the article from which it came, which is the first article I ever published that anybody ever noticed (mostly they noticed to say cruel things about it), was "Come Back to the Raft Ag'in, Huck Honey." Even Philip Rahv, who was the editor of *Partisan Review* and who accepted it, said after *Love and Death* came out, "I didn't realize you took those things seriously. I wouldn't have printed the thing in the first place unless I had thought it was intended to be a *boutade*, a put-on, a joke."

Diane: Did you believe him?

I guess I believe him. I don't understand why he printed it at all. I think it was printed over his head or behind his back or something. I had said some unkind things about his own criticism in print in between, and maybe that had something to do with it. It was before I had my complete falling out with the *Partisan Review* over that article called "Dodo or Phoenix?"

Diane: Did it have any progenitors as far as you were concerned?

This book? I think I acknowledged it in a preface. The book which most influenced me was *[D. H.]* Lawrence's *Studies in Classic American Literature*. That for sure was on my mind, except that I wanted to move it further. The interesting thing that occurred to me as I sat and pondered some of the things that Lawrence said in *Studies in Classic American Literature* was that Lawrence had not dealt with a single American book which had in it a Black character. Not one. As far as he was concerned, America had only two colors, Red and White. He says someplace, "I came to America kindled by Fenimore Cooper." And he finally found the place to live in the country, in the Southwest, where he could live close to the Indians. He didn't write about Mark Twain. He stayed away from almost everything.

Later on it occurred to me that there was another lack in his *Studies in Classic American Literature*, but I sort of fell into that trap in *Love and Death* and have only been trying to make up for it since: it's a book which deals with American literature without dealing with a single book written by a woman.

One of the strange things that happened long after this book came out is—you know a little about this, I think—I had a series of nasty letters from Gershon Legman, insisting that I had cribbed some of his ideas in the book. But actually, I had written about Gershon Legman to say all the ways in which I disagreed with him. It was a rather insulting piece. And what was much on my mind were the places where he and I were wide apart. If his book had any influence on me at all, it wasn't in the front of my mind when I wrote. I was attempting to occupy a space it seemed to me he had neglected, too.

I think I insulted Gershon Legman, because in the early days he signed his articles "G. Legman," and the letter I wrote to him first was addressed to "Miss" Legman. I assumed that the reason for using the single initial was that he was a woman trying to disguise it. He didn't seem to like that. It was not meant as a deliberate put-down of any kind, but it was an unfortunate incident.

It was also a book written against the books about American literature which I had read before reading it. I thought American literature was immensely interesting, but the only book about American literature, which had been written before that was interesting in itself, was Lawrence's. The other books made American literature sound as dull as they were. Matthiessen was a little on my mind, but his book was not much use to me one way or the other. He was going in such different directions. As a very young man I had read Parrington a lot, but it took a long time before Parrington really worked on me because that kind of populist approach —

Bruce: I haven't heard anyone mention Parrington in years. I really liked him.

Matthiessen acknowledges in a footnote in his own book that he was influenced by Parrington.

Parrington was a Western writer, so I felt very close to him. In the years that I lived in Montana, Seattle was the nearest big city. That was where he held forth. There was Parrington Hall, in which the English Department was housed, but somehow he had disappeared from sight. I still have a copy of Parrington around. It's a book I look at from time to time. It's full of crazy stuff. But even when it's crazy, it's useful and fruitful. It takes you in certain directions.

Love and Death had progeny, because really I think of this as the first volume in a trilogy, and perhaps even in a tetralogy. It was followed by *Waiting for the End*, which brings the book a little bit more up to date. This book stops at about 1950. And then *The Return of the Vanishing American* is the third book. And maybe even *What Was Literature?* can be thought of as the fourth book in the series. I would like ideally for the thing to be brought out in three volumes together.

[*Love and Death* is the book] that most people know and read, and by now it's rather disconcerting. People approach me who seem to be elderly, with gray hair, wrinkled, and so forth, and they say, "I read your book when I was a freshman in college," or "I was introduced to it when I was a sophomore."

It's the same effect that my family has on me. I never feel how old I am, even looking at myself in the mirror. But when I look at my kids, then I know.

Other people have been influenced a little by the book; they've done the proper thing with it. I'm a teacher who really hates to have anybody as a disciple or follower; I want them to find themselves. I think of Jim Cox, who was my student to begin with, as being, in a way, my cultural or spiritual descendant, thought when he wrote his book on Mark Twain, he wrote it against things which I said. But at least I had defined the questions for him.

Diane: What about the questions here in Love and Death? *Do you think that they still read and hold in light of the current feminist readings?*

I think the people who have stolen most from me without acknowledgment are the feminists. The only one who actually came out and said it—but she's never said it in print, but in some letters to me which we began to exchange—is Ann Douglas. But she's been learning from my new book, too. She's been thinking hard about the pop literature and her own contempt for popular literature, even when it was written by women, even when most of it was written by women. I think she's a person who's read a lot of books and read them hard, and she says some good things from time to time, but essentially she's inherited a kind of elitist point of view, which actually comes from a WASP male, straight, parochial point of view. And she's beginning to know that now. Some of her more recent things are really interesting. She's trying to come to terms with some of those popular feminist novels of the middle of the nineteenth century and just after the Civil War.

I think some of the newer feminists are interesting. They begin to write seriously about writers like Fannie Hurst and Edna Ferber, instead of writing one more goddamned article about Kate Chopin, who comes closest to fitting the old standards.

Diane: Are you writing about any of these women?

The one I've written a lot about—because I've got a particular hang-up on her—is Margaret Mitchell. *Gone with the Wind* seems to me a book that one has to come to terms with. And it just stays there; it won't go away and die. You can ignore it, you can say nasty things about it, you can put it down, but it persists.

Bruce: It's in the airports.

Right. It's still the best-known book in the world. You can't tell where the knowledge of the book stops and where the knowledge of the movie begins, but it's known better than anything else.

I write about it in some length in *What Was Literature?*, in which I point out that at the Trial of Four in China, it came out that Jiang Qing, the last Madame Mao Tse Tung, suggested that teaching of literature be revised completely in the universities; that they not study the Chinese classics, much less Western classics, but the model for the novel of the future that they use be *Gone with the Wind*. This was reported by her enemies, but it's apparently true. It was said as part of the charges against her. Some Chinese friend translated an article about it for me.

Diane: What could have been her reasoning?

She thought it was a book which reached the broad audience. It was a book which instead of exacerbating even more the difference between the undereducated and the overeducated closed the gap.

That explained to me something else which had puzzled me. When the first cultural relations were set up between the United States and the North Vietnamese after the war was over, the first two films they asked be sent over to them, one was *Gone with the Wind*; the other was, I believe, *King Kong*, which was Hitler's favorite movie. It's the kind of literature which makes politics absolutely irrelevant.

I'll tell you one more *Gone with the Wind* story. I have a very good friend, the last descendant of an old, old Italian-Jewish family, who lived in Ferrara. His family has been there for eighteen hundred years, I think. When the Nazis occupied Ferrara, they captured twenty of the leaders of the Jewish community, one of whom was his father. They held them through a long night. They knew they were going to shoot some of them, but they didn't know how many or who. And he and his mother (he was then a boy of eight, nine, or ten) hid out all night long in a cellar, praying for his father and hoping for the best. And in order to cheer him up all during the night his mother told him at great length the story of *Gone with the Wind*. It's a story of survival.

Bruce: I'm giving a seminar in epic. It never occurred to me to include that in an epic seminar.

It would be interesting to try it. She was very conscious of the historical roots of the whole thing. She apparently did a lot of research for the book. What she really created, as good epics do, were truly mythic characters. There's no place I've ever been in the world where you can't say "Scarlett O'Hara" and "Rhett Butler" and not have an instant recognition. It's been a favorite book in China all along. That's why Jiang Qing could talk about it. The only book that compares to it is the other women's book, which I talk about at considerable length, *Uncle Tom's Cabin*. In some ways it was intended to be an answer to *Uncle Tom's Cabin*.

There are a series of books, which I myself, if you use the term epic, called *The Inadvertent Epic*, which were done by different writers. This would begin with *Uncle Tom's Cabin*, and then would go on to *The Leopard's Spots* and *The Klansman*; then to Margaret Mitchell's *Gone with the Wind*, and then to *Roots*, Alex Haley's book. They are interesting because they are all done by outsiders from the society: Blacks, women, rednecks.

Bruce: And nearly all of them achieved mythic treatment in film, too.

Right. *The Klansman* and *The Leopard's Spots* are not read as books, but *The Birth of a Nation* will go on forever.

Diane: Talking about epic: Sergio Leone died today. Sixty years old.

They're dropping like flies. He died of what?

Diane: Heart attack.

The Inadvertent Epic is a strange book. It happened to me by accident. I can say more about the history of it. I've already said that before I wrote the book, I did what is the center of the whole thing, the main substance of it in the form of the Christian Gauss lectures *[at Princeton]*; but even before that I did it as a series of lectures at the University of Rome, and the University of Bologna.

I had never been professionally interested in American literature, I always thought of this as a private place of mine. It was my own literature; I didn't want to talk about it. I never took a course in American literature in college or in graduate school. In graduate school we thought only second-rate minds took courses in American literature anyhow. I was in a very elitist English Department at the University of Wisconsin, where if you did anything after the seventeenth century you were frowned on. Nineteenth century was barely acceptable if it was English at least—but American?

Then I went to Italy as a Fulbright, and it turned out that the pressures on me to talk about American literature came from two places: on the one hand, there was the desire to teach for the first time courses in American literature in the Italian universities, which had not been permitted under Fascism. An interest in American literature was considered politically suspect under Mussolini. The nonacademics who wrote about American literature then were people like Pavesi and Vittorini, who were anti-Fascists, and in some ways they used what they wrote about American literature as kind of anti-Fascism. They wrote about it in Aesopian terms, as anti-Fascist.

The second thing which they assumed in their superior way was that as an American, the only thing that I could really talk about with any understanding and insight was my own literature. So they said, "Talk about American literature." And, for the first time, I had to talk about American literature. I had already written the little article "Come Back to the Raft Ag'in," and I sort of took off from that and opened it up. I read some things hard. It was a strange experience, because in some ways being in that country I felt as if I were standing outside my own literature and looking at it half from their alienated point of view because I tried to get in their heads. I discovered very early on all kinds of silly things that they thought of American writers with names which I didn't recognize. If I said Hawthorne, for instance, they would look at me with a look of "Who's he?" But if I said *Owtorné*, that was the Italian. So I talked about *Owtorné, Melvillé, Poae*.

There had been very great essays on American literature, written by Cesare Pavese, who also had translated *Moby Dick* into Italian. Just marvelous. He died just the year before I came. I read a lot of him while I was there and wrote about him while I was there. So there were those lectures and then I redid them for the kind of audience which came to the Gauss lectures, who were people who were very knowledgeable about a lot of things, not necessarily nineteenth-century American literature, but if you take George Steiner as an example, they were New York intellectuals mostly. I think Mary McCarthy turned up at one point. They were sort of the things to go to in those days. If you would venture outside New York, you wouldn't go to Newark, New Jersey, God forbid, but you could go to Princeton. It's only forty miles down the pike.

Bruce: Where were you then, the year you gave the Gauss lectures.

I had already gone back to a permanent job in Missoula, so I came back on a year's leave, mostly because of Blackmur. Blackmur I had met in that mad summer I had spent in Indiana at the School of Letters. That's the way the connection went. It's more of those academic "old boy" connections.

Diane: Did you ever publish on the Renaissance?

Yes. I published more on the Middle Ages, which was my first center of interest. I published a couple of things on Dante, and I have an essay called "Chutzpah and Pudeur," which begins with Provençal poetry, which I know a good deal about and have a continuing interest in. The one Renaissance thing I have ever written about at any length is Shakespeare. One of the earliest scholarly lectures I ever gave and published I did for the English Institute was on Shakespeare. It was mostly on the play within a play and about mannerist playing with illusion. And then the big book on Shakespeare, *The Stranger in Shakespeare.*

Donne I never published anything on, though I preserve my dissertation on him, which I am very fond of because it was the shortest dissertation ever accepted at the University of Wisconsin. It consisted only of ninety pages with three indexes, but it was so immensely learned with quotations from Old Gascon, and so forth, that nobody dared challenge it.

I'm very learned. I began learned and have been learning about how to become less learned.

Long before I was anything else, I was a poet. The very first poem I ever wrote (I don't know if I regard this with a kind of strange admiration or deep horror), which I wrote when I was six years old, is called "Mercury and the Invention of the Lyre." It was read to a whole school assembly. I was sunk at that point.

Diane: How long was it?

It must have been ten or twelve or fifteen lines. I probably have that someplace, too. I never throw anything away, but I file it away so that I can't get at it easily, lest I be tempted to look.

I'm sort of a poet who took a wrong turn some place along the line. I've written poems since I was six, and most of the first things I published were poems, as a matter of fact. I've published a lot of poems. The first volume of mine that was ever considered for publication, though at the last minute turned down, was a collection of my poems. Delmore Schwartz liked my poems and John Crowe Ransom sort of liked my poems. I'm still writing them. Still writing stories, which was the second thing I ever wrote. I became a critic only by mistake. I mean I would send a story off to a magazine, and they would write back saying, "We are sorry we can't use it but we are sort of interested in you. Would you be interested in reviewing such and such a book." I ended up writing book reviews, and then just things that came off the top of my head. I didn't publish much until I was thirty. The first things really began publishing in '47 and '48.

I think as early as '40 I had published some things in *The New Directions* anthology. James Laughlin, I think, was the first person who ever published me. It was a long poem based on Dante. When I was seventeen I started to translate *The Divine Comedy*. Very bold. I didn't get very far. But I used some pieces of it in the story and the poem is sort of a narrative poem, in which a teacher is teaching a certain section of Dante and then reflecting on reverberations of the thing in his own mind. They published my first story too. My first really successful poem that I felt happy about, and story both, as I told you last time, were brought on by the death of my closest friend at age twenty-three. It is a poem called "Oh, Al" and the story was called "The Fear of Innocence." "Innocence" has always been a favorite word of mine.

Fiedler on the Roof, which I talked to you about before, which is my next book coming out, is the first of three volumes of essays of mine which have appeared over the past fifteen years, which I haven't collected together. The third of the volumes—I'm not sure what the title of the second is going to be—is going to be called *Back to Innocence*. So it will go from *The End of Innocence* to *Back to Innocence* and it will all round out completely. The *roundeur complet,* as Walt Whitman would say.

Diane: Did you ever write about film?

This is something I've protected myself from. I think a lot about film. I've published only one article on film, on Russ Meyer's *The Immortal Mr. Teas*. I wrote that for some show biz magazine.

Bruce: Was that his first movie?

It's the first that got any attention. The first released that was publicly released to a semi-respectable audience.

Diane: You showed his Beyond the Valley of the Dolls *and you gave a lecture.*

Somebody tells me that he keeps a copy of my article on him over his desk. He's proud of having been recognized by a respectable critic.

Diane: What do you think of Leone? Do you know his work?

I know his work very well. I like the spaghetti westerns a lot. They're very good.

Jeff Simon [Buffalo News *reviewer*] called me the other day and asked me if I would like to review movies or television sometime. But television and movies, as I say, I keep as my private precinct. Maybe someday I'll write about them. I once wrote a long piece on writers who go to Hollywood and make movies, which was put in some collection of stuff about the movies called *What Shining Phantom*. It comes from a poem which somebody wrote about a writer selling out to Hollywood. I like old movies. Thank God for cable television.

Bruce: Do you get American Movie Channel?

I watch that a lot. TNT has some good things on it.

Bruce and Diane: TNT has too many commercials.

They do indeed. Arts & Education has movies sometimes that are worth seeing.

I've always wanted to write a movie. For a while there seemed a possibility that a novel of mine, *The Second Stone*, was going to be made into a movie. I actually got to doing a script for it, and we had a location for it. There were two that were considered. The other thing that really came even closer was *Nude Croquet*, and I was excited about that because a man called Schüfftan—what's called process photography is really called "Schüfftan process photography." He's the guy who invented it—[wanted to make the film]. But he never could quite make it in Hollywood. They wouldn't let him in. He was a German filmmaker. Then when we got a director, we lost him; and when we got him, we lost the money, and so forth, so nothing ever happened. The closest I ever got to movies was being an actor. But I would like to make a movie.

Actors intrigue me a lot. They are so fucking stupid in an interesting way; negative capability or something. I could never understand how they work.

Bruce: I never understand how they live between when they work.

What happens to most of them is they get a part they play called by the name under which they act and they're always "on scene." And that kills them, finally, because then when they get parts, they are playing a semi-imaginary character playing the part. That's called "ham."

Diane: Andrew Sarris told me a friend of his told him that he was offered a very fine career about to be launched by a very fine agent and the name was chosen and everything was set. But the guy had to be the fellow's lover. The name was Rock Hudson. This guy, the friend of Sarris, turned it down. So it went to somebody else.

Rock Hudson is the second Rock Hudson?

The actor I know best in the world, as I think I've told you before, is Carroll O'Connor, who was my student in Montana. We remained friends ever since. We were in Rome at the same time when he had a minor part in *Antony and Cleopatra*. He was off for thirteen weeks while they made love. I've followed him all his life. I saw the production of *Ulysses in Nighttown*, where he played Buck Mulligan. He was truly great. Through him I keep meeting all kinds of actors: Shirley MacLaine, Burgess Meredith.

Diane: What did you think of Shirley MacLaine?

I thought she was awful. She was name-dropping the whole time. "When I saw Fidel last, he said to me . . ." That was at a point when I was acting in a play, and she gave me advice on what to do with my hands. When I went out there, Sally came out to see me for a while, and Carroll threw a big party for her and he invited Shirley MacLaine and Burgess Meredith and various other people, and a guy who was just starting to make it called Larry Hagman. He was the most interesting, I thought. Sort of pretending to be a small boy, which he managed to do by having a wife who got ten years older every time a year passed, while he got ten years younger every time a year passed.

The only interesting person I knew and never got to know him very well—there was a woman we knew in common, and I spent some time with him in his house in Ireland—was John Huston. I have a picture of myself drawn by Huston on a cigar box cedar liner.

Bruce: Huston is one of my heroes.

He's a very great man.

Bruce: He's one of the great storytellers of the world.

He began as a writer, and you can tell it. He may be the son of an actor, but he really makes the pictures like a writer. He was fine, once we got past the first impressions. He couldn't understand what I was doing there. I dropped by. He had invited me to come. He thought I was going to get an interview with him, and/or ask him a favor to try to get into a movie. But when he discovered I just wanted to talk to him, he really talked. And we drank a lot, and we smoked many cigars, and he showed me his paintings. He was a very good painter. He had one compulsive subject. You won't be surprised to discover what it is: his daughter Angelica.

The second time I met him I was in Paris when he tried out a movie, the first movie Angelica ever made, I can't remember the name of it, but it was so terrible. Afterwards we had coffee together, he and Angelica and me and my oldest daughter Debbie. It was a little, tiny family scene and I tried to say nice things about the film, which was impossible.

The first time we mostly talked about Marilyn. I had been all set to go out and spend a little time on the set with her when they were making *The Misfits*. On my way out I got a telegram saying, "Marilyn in hospital. Don't come."

Diane: What did he say about her?

He said dumb things about her, like if she had found something socially useful to do, she wouldn't have killed herself. He thought she should have done public service of some kind. God only knows what. I don't think he liked her much, though he was being nice.

Diane: Did he like any women much?

Angelica.

Diane: In Chinatown *he plays the incestuous father brilliantly.*

I saw him under very peculiar circumstances. I went there with an Irish woman I knew, who came with her clothes in a paper sack. He was treating her like a servant. She happened to have a PhD from Oxford, one of the brightest ladies in the world. It's very hard for him to deal with anybody who is (a) Irish and (b) was a female.

[He asks Sally to get the Huston drawing.] The picture looks more like him than it does like me. It's one of my most precious possessions.

Diane: What year was this?

It was just before I met Sally. Let's see, Sally and I have been together for sixteen years, so that takes us back to the early seventies. Some place in there. Unfortunately it's not signed.

Bruce: You saw The Man Who Would Be King?

Diane: It's one of the best movies ever made. [Sally arrives with the drawing.] Wow. It really does look more like him than Leslie. Absolutely it does! He thought he was doing himself.

When I remember it's the cedar lining from a cigar box and that he died from emphysema, I begin to worry.

Bruce: That's a real treasure. I read an interview with him about two years before his death in which he was talking about remaking movies. He said he could never understand why anybody would remake a good movie. He thought it was the dumbest thing in the world. He said the only movie worth a remake is one that they failed at. The Maltese Falcon *they'd failed at twice before he did it, so that was a good one to remake. I haven't seen* The Dead *yet.*

I liked it a lot. The voices in it are just right, and he turned it into a movie, that's what some people don't like about it. It's almost impossible, since there's no motion in it. But the camera moves from object to object, caressing each one, every piece of furnishing in the room, every dish on the table.

He had a great desire to be associated with literature and literary people, though he sometimes killed them, the way he did James Agee. He was apparently a real bastard in many ways. He wanted everybody to be able to run as hard as he did, drink as much as he did . . .

Bruce: I read Hepburn's book about making The African Queen. *She says almost nothing in it. It's a small book with very large type unfortunately. Several times she talks about "John going off" with someone "scouting." They're obviously getting drunk for three days someplace.*

One of the most interesting books about him is semi-fiction by a man called Peter Viertel. It's called *White Hunter, Black Heart*. It's about Huston making a film in Africa. The character is clearly Huston.

Diane: His own autobiography is good. Did you ever read that?
No.

Diane: His documentary work is very important. He worked for the Army in the Second World War.

Bruce: You know Huston's film San Pietro? *It's one of the great war films. It was made by the Army and then the Army didn't want to show it. It's about taking this little town in the Liri Valley in Italy. Almost everybody in this battalion is killed. And he says in voice-over, "The ones who weren't killed this time were the next time." The Army didn't want to show it because, they said, it might depress the soldiers. Whoever was the general—it wasn't Eisenhower—it was the one who fired Patton. He said, "No, show it. They should know what it's like." We have a print of it. We can watch it, if you like. Huston narrates it. He has a great narrating voice.*

Diane: And he uses the Mormon Tabernacle Choir. Unbelievable!

Bruce: He was really good at that sort of thing. It's the only one of that group of films that isn't beating the drum. At the end, it's got great sentimentality about children being resurrected and the flowers coming out. But, aside from that, it's a wonderful film.

Diane: Another one he did was Let There Be Light *which was about men who were shellshocked after the war and being treated in a psychoanalytical manner in a war hospital or a veterans' hospital. That was suppressed for over forty years. We saw it for the first time only a few years ago.*

Bruce: The reason it was suppressed was because it showed soldiers crying.

Diane: That's what they said. It showed men who were garbaged by war.

Maybe I'll end up writing about movies. If I make it past eighty I will. That's a promise.

I'd like to write something about Huston. He's a man without any sentimentality in him at all. I can't think of any place where it shows up.

Diane: It shows up at the end of San Pietro. *His* The Man Who Would Be King *is the most wonderful movie, but it has no weakness of sentimentality; it just has the dream.*

That one really works.

Bruce: I will never hear "The Minstrel Boy" again without thinking of it.

That's one we like a lot. Brilliant movie. Did you see *Wise Blood*?
Bruce: Yes. Scary movie.

Not many people have seen it. It's not widely exposed.
Bruce: He really gets her. [Flannery O'Connor, who wrote the novel.]

That's the one the Fitzgerald children did, right? *[Robert Fitzgerald was Flannery O'Connor's literary executor. Three of his children were involved in the film: his sons Benedict and Michael Fitzgerald wrote the screenplay; and his daughter Kathy and Michael produced it.]*

Bruce: Yes. They were friends for a long time. Fitzgerald and he and Agee were all friends from those years.

Wise Blood was a special movie for me because I knew those kids when they were little.

Bruce: The Fitzgerald kids?

Yes.

We spent some time together in Italy in a strange petit bourgeois beach resort at Fano, where the kids roller-skated all the time. I loved that beach. It was a great beach. The women wore underwear under their bathing suits. The Italian ladies. The best time to go to the beach was exactly at twelve o'clock because the beach was deserted. The pots would be boiling at home and on the beach a cry would go up, "Butta la pasta": "Throw the pasta in." And everybody would disappear. It was marvelous.

It had a strange feeling. It was Browning's favorite beach. But though it was very romantic, it was extraordinary for him because it was full of ordinary people. It is just down by the sea from a marvelous Renaissance town where we were, Urbino.

Diane: Wonderful town. With that ducal palace.

Sally and I spent a while there. I did a course there. There's a university in Urbino.

Diane: That's a perfect Renaissance building.

The whole town you can't believe. It looks like it's a movie set.

Diane: With all those perfect little Giotto trees along the way.

What a great place it was. It was Sally's first look at Northern Italians, and she was a little startled.

Diane: The light there was spectacular.

A bunch of rich kids gave us cars to drive around in.

Bruce: When was this?

Sally: Sixteen years ago. A long time ago. It was our first summer. There was a conference there on semiology.

Bruce: He was my Epic teacher. Fitzgerald.

Was he?

The Fitzgeralds are close, close friends of one of my oldest and best friends, a woman called Teki, Teki Clark, who is known as "La Principessa Americana." That's what Ralph Ellison calls her because when she was a kid her father owned the biggest department store in Oklahoma City and Ralph Ellison was the chauffeur who drove her around. Teki since then has married four, five, or six times. She lives outside of Florence.

Bruce: The Fitzgeralds lived in Fiesole.

They were close neighbors and lived in a house which was quite appropriate for them. It had a beautiful old chapel, absolutely preserved.

Diane: Did they get a priest to say Mass?

Bruce: They had enough children to.

He left his Sally behind, and he had another woman in his life. I think he actually married the last one. That's a great name for a wife, Sally.

Diane: What was the new wife's name?

I don't know. I never met her.

Diane: We were intrigued to see that Sondra Locke and Clint Eastwood are splitting. We met them in Sun Valley. Two abortions and a palimony lawsuit. It's not going to be pretty.

Bruce: "You promised to support me for life."
He probably did at some weak moment.
Diane: They've been together for over ten years.
He *should* support her.
Diane: Everyone talks about how tight he is. He brings his films in under budget. He's very, very careful. He was poor for a long time. He was utterly poor when they were doing the Leone stuff. He tells stories about how they used to stop filming because they ran out of film. Leone didn't have any money, nobody had any money, and people would go —
Bruce: Leone was making his films for $150,000.
He made some money on them, finally.
Diane: Finally he made a lot. And also on Once Upon a Time in the West.
Bruce: Once Upon a Time in the West. *That's the one with Henry Fonda. Did you ever see it?*
I don't think so.
Bruce: You have a VCR. I'll lend you a tape of it. In it, Henry Fonda is the most evil badman.
Diane: It's wonderful, fantastic.
Bruce: Those blue eyes. Those sincere American blue eyes are the most evil bad guy you have ever seen. He kills babies!
Diane: He does, he does. And Claudia Cardinale is unbelievable.
Bruce : Claudia Cardinale, Charles Bronson, Jason Robards Jr. —
Diane : and Henry Fonda.
Bruce : And the way he uses music.
Diane: To die for. It makes me cry that music. So beautiful.
Bruce: Leslie, can we do this next Sunday? The week after that, Bobbie Louise Hawkins is staying with us for a week.
Sally: You get along with both *of them?*
Bruce: Totally separately.
Sally: I can imagine.
Bruce: This happened quite by accident.
Diane: My big mouth of course.

Figure 12. Leslie and historian Lawrence Levine, Atrium of UB Center for the Arts, 1997.

4

May 7, 1989

Bruce: In your discussion, you talk about some of the whaling stories about buggery on the ships, and people talking about this being something that happens only because of the absence of women, and you suggest that perhaps one of the reasons for going to sea was so you could be in a place where that would be ordinary and you'd have the excuse. I met guys in the penitentiary who I'm sure went back to prison just for that reason. It was a place where they could take on those roles without opprobrium. They didn't know how to do it on the streets. There's no way they could get fucked in the ass on Mulberry Street, but in the penitentiary it was okay. Going to prison gave them a context in which they could behave in the way they really wanted to behave and have relationships they really wanted to have.

I've often thought about the ways in which ships and prisons are alike. They're the two places in the world where people read long books. I've seen sailors go into a bookstore and say, "Give me the fattest one," and end up with *War and Peace.* And it was only on shipboard that I managed to read through *Finnegan's Wake.* I was once at sea for sixty days, so I figured I might as well be *totally* at sea for sixty days.

Bruce: A friend of mine's father, he became an English professor, was in the submarine service during the war. One of the books in the ship's library was Ulysses. *It drove him crazy. For two years he tried to get through* Ulysses. *The war ended, he went to school, he went to graduate school, and he finally became an English professor at University of Florida.*

That's better than chipping paint.

That shipboard experience was an important experience for me.

Bruce: Why were you at sea for so long?

I sailed on the command ship for the fleet that went into Iwo Jima. It was my job to do the interrogation of prisoners, which I eventually did. We sailed evasive maneuvers, heading for various places, but only putting ashore for a few hours at a time. So I read and played poker.

We were actually straddled by bombs one night. It was one of the great experiences of my life.

Bruce: You were on a battleship?

The ship was what is called an AG-C, which is a command ship. We had everything on it: three-color printing presses, all kinds of radar equipment. We would get intelligence reports and then turn out leaflets with the latest information.

At first they brought the prisoners out. We would lie fifteen hundred yards offshore and I watched the whole goddamned battle of Iwo Jima, like somebody sitting before a newsreel in a theater. On the third day I went ashore to pick up some prisoners.

Bruce: Was there sound or did you watch it silent?

A lot of the sound was coming from us.

Bruce: Right: you were shelling.

The admiral insisted on flying his three-star flag, which attracted the bombers. He was a very vain man. He was a lovely, typical Navy man, who had heard I was a writer and asked me up to his cabin one day. I thought, "God knows, I'm in trouble." He wanted to show me a book he had written and privately printed, called *Maryland's Colonial Charm as Shown in Her Silver.* We had this charming conversation, in which he said, "You know, we commit atrocities sometimes, too." And I said, "Yes, I knew that."

The first prisoner who was brought out to the ship—we couldn't get any for a long time because, you know, the way Japanese are conditioned. Somehow the Marines who brought them out had found a baseball bat, God knows where. And as they came out they were swatting them; not very hard, but first on one side of the head and then on the other, just to make their point.

Diane: Were they capable of talking?

The only people we had as prisoners were traumatically wounded to begin with. That's the reason they became prisoners. Once taken prisoner, they were sure they were going to be—they had heard all kinds of stories—they were going to be castrated.

Bruce: Which was one of the reasons it was so hard to take them prisoner?

That was one of the reasons. The other was they had been told that Japanese were never taken prisoners, period. So when you got a prisoner, he would sing like a bird because they hadn't been conditioned for how to behave *after* they were taken prisoner.

One of the first things we did with them was to shave all their body hair off of them. They had lice. They were *sure* they were going to be castrated. I always remember one guy got so scared when that razor came close that he began to pee. And then he was shamed: "My piss is trickling out!" And then he kept trying to commit suicide. He grabbed somebody's knife, he tried to jump over the side of the ship. And afterwards we looked at the pictures of his wife and his kids. He was one of them who fell in love with me.

That's the other thing that happens. You heard about the Stockholm syndrome, but I've seen it from the other side: "I love you, take me home with you."

I had no training whatsoever before I went. I was working, translating documents in Pearl Harbor, and I finally couldn't stand that. I thought anything else was better, so I volunteered to go out on the next thing, whatever it was. It turned out to be Iwo Jima. I said to our commanding officer, "Look, I don't know what to do. I never had any combat training. I don't even know how to scramble over the side of a ship." His first response was the response to anything you ever asked him, "Go shit up a rope." And the second response was, "Do whatever the guy in front of you does." Which I did. But it was a hard experience because all these interrogations went on in sick bay, because these guys were badly wounded. One had both legs shot off and some were dying.

Diane: What were you supposed to try and get out of them?

Where their gun emplacements were; where and how many men they had; which part of the beaches they had covered and how. We found out a lot of things a day late. We could have helped a lot if we had known sooner, but we turned out beautiful little pamphlets showing the layout of their guns once we discovered them.

It was a very strange experience. The ship was overloaded with brass. They had a Marine Corps general, two admirals, as well as the captain of the ship. General "Howlin' Mad" Smith, a famous Marine, was on the ship.

But, on the other hand, we lived like kings on the ship. We were waked up in the morning with little tinkling bells. We had beautiful cabins and good food. We had to wear ties the whole time.

Bruce: You had to be spit and polish?

All the time. The admiral on our ship was a guy called Hill. He was not in military charge, but he was top man in charge of supplies and logistics.

Diane: How did they treat you?

I had nobody over me. I was sort of independent. There was a chief intelligence officer on the ship. I worked under him; he was a Marine. He was rather stupid. The Marines put the most stupid people in Intelligence.

Met some smart Marines, including a guy who has been a congressman ever since: Jack Brooks from Texas. He was known as Babbling Brooks in those days. He was bound to become a politician. He was with the signal battalion of the First Marines. I was with him in China. I was attached with the Marines at that time. They put me in a Marine uniform, and we went ashore together and we had been there one day and Jack Brooks had complete furnishings: desk, beautiful Eurasian girl. I figured he was bound to be a congressman someday.

He was the smallest Marine. He never went out without brass knuckles in his pocket. He's smart. Highly articulate. He had a tailor-made uniform, and the rule was when we traveled the streets—we were in Tientsin—we were supposed to carry a gun with us at all times, a .45. It made too much of a bulge in his uniform. So I was always the one who carried the gun. That was no protection for anybody.

Diane: Were you terrified to be roaming around there?

No, I really wasn't. I'm very stupid. I never believe anything is going to happen to me. I was one of the few people who would go into the Chinese city, a city much like Shanghai, Tientsin had foreign settlements. There was an Italian district. Our headquarters were in the Italian district. They had a big jai lai palace. They had imported Basque jai lai players. The Chinese loved to bet on jai lai, and they used to go from Shanghai to Tientsin and to Beijing.

I would walk into the Chinese city and when they would see a White face, they would make this sign, which means they thought I was a Russian Communist. That's the Eighth Route army, right? *[The Chinese Communist Army that fought the Japanese in World War II.]* They thought the only White man who would be stupid enough to walk around a Chinese city would be a Russian.

Diane: Did they hate you?

No. We were hailed as conquerors when we came. People were kissing us, throwing flowers at us, since we presumably drove the Japanese out. It took about ten days, and then they decided we were the new oppressors. So there was trouble. But there was nothing bad. The only real threat there was venereal disease.

The sailors thought the war was over. I hated it at first, because I was supposed to go home. The war was over, right? And I had been out twenty months. But I was low man on the totem pole because I was in the Navy and attached to the goddamn Marines, and they put the Marine officers ahead of me. So I stayed for three months.

There were a half-million Japanese still in North China and Mongolia and the treaty agreement was they had to be repatriated. They were only allowed to carry out thirty-five pounds of stuff with them. And rather than sell the stuff, for which they got nothing, I got many presents, including a prize picture, including that great Utamaro. It's a prize picture, perhaps the most valuable item in my house. It's called "The Abalone Fisherwomen."

The Japanese who gave it to me thought of it as a pornographic picture. It's presumably a very early print.

. . . I figured that night I was dead. A bomb dropped in front of us and a bomb dropped aft of us.

Bruce: And you figured the next one had you.

They had a guy on watch way up in the crow's nest, and he screamed, "It's coming down on me." Now I knew in my head if he saw that plane over him, the bomb wasn't going to hit us. But my stomach didn't quite believe it.

The only time I was actually in danger, we got one person who was all wrapped up and the doctor and I worked on him and we unwrapped him very carefully and way inside, after we had touched him, was a little sign somebody had written saying, "gas gangrene." So the doctor shot us both up with a presumable antidote. He got a little sick, the doctor, but I didn't. It's highly infectious. People should wear rubber gloves when handling such cases.

When I saw the movie version of *M*A*S*H**, it felt right at home to me. I'd been there. I spent most of my time in sick bay. The Japanese were incredible. The guy who had his legs blown off insisted on coming up the side of the ship on the ladder on his stumps. He wasn't going to be hauled on the ship; he would have lost face doing that.

So I ended up, it worked both ways: I totally identified with the Japanese, especially when I was with the Marines.

Diane: Were they particularly bigoted?

No. Well, you know. A typical thing, to give you an example of what they were like, ordinary enlisted men, Marines or sailors. You would bring a prisoner over the side of the ship. The guys on the ship are never in a war exactly, they're just machine tenders. This was their chance to show how macho they were. They would all scream, "Kill them, kill the son of a bitch," and pull out their knives and so forth. And three days later they're down swapping pictures and American money for Japanese money. After all, it's just another human being. In bad trouble.

Bruce: Did you ever know Alvin Josephy? Alvin used to be editor of American Heritage. *He edited a book called* The Indian Heritage of North America *and some other Indian things. Alvin was there—at Iwo Jima—too. In fact the Marines who were there on the summit made themselves up special ID cards. Alvin had one.*

I saw them put the flag up twice. The shot didn't come out the first time, so they had them do it again. It was a strange place. I sort of wanted to go back some time. It's an American naval base. It wasn't much of an island to begin with.

Bruce: It's a small island, isn't it?

You could see the whole damn thing from where we were. Another Japanese name for it is Piposhima—Pipe Island. It looks like a pipe: a long thin island and then the mountain comes up. *[He misremembers: The name is Iōtō—"Sulfur Island." It's turnip-shaped.]*

I went swimming on that beach when I did get ashore. I go swimming whenever I can. It's a black lava beach. There were all kinds of spars and bodies and so forth floating about. One of the problems was about what to do with bodies. The day I got ashore they were burying a bunch of people. There must have been a thousand of them, Americans, Japanese altogether. They just bulldozed them all into it. A lot of people died.

Diane: What was the significance of it, of Iwo Jima?

That won the war, actually. Once they got there, they were in an easy airplane range of Japan. So it was an absolutely vital island. They jumped from there to Okinawa. You're really in Japan from there.

Bruce: The B-29 raids were from Okinawa.

Those B-29s were coming over us when we were there. From Guam or someplace. I was on Guam for a while too.

On Tinian I met a Shinto priest and an old lady, and they insisted on doing a tea ceremony for me, with rusty old tin cans. And the lady said to me in elegant Japanese of a woman speaking to an officer, "And how many women have you raped in the great war?" It was no joke, it was just considered something that one does in the great war. I denied that I had raped anyone in the great war. And she tittered and said, "Gojo gandisho," which is what you say to someone when he says something improbable: "You're making the honorable joke perhaps?"

Diane: Was that a proper question?

Yes, it was. She thought it was complimentary. She was praising my machismo.

Diane: Did Japanese men rape in the Great War?

Yeah. They didn't have much chance, but they did when they could.

Bruce: They weren't in very sexy places, were they?

No, they weren't. On the island of Iwo Jima, there was nobody available. There were only Japanese, and the first prisoners we took all turned out to be Korean. They were sort of slave laborers who dug the holes for them.

Bruce: Did you learn Japanese in the Navy?

Yes. At Boulder, where they had a special Japanese language school. I was there fourteen months. It was kind of rough.

Diane: How many people were with you?

Our class must have been about 150. There were more to begin with, but almost half of our class got thrown out when they were investigated. We entered as yeoman second class and when we graduated we were commissioned. Before you could be commissioned, you had to be investigated. And they were political investigations. Finally, I would walk past the commanding officer's headquarters and hear some guy protesting he had just been told he had to go, and the kid would say something like, "But, goddamn it, everybody was a Communist in those days."

Diane: Why did they pass you?

Finally, everybody in the goddamn thing had either been commissioned or thrown out except me. I was the last one left. And I heard later what happened. They sent the investigators. One they sent to Newark, and he made a mistake. He stopped a woman on a street who was pushing a baby carriage. She was the sister of a good friend of mine, who had hated me like poison all my life long, as she hated her brother before me. But when he asked her about Leslie Fiedler, she threw back the hood of the carriage and she said, "If this boy grows up to be like Leslie Fiedler, I'd be proud." Then they went to Missoula and ran into Baxter Hathaway, who was an old friend of mine, who ended up at Cornell, where he was for many years. He ran a little magazine called *Epic*. A very interesting fellow.

And they said to Baxter, "Is it true that Leslie Fiedler was a Communist?" He talked very slowly. He'd put down a word and then walk around it for a while. "Well," he said, "I think he may have been a Lovestoneite at one time or another." And the guy said, "What?" Baxter said, "A Lovestoneite," and the guy said, "Aw, forget it." It was a little too difficult for him to deal with.

So I was commissioned. It was weird. They would turn somebody out because he had once appeared at a Quaker symposium, talking against the war. Then the guy who was the actual organizer for the Communist Party while we were there went through. Of course, they were our allies at that point, so I don't know whether they knew what to do. A lot of the people were Leftish.

They had nobody who knew Japanese, so what they did basically was to go to all the best schools in the country and asked who the best graduate students were. They went to Berkeley and they went to Harvard and they went to Yale and they went to Princeton. And then there were some people who volunteered along the way, like me. And they creamed them all off. The place was badly divided into groups: the Harvard people only talked to the Harvard people and so forth. Then there was what was called the "salami goumie," the salami club. These were a bunch of Jewboys, real smart Jewboys from New York. I associated with them. Then there was the gay goumie. And they wrote Japanese poems to each other. I was married and had kids, so I could live off base. The others had to talk Japanese day and night. On Mondays for relaxation we were shown a Japanese movie.

Diane: Was it a good school?

They had a method of intensive training. You learned fast. But the people who taught us, you know, you had all these super graduate school people and the teachers were Japanese, Nisei, who had been gardeners and fruit peddlers. It was a rather strange relationship we had with them.

Bruce: You must have had a strange vocabulary when you started interrogating prisoners.

They tried to teach us military terms and so forth. We had a little practice interrogating prisoners back in Pearl Harbor. That's where the translation operation was based. A strange organization. All these organizations had strange names. It was called JIC POA: Joint Intelligence Center, Pacific Ocean Area. Then I was moved to one with an even stranger name, where we did code stuff. It was called "FRUPAC: Fleet Radio Unit, Pacific Area." And most of the cryptographers were fruits, in fact; it seems to go with the profession. That was a great unit, FRUPAC. I have a unit commendation. They're the ones that broke the Japanese code. I didn't have much to do with it.

Diane: Was it very repressed and quiet? Wasn't it forbidden?

No: there was nobody there but us. We lived practically by ourselves. It was a good life on the island. I fought hard and I finally got the watches I wanted. I worked from three in the afternoon to twelve midnight. And after twelve midnight you could do what you wanted—get a little sleep and spend the middle part of the day on the beach.

I got to know some of the local Japanese. It's funny, the Japanese were rounded up everyplace but in Hawaii. There they weren't sent to internment camps, because the whole economy depended on them. I used to go out with this guy who had a little farm, I used to go out and milk his goats.

Diane: Is this in Oahu?

Yeah. Shinjewan, the Japanese called it. That's Pearl Harbor. Honolulu, is a nice place. We didn't lose a single person who came out of the Japanese Language School. One guy committed suicide. He was accused of molesting a newsboy.

I had all kinds of strange associates. One came to visit me last year. His name is Reed Irvine. Does that name mean anything to you?

Diane: Accuracy in Media?

Absolutely. Reed came to see me and we talked about the good old days.

Bruce: He was in your unit?

He was in my little, tiny class when I went through Japanese Language School. There were only five of us.

Diane: And what happened to him?

He was a Mormon to begin with, married to a Japanese woman. He was very smart. We talked about Iwo Jima, the Corps. We had our choice at the end of either going into the Marines or into the Navy. He went to the Marines.

Bruce: What did you come out as?

Lieutenant JG. One rank up.

Diane: What did he then do—Reed Irvine? What was his profession?

I think he went to graduate school some place. I think he became a lawyer; I'm not sure. We didn't talk about that much; just the good old days. Sally was very surprised that we had a congenial conversation. But, what the hell.

Diane: He didn't say anything political to you?

He was here for something official, but we didn't talk politics

Bruce: He's doing "Accuracy in Education" now, which is a scurrilous newsletter.

I've never seen it

Bruce: It's horrid.

He was a good Latter-day Saint when I knew him.

Bruce: When did you first go to Japan?

I never got to Japan in the war. I was in Guam and I was in Saipan, I was in Iwo Jima, I was in Okinawa. And then I went to China. For a long time, I didn't want to go to Japan.

Diane: Why?

I wanted to forget everything. The first thing I did was to forget all the Japanese I ever knew. I had bad feelings. I must have first gone to Japan twelve or fifteen years ago.

Diane: What kind of feelings did you have when you went there?

Odd. I had some strange experiences that would flash back to me. I would look at a poster and I would have read it before I said to myself, "You don't remember anymore." I had known a lot of characters, three thousand. And then it would be gone again. And then driving from the airport, traffic was terrible, and I found myself saying to the cabbie, "Tien doha"—"It's awful, isn't it?" I can't really do Japanese anymore. And the thing I can't remember to save me is the word for battleship or gun.

Bruce: Did you learn kana or just characters?

I learned everything. We learned conversation and reading and writing. At the end of it all—I may have said this to you—we went to the General Intelligence school in New York, called ANIS—Advanced Naval Intelligence School—which was absolutely ridiculous. But it was a month in New York before I left. And then they divided us up. Some went to Pearl Harbor, some went to Australia, and some went to Washington.

Diane: After fourteen months, were people basically competent?

Yes. Some of them were very good. A lot of those people have stayed in Japanese. A lot of translators of Japanese novels these days come from the Japanese Language School. The very first class were the really sharp ones. We were the second group that went through. Some of them sort of went native and refused to go home. The best guy in the school married a Japanese woman and he's been living in Honolulu ever since. I think he has a fishing boat. He was a very California type. He had a very California-type wife, who would send him pictures of her standing next to her plane or something, and he decided to drop her for a nice Japanese girl.

Bruce: I was at a symposium in Germany a few years ago—German translators who were translating Black American literature into German. One of the prime guys in that group had learned his English in an American prisoner of war camp in New Jersey during World War II. He was allowed out of the camp for work.

In Missoula there was a camp of Italian internees, they were civilian internees, and they wandered around any place in town. Several married into Missoula families and stayed, ran the local grocery store, members of bands and so forth.

Bruce: At the beginning of The Godfather *there's a character who comes for help because his daughter has been knocked up by a German internee. He wants the Godfather to arrange for the German to stay after the war so he can marry his daughter.*

One of the last times I was in Japan I ended up at a bar late at night and there were a bunch of Japanese men of my age and we began singing songs we knew in common. The famous popular song, which is called "Shina No Yuru"—"Those Beautiful Chinese Nights" or "Those Rainy Chinese Nights," sung by a woman who is still alive and who is the Japanese kind of Dinah Shore. Her name is Watanabe Hamako. I actually knew her in China; she was entertaining the troops there. That was a bit of nostalgia.

Bruce: "Shina No Yuru" was the song I heard more of the old-time Marines talk about than any other. Doesn't someone sing it in Year of the Dragon?

[Leslie sings some of it.] "Those rainy nights." Yeah.

I sort of fell in love with Watanabe Hamako, but I was very young then and when she told me she had a son old enough to be in the Japanese army, it kind of turned me off.

Diane: How did you meet her?

I worked with the Japanese population in China; I was helping to repatriate them, so our social life was all with the Japanese.

Have I told you about the great occasion for the party for fifty of my closest friends? One more story and then I'm through with war stories.

I was walking down the street and this Japanese came toward me. He looked like the comic stereotype of the Japanese: his teeth hung out and he was wearing glasses that were patched with adhesive tape. I got in conversation with him and discovered he was a scholar, a political scientist. I went up to his room and he showed me his books; some of them were in English and some were in Japanese. I said, "Is there anything I can do for you?"

He said, "Yes, I'd dearly love some coffee." So I got him a pound or two of American coffee and I gave it to him, and he said, "In return for this, I would like to give a small party for you and fifty of your closest friends." I didn't have fifty close friends. I had a couple close friends, so I invited them and forty-seven Marines.

It turned out that this guy must have been the head of the local Black Dragon Society. It was a great power and what was left of the Japanese community. They all got out their best lacquerware. There were fifty settings and fifty high-type geishas, one for each of us. These were the geishas who had been up with the general officers in Northern China and Outer Mongolia. They had painted scenery, and they did classical Japanese dances, and served us elegant food. It was all going very stiffly but very well, and right in the middle of it, one of the goddamn Marines couldn't stand it anymore and he grabbed the girl behind him and he yelled, "Let's make the Big Love, baby." And everybody leaped, and the whole place turned into a shambles in about five minutes, and I, like a coward, fled.

I came back a day later to see my friend and prepared to apologize. Before I could open my big, stupid mouth and say my apologies in halting Japanese, he said, "This is an occasion we'll never forget. You honored us with your presence." And I figured, What the hell, I'm a barbarian, and I said, "You're welcome."

"Let's make the Big Love, baby." These were high-type geishas; the most elegant women you've ever seen.

Diane: What do geishas do? Are they like companions?

Think of a geisha like an airline stewardess. They're there to serve you and to make conversation. And if they like you, they'll sleep with you.

Bruce: But it's not "Let's make the Big Love, baby?"

No. *Geisha* literally means "talented person." They can dance and they can sing, and they can look elegant—if you don't mind the smell of fish oil which they used in those days on their hair. They powder themselves a beautiful white color.

Japanese classical dancing is very strange but very beautiful. They were playing the Koto, that long, thirteen-string instrument. The first couple of times I heard anybody play it, I thought now he's finished tuning up and he's going to start. And it was over apparently. They do keep changing pitch.

Diane: I suppose it's a very different place now.

I've been back a couple of times. It had begun to change earlier. The Japanese adapted very readily to Western technology. Kyoto is a strange city to go to, because it's one place where the old Japan is preserved, but side by side with the brand new Japan. You know, the telephones work better than ours, the television pictures are better, and you go to get in a cab and you reach to open the door, and you discover that the door opens and closes automatically. You figure you come from a technologically backward country. But on the other hand, there are still buildings there that were there in the heyday of the samurai. And the last geisha houses were there. They're running out. They can't persuade girls to enlist and be trained any more. There is a White geisha in Kyoto: an American female sociologist who came over to study the geisha and decided it was an admirable way of life and became a geisha.

Bruce: It sounds like another opera.

Diane: I wonder if the Japanese like Butterfly.

I don't know. It's very anti-American and pro-Japanese. The original story had a happy ending: She recovered from her suicide attempt and lived happily ever after. It was changed even by the time the play was written.

Diane: In the opera, she dies.

Yes: betrayed by the cad.

There's only one good book ever written about the non–meeting of minds between Westerners and Japanese, and that wasn't written by an American. It's a book called *The Honorable Picnic.* For a long time it was a banned book in Japan. It's a book which must have come out in the late twenties or early thirties, and who wrote it I've never been able to find out. It was written in French originally, and the guy signs himself Thomas Raucat. But if you said *toma raucka* in Japanese, it means "Shall we spend the night?" It's a book whose basic story is a little like the story of *Madama Butterfly* about the complete series of misunderstandings between a Frenchman and the Japanese girl, which ends with her suicide. This one is absolutely faithful to the way Japanese minds really work and the way Western minds work when confronted by Japanese customs. It was a popular book in its English translation in the thirties.

One of the places where Japanese and Americans simply don't think alike is in terms of sex and love.

Diane: Do you like Ruth Benedict's book? [The Chrysanthemum and the Sword: Patterns of Japanese Culture, *1946.]*

It's kind of interesting; as far as it goes it's okay. It pretends to understand. The only really honest book would end up saying, "I'm baffled."

Japanese have this great love for Americans, and they are soaked in American popular culture especially. The first question I was asked by a young Japanese girl in China, when I could talk to somebody face to face, was, "What has been happening with Gary Cooper?"

Bruce: Do they know Twain and Melville?

Yes. They know classic American literature a lot. What they especially know is American movies. As you know, even Kurosawa did a western. Westerns they love. That's one place they feel close together because the samurai tradition is not so different.

Diane: Do you think it is?

No. The ronin, you know, were the independent ones; they were loners, like gunmen in the West. They're not exactly alike, but enough alike. There are a lot of Japanese comic books, which are just like western comic books, about the ronin.

Japanese comic books are fascinating. They have a tradition that is as old as the western tradition of comic books. They sort of invented them independently, and of course they have been influenced by ours a lot; but they have their own. Theirs never come over. There was a famous one done by a woman, Riyoko Ikeda, called *Berusaiyo no Bara—Rose of Versailles*. Its heroine is a Western woman. It takes place in seventeenth-century France. She's round-eyed and has blonde curly hair. She appears either naked or dressed in a man's uniform. She's a heroic figure. It was done in a music comedy too. It was very successful on the Japanese stage just a few years ago. Riyoko Ikeda was fifteen or sixteen when she began writing these things.

When I was in Kyoto I got bored with the Zen gardens and I said to a guy, "Show me Japanese popular culture." The first thing he did was to introduce me to—this was a professor at Doshisha University there—Japanese comic books. He said unfortunately his own collection had been stolen by a favorite student of his, one of the founders of the Red Brigade or whatever the hell they're called. He took them when he went underground. Then he took me to a striptease, but it turned out to be an audience participation sex show.

Bruce: Would you care to say more?

Yeah. All kinds of things go on on the stage: straight sex and homosexual sex, mostly women. I saw a double dildo there for the first time in my life, a two-ended dildo. They invite the audience to come on up the platform if they feel like it and participate. They told me that they often take their distinguished visitors to see this when they decide they can stand it.

They took Saul Bellow there, they said, and he said, "This is the first thing I've seen in Japan that interests me." And they took George Steiner there and he said, "This represents the ultimate degradation of the human spirit." They were amused by that.

Bruce: What did Leslie say?

I didn't say anything. The guy behind me tapped me on the shoulder and blew my mind. He turned out to be Jay Cocks. I asked him what he was doing there, and he said, "Studying popular culture—like you."

Diane: Do only men go to those things?

Yes: only Japanese men go to those things. There were a couple of American women there, keeping a stiff upper lip. It reinforces the stereotype, though: Japanese men are indeed short peckered; they leave you feeling superior. The audience was very interesting. There were all levels of society: there were university students, university professors, and taxicab drivers and factory workers, and clerks.

Bruce: Do they have this kind of joint in Tokyo and other cities?

I don't know. This is the most famous one, they tell me, in Japan. But there are probably others. They probably do.

So I saw Japanese in extreme situations. I think I know them in some ways better than most people get a chance to know them.

[During a break, Leslie mentions a forthcoming conference in Spain.]

Bruce: Who else is going to be participating in this conference?

There's an Italian professor, whom I don't know, who is running their side of it. And he's invited some people. Ihab Hassan is the other American participant. Ihab has been going a lot to Japan; but he always brings his wife with him, which puts him in a bad relationship with the Japanese. Because you can't really talk to Japanese men, except alone. Ihab also does the unforgivable thing: When his wife is not present, he's always praising her. That's really bad form. That's like boasting about yourself. You're supposed to put her down. If you say something nice to a Japanese about his wife, he's says, "My foolish wife, she can't boil an egg."

Diane: Do the women say anything?

They don't say much. Ever since the twenties there have been attempts at the woman's movement in Japan, but it's awfully hard to break through. Women live, I gather, at second and third hand, a very busy social life of their own. There's a lot of lesbianism in Japan. There are women's theaters, with all-female actors, just as there are men's theaters—they're all male.

Diane: Has this always been true in Japan?

I think so. Except in the very upper circles of Japanese society, where the women . . . It's like England in the Renaissance, where women participated in the intellectual life. The first great Japanese novel was written by a Japanese woman *[*Tale of Genji, *by Murasaki Shikibu, ca. 1021].*

But the geisha do the talking. And bar girls do the talking. I saw a lot of the bars one of the times I went there because I ran into an old friend of Kurt's, whose name is John Nathan, who knows more about Japan than any American, I think. He was trained as a Japanologist at Harvard; and then he taught at Princeton. He couldn't stand academic life. He married a Japanese woman and went off to Japan, where he made documentary movies. But he's also the translator of *[Yukio]* Mishima, and he wrote a book on Mishima, which is a very good book. He took me around to some of his favorite bars in Tokyo.

Diane: Do geishas ever marry?

No, not while they're working. They can quit and get married, though that's a little tricky.

Nathan's an interesting guy. He speaks Japanese perfectly, the only American I know who does. But he's absolutely not at home in Japan because he stands about six foot two and weighs three hundred pounds, so he walks like Gulliver among the Lilliputians. He's actually had parts in Japanese plays, where he plays the visiting foreigner. *Gaijin* in Japanese means "foreigner" or "outside person." This is the polite word. "Hairy barbarians" they called them first because they came with beards.

Japanese are pretty hairy, too, as compared to most Orientals. They can grow pretty good beards if they want to, but it's against the tradition. But they're not sparse-bearded, like the Chinese or the Koreans, especially. Koreans call the Japanese "dwarfs."

Diane: Are there any tall Japanese?

The Sumo wrestlers are big, not just wide, but every way. And they're getting taller all the time now, since their diet has changed. So you see some bigger kids. But they're still human size. Not like those Black and White barbarians who grow so grotesquely. Mediterranean size is what they'll be primarily.

Japanese religion is absolutely impossible to understand, because they have this overlay of Buddhism, but underneath, the old animistic faith with animal deities still stands.

Bruce: Pre-Buddhist?

Yes. Shinto is the official national religion.

Diane: Those myths were suppressed. Because of the identification of the emperor with the sun god. And in Shintoism, the emperors had to receive the power of the sun goddess. She had to come into the Shinto shrine and enter. It was part of the investiture of the emperor. One of my Japanese students was telling me that as part of the investiture of the emperor, he goes into a period of four or five days of absolute seclusion at which point the spirit is supposed to come upon him. There's a big discussion now about whether the current emperor did perform this—the tradition and rituals would have him not be really the emperor if he didn't do it. If he does do it, there's a worry that it will be insufficient.

I have the impression from things people have told me that he's impatient with the old stuff himself, that he'd just as soon cut loose. But he'll still write poems, I presume.

Those poems are really part of the Japanese. They play a game in which if you get half of a classic poem and you have to match it to the other. It's one of the parlor games that are played by people you would think of being pretty low on the scale of literacy. The poems are haiku. Everybody knows Bashō. Only recently have they been allowed to admit that he was gay. I used to know the most famous ones.

Diane: Do you know those in Japanese?

I used to know the most famous ones. *[He speaks in Japanese]* "Sound of water . . ." *["An ancient pond! / With a sound from the water / Of the frog as it plunges in."]*

The first things that came out of Japan to the West were these paintings and prints—the *ukiyo-e*, which means "floating world" paintings, that is to say secular, rather than religious. Not the eternal world. In Japan they were pure pop culture. They were sold for a penny. Everybody bought them. The Americans turned them into high art. The great collections are all in the United States. The Japanese despised them for years, but then through the West they rediscovered them. Now they're fighting to get them back again. They just drew the current favorite actresses and whores and "beauties," like pinups. I got much interested. I have a great collection of them. I have a [Suzuki] Harunobu in my bedroom. He's the guy who does the very narrow ones. He's a very strange artist. All his female figures are sixteen years old, even when they're supposed to be old women. He only liked that type.

A Japanese came to visit the other day, a man who's been here for a while, and he brought me a Utamaro print. But I know better than to try to give him anything back because next time he'll invite fifty of my closest friends . . .

Diane: That's so embarrassing.

Bruce: It's a wonderful story.

I sent a telegram to Margaret just before I came back saying, "Bringing home No. 2 wife." To which the response was, "The hell you are."

Bruce: A lot of guys did this after World War II.

Diane: Did the government try to stop guys from doing that?

They discouraged it, but nobody stopped it. In the deep American psyche, there's really no miscegenation feeling against marrying Japanese women. They're considered erotically okay.

Bruce: It's not like marrying a Black woman was then.

Right. Or even an Indian. In some ways, their ideal female beauty fits with our own; although really it's quite different. Breasts mean nothing to the Japanese; it's all ass and nape of the neck.

The first time I went to a polite Japanese home, the wife of the family took me to the john and stood by to see that I didn't miss. I felt deeply embarrassed. But that was okay. That's gone now in Japan but it used to be the custom. Her eyes were cast down, to be sure.

Diane: How could you miss?

She was just there in case you needed anything, a towel, god-knows-what.

Long before that I got used to . . . you know, women would wait for you to pass in front of them.

Diane: The bathing stuff is . . .

They don't have a nudity taboo.

I grew up in a household where no glimpse of my parents naked was permitted.

Diane: Even your father?

Even my father. Except when we went swimming. But in the house itself—no.

Bruce: I remember my father taking me to a place where you had to swim naked. It was horrible. You just grew up never seeing other people naked.

My father was an immensely, ferociously puritanical man. He was absolutely convinced—in the twenties when I was growing up and he had his first influence on me—that the world was going to hell. He would write letters to the newspaper about short-haired women and long-haired men, and confusing liberty with license. The first essay I ever wrote when

I was ten years old, was an answer to my father defending the styles of the flapper.

Diane: What were your grounds?

I had an aunt I loved dearly, who was my piano teacher and who was into the spirit of the age. My father was fierce. He thought he'd become a real honest-to-god American, and an American to him meant a puritan. Two things it meant: atheism and puritanism. Rigid morality and the hell with all the old-time religion. The first books he ever urged on me to read were by Bob Ingersoll and Tom Payne.

Diane: I thought that bit you did about westerns on the Today *show where you talked about anti-Christianity being at the heart of it was really brilliant. Most people don't say that.*

I don't say it either. It seems so evident.

Bruce: It's evident now that you've said it. I've thought about westerns a lot and I don't think I ever thought about it until you said it.

Especially if you think of *High Noon*.

The Code of the West is much closer to the Japanese heart than Christianity. They never took to Christianity at all, unlike the Koreans, who are mostly Christians at this point. I think the majority of the population of Korea belongs to a Christian sect, one kind or another. Those other religions never appealed to them very deeply. There's their old religion, the old animist religion; there's Confucianism, which leaves plenty of room for religion to slip around the corners.

Diane: Militarism is at the heart of Japanese Buddhism, I think.

Maybe it's no more difficult than militaristic Christianity. Militaristic Buddhism seems a strange notion, but that's what Bushido is. *[Bushido: the Samurai code embracing honor, loyalty, and martial arts, partially grounded in Zen Buddhism and Confucianism.]*

My last assignment in the Navy, if the bomb hadn't been dropped and the war had gone on: I was already assigned to a battleship and my particular assignment was to pick up kamikaze pilots who had missed, or who didn't die, and to interrogate them. So I say without any shame whatsoever, when I sat listening to the radio on the island of Guam and heard that the bomb had been dropped, I cheered.

Diane: Did you have any qualms at all?

None at all. I thought, "The war is over." All I thought was "Lots of lives are saved." Not just American lives, but Japanese lives; because by that time I was convinced it would be a struggle right to last man and the last hole in the hills.

Bruce: Having been in that war zone, you had evidence for that.
Yes.

Diane: Did you interrogate any kamikaze prisoners?

I never had one, no. There were some around us when our fleet was coming in but I never saw any. I don't know how many kamikazes there were. They must have been a relatively small number but they made a big splash.

I feared them because the office I was in was right under the bridge, and that's where they would dive in.

Diane: Did they hit many ships?

They hit a few. They didn't take any down, but they did some damage. They destroyed the control of the ship. They aimed for the part where the ship is conned. *["Con" = direct a ship's operations. Eleven Allied ships were sunk by kamikaze aircraft. One—the USS* Bismarck Sea*—was an "aircraft carrier, escort"; the others were troop transports, cargo ships, and minesweepers.]*

The first officer I ever took as a prisoner was still saying over and over again, "Keep your head down, keep your head down. Don't put your head up. Keep your head down." They were pretty well protected, but they blasted them out with flame-throwers. I saw that done. The Japanese would be in a cave or a hole, and instead of trying to fight their way in with just guns and fire power, they would just blast the thing with a flame-thrower—a jet of flame. That would burn or asphyxiate them.

The day I was on the beach I saw a Marine, who, contrary to orders, had fallen behind his men and was digging the gold teeth out of a dead Japanese. They had lots of gold teeth.

On the other hand, those guys were so brave, you wouldn't believe it. Especially the junior officers. They really said what they said in the movies. "You sons of bitches, you think you're gonna live forever?" The men would be advancing, and the junior officers would be backing up with their backs to the enemy ahead of them. The officers would go ahead. The thing that impressed me was their backs were turned. An awful lot got killed. Two divisions were almost completely wiped out of the four that went in. I think there were fifty percent casualties, including wounded and dead. It was impossible. The enemy was in an impregnable position. They had been preparing for years.

Bruce: The Navy shelled it for days.
And the bombers went over.
Bruce: They were dug into rock.

Soft lava rock . . .

It was a strange war; it's like all wars. I see these Vietnam movies; they drive me a little crazy. It's as if it's the first time that the troops didn't know exactly what we were fighting for and everybody ended up wanting only one thing: for it to be over and to get home. But *all* wars have been like that.

The worst war story I ever heard was when somebody told me that on the battlefield at Gettysburg more than half the men found dead had never fired a single shot from their guns. They just walked out and got killed.

Diane: You know that line in Reds, *I think it's Adele St. John talks about how "Men love war: don't be silly dear. They love putting on those uniforms and going out and doing it." Did you see* Reds?

Yes. It moved me a lot. I felt that way when we moved into Tientsin, when I was the conquering hero. I wasn't exactly wearing a helmet; that was too hot and heavy. But I was wearing my helmet liner. There I was in that Marine uniform which I never quite believed in. And we were the deliverers and people were showering us with flowers.

Bruce: In Tientsin there were a lot of émigrés from Nazi Germany.

There were a lot of Europeans, but they were mostly émigrés from Bolshevik Russia. They had come much earlier, as far as Mukden in Manchuria, and then had come on down into China.

I met a lot of Russian Jews there. I used to go to the Imperial Hotel on Sunday mornings and have bagels and tea. All the Jews were *luftmenschen [Yiddish: an impractical person, one with no regular income or business]*. They were living by changing money or running sleazy nightclubs or doing a little pimping. There was one favorite money changer I had one day. I gave him an American five or ten dollar bill—and he gave me two thousand or four thousand or six thousand in yuan—Chinese money. And I said to him, "Thank you." He looked up at the heavens—a classic Jewish pose—and he said, "Look at him. He gives me good American money, and I give him shit paper, and he says 'thank you'?" I thought, "The Jews will never die."

A lot of them went to Japan afterwards when the Communists came in. Some of them stayed there for a while. The Japanese were not used to dealing with Jews.

Diane: And how did they do?

They did all right for a while. But I'm told that very recently, some anti-Semitism has developed in Japan. It never existed anyplace in the

Orient, actually. India it hasn't touched yet. In China there's no feeling of that kind. And the times I went to Japan, the feeling was very good about Jews. Their religion is even older than ours.

Bruce: There's a kind of Oriental respect.

Yeah.

There were three clubs of the Russians in Tientsin. There was the White Russian Club: people were still faithful to their old Czarist ideals. There was a Red Russian Club: mostly the children of the people who were in the White Russian Club. There was a club of the Russian Jews, which was called the *Kunst* Club, believe it or not: The Art Club. But the only art practiced was money changing.

It was a fascinating city. It was full of everything. There were these French, these Turks, and these Basques, who had been brought in to play jai lai. We used to sit with the Turks sometimes, and we would plan to come back and go on a caravan afterwards. I said, "They all speak Turkic languages through central Asia." And the French were eager to sell you their wives. Everybody was acting according to ethnic stereotypes. And the Italians, of course, had put up a statue of Dante in the middle of the square in their part of the city.

My job was to translate into readable English all the local political newspapers that were being published in Chinese and Korean and Japanese. I could read Japanese, but I would say to the Chinese translator—we were doing the Communist newspapers—"Read me the first half of the first sentence, and I'll tell you the rest of the article." We'd bet on whether I could do it.

The Koreans were absolutely marvelous. They were prisoners, and we turned them loose. They immediately divided into three political groups and began shooting at each other. Koreans were tough beyond belief.

Bruce: You're how old?

In 1945 I was twenty-eight years old. I was feeling young. That's one of the things the war gave me a chance to do, to be young again. I had two kids and a regular job, and I was suddenly loose again.

Diane: Did Margaret envy you?

I don't know.

Bruce: Did you tell her how much fun you were having?

The only time she seemed deeply disturbed was for three months I spent on Guam, in which I was not sober for one day and it apparently showed in my letters home. First beer call was at 11:00 am in the morning, but we would always buy a bottle of Pastis to have for breakfast, to give us a start. When the Marines landed in China, the first thing they unloaded was the whisky.

There wasn't dope yet. The rickshaw drivers would offer it to you. There were still old-fashioned rickshaw drivers in those days, where you had a naked back pumping up and down in front of you. The Marines couldn't stand it. They would want to put the rickshaw driver in the seat and they'd pull it.

Bruce: The boys showing off?

The boys. All this stuff about male bonding. And the army is a little like ships. They would spend the first part of the morning rubbing each other down—the Marines. They would strip naked, lie out on a cot and guys would take turns caressing each other's beautiful bodies.

Bruce: That was gone by my day in the Marines. Somebody must have told them what it meant.

They were far from home; nobody was watching.

Diane: And fear of venereal disease. It wasn't curable then.

They used to do prophylaxes; you know, they'd inject something. That was the other great morning exercise, milking down their penises after they shot something up.

Kurt *[Leslie's son]* was in the Marines for a while, too. That was after his experience at Harvard the first time. He went there and had some wise-ass young instructor in the freshman class in English. Kurt sounded off one day and the guy said to him—the worst thing he could have said to Kurt (he must have known)—he said, "Kurt, if you'd talk for yourself, instead of repeating what your father said, you'd be better off." Kurt walked out of the class, walked out of Harvard, and joined the Marines.

Diane: What a mean thing to say.

Isn't that shitty? You can be sure he wasn't echoing me. That's the last thing in the world he'd do. Kurt got busted twice out of Harvard. He tried twice at Harvard, then went to Reed College for a while. At Reed he suddenly discovered he was only two months away from getting a degree and he couldn't stand that. That's where he met Emily, who became his wife. He picked up and took off and he ended finally beachcombing in Fiji. He was at that point twenty-six, twenty-seven years old. And then suddenly his life sort of turned around. He decided he could figure out something he wanted to do. He came back to the states and went back to school, right on through medical school. He finally finished college at the University of New Mexico.

Diane: He and Emily are divorced, now, right?

Yes. Kurt's been married again for quite a while now. He married a marvelous, marvelous woman. At the point he married her she was thirty-three years old and this was her seventh marriage. Sounds incredible, doesn't it? She had had three kids somewhere along the way, but had kept in touch with only one of them. The others were turned over to the parents of the husbands, I think. But she's turned out to be very great for Kurt. She's a girl who grew up on a ranch in New Mexico. Very solid, very beautiful. Hardly gone to school at all. She's going back to school now.

Diane: Have they had kids?

No. But Kurt's two kids are with him basically. One of his wife's kids must be twenty-seven or twenty-eight by now.

Emily went completely to pieces after the breakup of the marriage; sort of disappeared from the world. She couldn't work; she couldn't function in society at all. She was terrible with the kids. She would keep the younger kid home from school watching TV with her. So Kurt went through a series of brutal battles and finally got the kids. She was an awful nice woman, but she couldn't deal with it.

Diane: Was she a Mormon?

No. She's half-Jewish, and her father—her name was Wirtz—came from an old Illinois family. He was the black sheep of the family, who the day he married her mother was put into jail for leading demonstrations of the unemployed in Chicago. He never had any education, but he was a man of great intelligence and great ingenuity. Kurt and Emily lived for years on a device he invented for rectifying type which was used by small printers, and he had the royalty on it. And then he wrote some of the first series of new math books which were used in schools and made a load of money.

Bruce: An interesting guy.

His family is an interesting family. His brother, Willard Wirtz, was a cabinet something-or-other at some point.

Emily's father had been president of one of the branches of the University of Illinois. Her mother came from an orthodox Jewish family. She committed suicide after her marriage broke up.

But Kurt has finally found something he enjoys doing, though he keeps changing his mind from time to time. At first he thought he was going to be a family, country doctor.

Bruce: What kind of doctor is he?

He went back to school for three years to study spinal cord injuries. He's presently in charge of a whole little thing which has been set up for him with special buildings built for him. He's in charge of fifty paraplegics. Half sponsored by the VA and half by the University of New Mexico. It's a little tough. The last time I saw him one of his patients—he won't call them patients—one of the guys he works with had committed suicide.

Diane: Does he do research? Is he trying to do electronic stimulation and all this stuff?

Kurt's a little scornful of the theoreticians. He thinks of himself as their family doctor and adviser. And he helps them cope.

Bruce: So he did wind up being a family doctor.

He talked to a lot of people, and he finally talked them into putting up an awful lot of dough.

Diane: Good for him, good for him. Do you know Ange Coniglio? You see him out at the university. He's in a wheelchair. He's in my class now.

Bruce: He's a friend of [our son] Michael's. When Michael did that book about kids who used drugs [Doing Drugs, 1983] Ange was the kid who was most fucked-up. He was dealing everything, using everything. Then he cleaned himself up. He stopped using everything. A short time after he cleaned himself up he was playing hockey. He went against a wall, broke his neck, and is now paralyzed from the neck down. That was about seven years ago. He's been going to school at UB. A very smart kid. It's like one of those sentimental novels.

Sally's niece just married a "wheelie." We went to the wedding. He's a paraplegic; a super-handsome, super-macho guy, who at age twenty smashed himself up in his car. He has no use of his legs at all, limited use of his hands. But he's got a job; he works with computers. And he took on a wife with two kids.

When Kurt went to Harvard he went through school with a guy called Bill Kelly. Does the name William Melvin Kelly mean anything to you? He's a Black writer. He came to see me one time. We had a long conversation. He said, "You've got to understand, Kurt is good. I don't know, and Kurt don't know what he's good for, but he's good." Finally, Kurt figured out what he wanted to be good at besides building and playing musical instruments. Kurt can build anything. He came here one summer and said, "You need a slide in the pool." So he organized the whole family, laid out the plans, put them to work, and they built the slide into the pool. He loves to build.

Diane: Is it true that Margaret said he failed her because he went through school?

Yes. Margaret was very bad with him. At his wedding she really insulted him. The two things she didn't believe in were jobs and marriage at that point. They asked her how she felt about the wedding, and she said, "I want to puke." So for a while Kurt wasn't talking to her, but he is now.

You were going to ask me something.

Bruce: I was going to ask, After your experiences in China, when you read Malraux's Man's Fate, *you must have been able to approach that with a very different take than you otherwise would have.*

Yes.

The feeling I came out of China with was the feeling that its problems were essentially forever. It would always be happening. There were simply too many people. And built into the Chinese system there is such deep corruption, which I take it they still have to wrestle with under the present regime. And that's what the students are hollering about now. One of the first words I learned in Chinese, which is not a Chinese word at all, is *cumishaw*. I think it comes from "commission": It means a bribe. In order to do anything, they reach out their hand and say, "Comishaw"—"Pay me off."

Bruce: When I was in the Marine Corps, the word for stealing things was "comshaw."

It's probably the same thing. It probably comes from the old China days. It probably goes back to the Horse Marines.

All those goddamned people! I used to walk down the road and get to feeling that if they push me a little further, I'm going to walk through with a swagger stick. You just brush them aside.

Diane: They're really wrestling with it now.

Not successfully. The population is creeping up too fast for them, much beyond their predictions. Because they'll cheat. You're talking about birth control. But they did it in such repressive ways—late marriages.

Diane: And forced abortions.

And then if you limited a family to one or two kids, and they get a girl child, they'll kill it.

But the other thing about China that drove me crazy is, it's a very strange feeling for an American to walk into a group of people who, collectively and individually, think they are better than you think you are. The Chinese can condescend to you beyond anything in the world. The people will be here, the central kingdom will never perish from the face of the earth.

Diane: Phil Habib told me that the Vietnamese were like that, too. He was part of the delegation that negotiated the Vietnam peace. My aunt was with him in Paris while it was going on. He said the head of the Viet-namese delegation asked him what year he was born. Phil told him and he said, "The year of the Monkey." Philip said, 'Yeah." The Vietnamese laughed and said, "Ah, yes, the monkey. He swings through the trees and then he falls down and into the river." And he laughed. Then Phil said, "And swims to the bank and swings into the trees again." And the Vietnamese bowed to him and he said, "I perceive you're not like most Americans." He had answered him in a story. He said, "Most Americans don't understand. They think we're barbarians. They think our culture is so ignorant, we have no stories, no traditions, no history, no common sense."

The Vietnamese were never able to assimilate the Chinese. That's one of the worst forms of racism in the world, the way the Vietnamese feel about the Chinese. That's why most of the people come out, people refer to them as Vietnamese, but they're always Chinese, almost always. Ethnic Chinese, whose lives have been made miserable. They were a large part of the population.

One of the strangest experiences I ever had with the Chinese was the time I arrested my only war criminal. At the time I was in Tientsin, it was an absolute interregnum. I mean, the Japanese had been driven out, the Americans were there for a little while, the Communists were already on the borders of the city, and had interpenetrated, and the Kuo-mintang *[Chinese Nationalist Party]* had moved their official troops in. Two of these young Chinese officers, in absolutely immaculate uniforms, looking down their noses at me, said, "We would like you to help us. We've just been informed that hiding out in a factory here disguised as a Chinese is a Japanese, a former factory owner. A, he's reported to have once castrated a coolie in a fit of anger, and B, he also has (and their eyes lit up) a large fortune in gold buried someplace in his backyard. He doesn't speak Chinese."

They spoke English and I was to be the interpreter. So we went to see this poor guy, who turned out to be a miserable, scared creature, who was indeed wearing Chinese clothes, where the Japanese mostly wore Western-style garb there. And they hauled him off and there was a little girl with him, who he kept introducing to me as his daughter, but it was obviously his mini-mistress, who kept weeping and screaming. I felt like I'd suddenly turned into the Gestapo. I hauled him down the stairs with the two Chinese officers. He was taken off to prison. And they dug in the backyard and found no gold, and I began to think, how reliable was the informant? Maybe there never was a coolie who got castrated at all.

So I went to the prison where he presumably had been taken to talk to him again. After many cups of tea and an hour and a half of avoiding my questions, it was reported to me that no such prisoner had ever been arrested, much less confined in a cell in that prison. They knew nothing about him. He obviously was dead a minute after he arrived. And whether he was guilty or not I'll never know. But I couldn't ever penetrate that Chinese official cool. Lots of bowing. Lots of tea.

I have a picture I drew of him. *[Sounds of things moving around.]* These are my Chinese pictures. I learned to use a Chinese brush. These are all from Tientsin. This is my war criminal. The way sheer manpower is used: that's one of the things that hasn't changed. A beggar woman.

Diane: These are wonderful.

Bruce: Leslie: this is a whole other aspect of you.

I thought seriously of painting and drawing for a while.

Bruce: Outside the jai lai court.

Diane: So what do you think was the story about the war criminal?

I think there was no "due process" in the whole business at all. And I can't tell you how I felt. Like, what am I doing here? I felt like a Nazi dragging a Jew off who's been accused of desecrating a host or something.

This is my one piece of Japanese pornography. You can see they're overcompensating. All Japanese pornography shows men with immense cocks. I really enjoyed working with Chinese ink and brushes and so forth.

Did someone teach you that?

No I just sort of learned.

I worked with a couple of Chinese translators, but the only thing I did with them was to start to read the *Four Books [of the core values and beliefs of Confucianism].* They started to teach me a little Chinese. I never got past the first sentence, it moved me so deeply: "To learn and to learn again. Is this not the greatest of all pleasures?"

I got two presents, books, when I left. One was a copy of the *Analects [The Sayings of Confucius],* in a nice old wood-block form. And the other was the *Principles of Marxism,* which was given to me by a young Japanese I knew who was going back to reform his country.

I was quite serious about art for a while. We got together when I was seventeen or eighteen, and we used to hire a model. I even started going to a local art school in Newark. I was discouraged because the first thing I ever produced in class, the teacher looked at scornfully and said, "I wouldn't hang that on the wall of my living room." That was not the point of the production but I was a bit discouraged.

I really wanted to preserve some of that visually, because lots of my impressions were visual impressions. And the ironies of the whole thing . . . That really was a shop sitting there.

Bruce: My friends who were in Tientsin when you were there, their parents were both German doctors and they were brought by some missionary group to escape the Nazis. They were immediately interned by the Japanese. But they had a fairly decent life because they were doctors to the Japanese, too. When the war ended, they said, the Communists were coming in, and it was the American Navy who rescued them. Her whole family absolutely adored the American Navy. Not because of the Japanese, but for saving them from the Communists.

Some of the people I knew in China had been in the Shanghai internment camp, which was the really big one. They told me a million dollars' worth of business was done every day between the Jews inside the camp and the Chinese outside the camp. There's much in common between the two cultures.

Diane: As George Steiner said, the Jews and the Chinese. You heard that story, didn't you?

No.

Diane: We were visiting George Steiner and George is going on about "Only the Jews and the Chinese have kept their gene pools pure. They're the two extraordinary races."

Bruce: George's knowledge of history has a few gaps in it.

He's willfully ignorant on some things.

Diane: So it was very clear as he began—he did a whole thing on chamber music and chess —

Bruce: That only Chinese and Jews can do both well.

Diane: It's very clear as he's doing this that he presumes that I'm Jewish. And for the first time in my life, I'm going to kind of let it go. I'm usually running after Bruce and saying, "Oh, no, he doesn't really mean that, don't take him literally." He goes on about how wonderful it would be to be a Chinese Jew. And then he says, he can't imagine anything worse than not being born Jewish. I, in this moment, am thinking, "I am gonna let this go. Sometime Leslie will be visiting this guy and he'll say, 'Not only is she a shiksa, but she used to be a nun.'" And George Steiner is going to learn something. I'm feeling really wicked. At the line where he says, "I can't imagine not being Jewish," there's a pause and I'm feeling really, really wicked, and Bruce says, "Well, ask her. She's a shiksa." I wasn't willing to lie on the face of it, and he looks at me, sees my face and knows it's true.

Bruce: And within five minutes we were out of the house. He took us to a nearby bar where he said the poet Rupert Brooke spent time before dying in the First World War. He orders two beers for us, said we'd love the atmosphere of the place, and he hoped we'd have a good train trip back to London. And he was gone.

5

June 10, 1989

Bruce: The fellow who wrote the Twayne book about you—Mark Royden Winchell. Do you know him? Do you have a relationship?

No. We started a relationship through the mail. When he first wrote to me, he was teaching a course on me and John Crowe Ransom. He's a very strange fellow. He's about as different from me as he can possibly be: (a) He's an absolutely hardcore right-winger; (b) he's a goy and a Southerner. All his jobs have been in Mississippi. He did a book on Buckley and one on Joan Didion.

He writes like crazy. His most recent book, which I think he got paid to do, is on *[Herman E.]* Talmadge. He's an interesting fellow.

Diane: Did you like the book?

It's all right.

Bruce: He seemed annoyed that you'd chosen Roots *over* Miss Jane Pitman. *He had his own little list of preferences.*

He's a strange and interesting guy. He's very young. And he's already a full professor at Clemson. When he wrote this book he was at the University of Mississippi or Southern Mississippi. He's a real Southerner.

Bruce: I couldn't tell from this if he'd had a lot of conversations with you or if he'd just done it from the outside.

Pretty much from the outside. We had a little conversation, but not a hell of a lot. What I said to him was, "It's your book, you do it."

At that point I thought I was going to do my own. But now I've pretty much decided not *[to do my autobiography].* Unless I can get an inspiration and can see how to shape it. I explained to you that I wrote fifteen thousand words. It was supposed to be a fifteen thousand–word autobiographical piece I was doing. And when I reached fifteen thousand words I was only seven years old. It turned out to be more about Newark than anything else.

Bruce: Gershon Legman is writing about his life. I think he said he had fifteen volumes. The title is The Peregrine Penis.

How old is he?

Diane: I think he was sixty-nine—although he might have made that up for his own purpose—when he was here in 1986.

He's been writing for a while.

Bruce: A long while. I got a mailing from him not long ago. It was a form letter and it was printed and mailed from someplace in New Jersey. He'd obviously sent it to someone who'd reproduced it and sent it out. It said that this would be made available to a very small group of individuals and if you want to be one, please contact Gershon Legman. So I wrote him.

He's selling it by subscription?

Bruce: Yes. I asked, are you giving these away, is this by subscription, are they awards for certain kinds of things? What's the story? He wrote back: It's none of the above. He's decided no one will ever publish it. So what he wants to do is get fifteen people, each of whom will be responsible for getting one volume typed in fifteen copies, and they will send the other fourteen copies to the other fourteen people.

Diane: We're in it. He stayed at our house and we almost killed him.

Bruce: I just said *I was going to kill him. He said this was going to be his version of* My Secret Life *[eleven-volume explicit sexual memoir published 1888–1895].*

This is going to be great!

Bruce: Are you writing now?

Yes. I'm doing short things. I'm just finishing a piece on Steinbeck—on *Grapes of Wrath* fifty years later. I gave it as a talk on a conference that was held in the heart of Steinbeck country in San Jose, California. I ran into a lot of grief there. It turned out to be a bunch of Steinbeck fans, who wanted to be told that his reputation had been put down by the Eastern establishment; that he was really very good. And there I was, this mouthpiece of the Eastern establishment. They meant Jews, right? On the other hand, I had lived in Montana for a long time, so they figured this might have redeemed me.

I finally enjoyed writing it.

Bruce: Do you find the novel holds up?

The parts of it which I originally hated the most, like the scene at the end, the young woman suckling the dying old man, I really liked this time through. I thought that sort of saved the book at the last possible moment, from his politics and his determined optimism. But you get all this half-baked Emersonian transcendentalism, oversoul shit, and it's just unbearable.

Another possible ending is the one John Ford used in the movie: to end at the government camp. A happy New Deal ending. But he passed that one by and he passed the soap box speech of Tom Joad. That [speech] could have been written by Clifford Odets.

It's one of the great memories of my life, Odets's *Waiting for Lefty* play. I played in it when I was a student in college. I was the guy in the audience who yells, "That son of a bitch is my own lousy brother." I still remember my line. I also yelled when the speaker says, "Time's ain't right boys, just like the fruit don't fall from the tree till it's ripe." I was the guy in the audience who yelled, "Sit down, you brute!"

For the record, it must be made clear I did not play in it at Harvard, though my name is listed on the program and given by a YCL *[Young Communist League]* Harvard production of it back in the thirties. I had a friend there whose name is Al Eisner, who decided to use my name as a pseudonym. I think I told you about that. So I've had long connections with that play. I saw the original play.

I saw a recent production of it. Odets has a kind of baleful fascination for me. I kept going to see everything. *Awake and Sing.* There were great actors in theater in those days. One of my favorite headlines is the review of one of Odets's movies, which says, "Odets, where is thy sting?" I think that was *The General Died at Dawn.*

You should take a look at that movie someday. Akim Tamiroff, I think, plays the Chinese general.

As I said, I've been writing a lot of shorter things lately. It's part of this project I have, which I think I've talked about already. I've gathered together these fugitive essays of mine which I haven't collected for ten or fifteen years. There's a lot of them I want to do. The first one is now set to come out, I think. I've got a new publisher, David Godine, who'll do a nice book, and who really understands what I'm about. He would like, if possible, to bring back into print some of those old Stein & Day books of mine. But BookCrafters, the outfit that's taken over and now wants to set up as a publisher, aren't willing to surrender the books. They want to put them back into print and circulation again.

Bruce: And they own all the rights to those books?

Yeah. They actually own some of the books, the ones still in stock.

Bruce: Our Death Row book was published by Beacon. I wrote Transaction books and said, "How about bringing out a paperback?" They said, "Fine. We'll contact Beacon." What they did was, they contacted Beacon and got their whole stock of hardbacks for $1 each, which were selling for $14, raised the price to $20, and issued it as their own hardback and never released the paperback because they didn't want to do it until their stock of hardbacks was gone.

That's disgusting!

Diane: And when we wanted some copies, they wanted to charge us the higher amount!

Beacon was my first publisher. Sol Stein was then an advisory editor for them. Sol was a high school pal of [James] Baldwin's. In the Bronx someplace. A good high school *[DeWitt Clinton High School]*. Not a top-notch school like Bronx Science or Stuyvesant. Stuyvesant is where my ex-father-in-law taught most of his life—Joseph Shipley.

Bruce: The guy who did the book on world literature?

Yes. He did all kinds of things, like an encyclopedias on world literature. Bud, we called him. He was Margaret's father, whom she never met after he left her mother when she was age four, until I introduced her to him. She got very fond of him, finally. He was a very charming. He just died at age ninety-two or ninety-three.

Bruce: Those survey books of his were great for preparing for PhD exams.

They were.

One of the first things I ever wrote was for one of his encyclopedias. I knew him before I knew Margaret. He had been an original contributor to a strange and wonderful magazine published in Montana, called *Frontier and Midland*, by H. G. Merriam, who was the chairman of the English Department, one of the first Rhodes scholars who went from America. I've mentioned him to you before.

An interesting fellow, H. G. Merriam. Students all insisted it stood for "Holy God" Merriam. He acted as if it were. He was an old-fashioned head of the department. For life. More powers than a pasha. He also lived to be ninety something. Those guys just wouldn't die. What Bud wanted to do was outlive his most famous student at Stuyvesant, who was James Cagney.

Bruce: I went to Stuyvesant. I thought, when I read that Winchell thing, I never knew that Margaret's name was Shipley and I was going to ask if she was any relation. Then I thought, "Nah. That's ridiculous."

The person who was closest to Margaret all her life, and still is, and is now eighty-nine, is her Aunt Ruth, Bud's sister, who is very proud and goes to the Shipley family reunions. They arrived in 1602 or something. That was a very weird family. Margaret's grandmother was Jennie, who was the daughter of a boardinghouse keeper in Brooklyn. One of the guys who stayed there was a law book salesman named J. Shipley. The name that runs through the Shipley family is Joseph Twaddell Shipley. It had been abbreviated in his case to J. R.—the initial standing for nothing—Shipley. And they ran off together. A nice Jewish girl from Worcester, Massachusetts, by way of Brooklyn.

Poppa Jay looked exactly like Rip Van Winkle. At age forty, his alcoholism required his retirement from life. He would walk down the road with his knotted stick and his tobacco-stained mustache and his dog. He was a little, tiny guy; must have weighed ninety pounds altogether. His wife weighed about somewhere between 250 and 300 pounds. She took over. She ran the family. She was a juvenile officer in the New York courts. My kids grew up raised by juvies. PRs *[perhaps Puerto Ricans]*, most of them. Some of those girls were mighty cute and tough. But Grandma Jennie was tougher than anybody.

Bruce: What else are you writing about?

The first volume that Godine is going to bring out is going to have the improbable title of *Fiedler on the Roof*. It's going to be a collection of things I've written on Jewish subjects, which is a subject I've sworn I would never write about again. The age of the Jewish-American novel is over, I said. Everything is gone. The awarding of the Nobel Prize to Saul Bellow is like a monument put on the grave of Jewish-American literature. The hell with it. I looked back and discovered that I had written things. For instance, I wrote a piece on Isaac Singer, on whom somehow I hadn't ever written anything before, called "Lost in America."

I do very, very few book reviews anymore, but it turns out I have actually reviewed three books with Jewish subjects: Styron's *Sophie's Choice*; Mailer's Egyptian book, that came out in some strange place, like *Psychology Today*; and then I wrote a piece—they put together a collection of essays by various Jews in once sense or another, Jews on the books of the Jewish Bible. I did *Job*.

The same guy has done another book on the Holocaust, and I did a piece for him, which will bug everybody who reads it. I called it "The Two Holocausts." I wrote about the one which destroyed the remnants of my family in Europe, and which I can feel very righteous about; and what pious Jews call the Silent Holocaust, to which I am a contributor. The slow disappearance of the Jews by intermarriage. I reflected on the fact that nobody will ever say Kaddish for me. That three of my male grandchildren have never been circumcised; that not one single one of my children has a Jewish mate, nor do I. It's all about the problematical sense in which I remain a Jew. It's a sort of a retrospective piece in which I talk about my long-term anti-Zionism; the fact that even after the original politics which spread it had disappeared, a sort of distrust remains. And why I refused really to let myself believe in what Hitler was doing until late, late, late, late. It's an essay I love very much, but I can't imagine anybody else who would like it.

It will come out before the end of the year in my anthology book, then in my *Fiedler on the Roof* book, which is due in 1990. David Godine *says* it will come out in 1990. I take it he's not very prompt.

Bruce: Did you decide that fellow who wrote you was just pulling your leg? The one who wrote and said: "I see your latest book . . . ?"

We finally worked that out. Finally got a letter back from the guy. We couldn't find a phone number for him. I guess it was unlisted. He said, "I made a little mistake. The book I was referring to was actually *The Fiedler Reader.*" Which is either true or not true. If he was trying to get away with something you'd see the book listed someplace. What he wanted was an autographed picture. That's why he wrote the letter to begin with.

The second volume will be a collection of things which were originally talks which I gave to health professionals of one kind or another. I've talked to nurses and doctors and people interested in medical ethics, gerontologists, and so forth.

Bruce: Is this a whole secret life we don't know about?

I've enjoyed it. One of those pieces which has the widest circulation in response is one which I originally gave to a bunch of nurses in Texas, at the medical school there. I talked about the image of the nurse in literature from Sariey Gamp *[in Dickens's* Martin Chuzzlewit, *1833–1834]* to Nurse Ratched *[in Ken Kesey's* One Flew Over the Cuckoo's Nest, *1962]*. It was a hilarious occasion because all of the nurses who came were in civvies, except one who was in an absolutely starched uniform and looked more like Big Nurse than Big Nurse *[in* One Flew Over the Cuckoo's

Nest] did herself. When the talk was over she came up and grasped my hand with enough pressure to crush the small bones in it and said, "I *like* Nurse Ratched."

This book will also include the keynote address which I once gave to the World Congress of Theologians. That was in Los Angeles. Sally and I were in Europe at that time and we flew to Los Angeles in a plane full of German theologians, who looked at me disapprovingly through the whole flight. And were even more disapproving in the audience. I gave a talk which was called "The Death of God and the Rebirth of the Gods." That was quite a long time ago—in the seventies. The reason I gave it was a sheer accident. At a cocktail party I had gone to, I ran into a man whom I knew slightly in Montana, which has always had a strong Department of Theology all full of Death of God theologians. We were both drunk and before we knew it we had agreed that I was going to give the keynote address at the next World Conference of Theologians. A lot of Sally's old Presbyterian ministers were there.

So I've done a lot of that talking.

And I have two essays on old age, which I gave to gerontologists and assorted psychologists. It turns out there are a lot of those things. Another one I gave to a group of doctors on the tyranny of the normal, which begins with some of the ideas—it was my *Freaks* book that got all these medical people interested in me originally—which begins with notions about healing freaks and repairing freaks and speculates about whether finally this will result in a complete abhorrence of any kind of difference. We'll eliminate fat people, skinny people . . .

The third book, which is going to bring an end to my whole writing career is going to be called *Back to Innocence*. It's going to be odds and ends about things I've written on popular literature and the popular arts in general.

Someplace in that I'm going to include a bunch of things I've done. I've been invited for various reasons to talk to groups of fans of various writers, beginning with James Branch Cabell and Robert Penn Warren, Faulkner, and so forth. They will probably be in that *Back to Innocence* book, where they really fit.

Somebody, when they introduced me the other day, said I had eight hundred bibliographical entries, but I think that's an underestimation. It may be closer to twelve hundred. Some years ago, in 1972, I think it was, a guy for his master's degree at the University of Louisville, did a complete bibliography of me up to that point. At this moment, a woman who's a complete nut and keeps disappearing and reappearing claims she's bringing it up to date. She's in Nebraska someplace.

Bruce: How much time do you spend on an essay?

I don't know what time I spend on it, since I have no schedule and I work erratically, under pressure sometimes for long stretches of time, and then I'll do absolutely nothing, usually convinced that I'm never going to do anything ever again in my life. I don't exactly block, but I sometimes end up with the feeling that I've said everything that I want to say about anything that interests me at all, and what's the point? And then somebody will say to me, "Will you do so and so?" And I'll say yes. Particularly if they call me up and they ask me. I always say yes on the telephone in order to get off as fast as possible.

Diane: That's how Bill Kunstler is. They have to keep him off the phone. If anyone can get to him, either on the phone or in person, he can't say no.

Bruce: They try to get to the phone before he does.

The only thing I've really persuaded myself to say no to are blurbs for books. I've stopped doing those.

At the beginning of July [1989] there's a conference in Spain, which wants to talk about the literature and films about Vietnam. I'm going to talk about *Rambo*, *The Deerhunter*, and *Apocalypse Now*. I'll call it "Mythicizing the Vietnam War." It's going to be an interesting conference. People are coming from all over Europe, somebody from the Soviet Union.

This is organized by a guy called Enrique something absolutely ordinary—Gomez, in Valencia. I was there once before under his auspices. Beautiful. It's the best food in Spain. That's where paella was invented and perfected. There are beautiful beaches close by. It's a nice place.

Diane: Won't it be horrid in July?

Yeah, but the ocean is there. And it will be air-conditioned.

Diane: [to Sally] Are you going to go?

Sally: I'm staying here with the granddaughter.

One of my uncircumcised grandchildren. The only one of my grandsons who's circumcised is Abraham Kwame, and that's because his father's religion requires it, too.

[My grandson] Seth's bris was one of the great events of all time. Bob Creeley was present at that. This was the one where all Kurt's hippyish friends attended, and we had a doctor who did the actual cutting, but I did the ceremony in English and for the first time the people heard what really went on. When you come to the point where you say, "In blood, in blood shalt you remember." And there's really blood to remember him by. And this gigantic goy who was standing next to me, looking like one of my ancestors with long hair, a long beard, and sandals (except for the fact that he wasn't Jewish at all), put his hand on my shoulder at that point and said, "Heavy trip, man," and fainted dead away. Then we had a grand and glorious party that seemed to go on for days. Seth is now twenty-two years old.

Bruce: Have those Vietnam movies replaced western movies?

Something has replaced western movies, though they're struggling to come back right now. *The Deerhunter* is a deliberate attempt to go back. That film is an absolutely fascinating film. I watched it again last night. It's without politics completely. *Absolutely* without politics. What happens is that the North Vietnamese turn into the Red Indians. There are goddamn Indians in that film. All there are, are these strange people who speak a language you don't understand with a culture which is incomprehensible to you, carrying on guerrilla warfare from behind the trees. And there's Natty Bumppo who can't shoot anymore. It's a fascinating film. Many people hated it but it's beautiful. Just as a piece of filmwork, it's magnificent. It had a great photographer, one of those refugee Czechs, I think *[Vilmos Zsigmond, Hungarian]*. And great actors. It's the first time Meryl Streep appeared in film. It's the one film in the world with working-class people in it that I believe in. I sat crying at the wedding scene and I said to Sally, "My grandmother always wanted to dance the *Kazatsky* at my wedding and she never got the chance."

Diane: What about the Russian roulette section at the end?

It isn't just at the end. That's the thing that binds the whole picture together from beginning to end. I think if you don't worry about ridiculous things when watching a mythological film like that is—"Did anybody ever really do that?"—and you let the image work on you, it's really very convincing. What it finally means when he turns that single shot on himself, not to bring down a deer or an Indian anymore, but *this* is the enemy that has to be killed: *Me.*

I always keep explaining to Sally that Russian roulette is not really very dangerous because if you have one bullet in the chamber of a gun, the odds are extremely strong that it will go past the one that the bullet will carry because of the weight. It's better than five to one. They say it's about a hundred to one.

So I'm writing about all the things I swore I would never write about: the Holocaust, Vietnam, the Jews, who I had sworn off of forever.

I may be going to Israel in January. I've been there six or seven times. What bugged me there the first time I went was not the relationship to the Arabs, which I knew something about, but the relationship between the White Jews and the Black Jews, which I knew nothing about. I saw a race riot in a working-class café outside of Haifa, between North African Jews and East European Jews, simply because they operated totally on different levels and their values were bound to bring them that.

Bruce: Do the White Jews look upon them as Arabs?

They're a permanent underclass. They're "niggers." They're really "niggers." Until very recently you had to pay to go to high school in Israel. You had to pay tuition. It was only *[Prime Minister Menachem]* Begin who changed that. It has recently been changed back again, I just discovered the other day, so that you only get a half day of schooling free, paid for by the state, and if you want to go for the rest of the day, you have to pay tuition, which keeps poor people forever stuck. They used to say to me at that point, "Well, they get educated in the Army." But this article which I just read says they won't even let them into the Army, because they can't pass the literacy test for getting in. The only kinds of jobs they'll give them are shoveling dirt. So it's really tough.

My Michael once went to Israel, and of course, he immediately joined a group of Black Jews and ended up doing a few days in jail. But he's been in jail in almost every country in the world. Most recently in Napal. It turned out it was just like a traffic trap in a small town. They arrest you so that you'll bribe them and replenish the local treasury. Fortunately, he had something to give them.

Diane: Was Margaret going there with the money? Is that why she went there?

Margaret got there and went immediately to the ashram of the Rajneesh and hasn't stirred from there since, so Michael had to meet her there. *Meshuga [Yiddish: crazy]*, as my grandmother used to say.

I hadn't realized how much more they were more Eastern Europeans than they were Jews. Even physically. When I've been in Eastern Europe, the faces I see remind me of my grandfather and my grandmother.

Both of my Erics have spent some time in Kibbutzim. The other Eric had a terrible time; he spent his time inoculating chickens against chicken pox and shoveling up the chicken shit.

I have very complex feelings about Israel. I have many good friends there. And I've gone back over and over for various things.

Diane: Does it feel racist when you're there?

What you feel is the racism that goes both ways. If the Jews are racist, the Arabs are super-racists. The one reason they think the Jews don't belong there is because they're White.

Bruce: Not because they're Jews.

Not because they're Jews but because their skin is the wrong color. They don't look like Middle Easterners. They say, "Go back to Russia, where you belong. Or Poland." There's strong racism.

The one person with whom I've had good conversations about this is Amos Oz, who is a marvelous writer. He and I spent a long afternoon on his kibbutz talking about how similar Jewish attitudes toward Arabs were to White American attitudes toward Indians.

Bruce: Do you think it's true?

It's pretty convincing. It's the same kind of fear and hostility and guilt, all tangled up together.

The one thing that protects Israel is that the Arabs have such strong nationalist feelings against each other. I mean everybody hates the Palestinians, who are in a way the Jews of the Arab world. They're too smart; they're too glib; they're too articulate. Syrians hate them; the Lebanese hate them; the Iraqis sure as hell hate them.

I had an uncomfortable conversation about all these matters with Ihab Hassan, who was one of the organizers of the conference in Japan that I went to. He's a strange kind of Arab who's suddenly beginning to feel that he's an Arab after all these years. He was born in Alexandria in a cosmopolitan community; he was sent to France to be educated. He's not been back to Egypt since he went off to college. On the other hand, he begins to be touched by what's happening now. He and Ed Said can scarcely speak to each other. They're so different politically. Ihab is very conservative, very American.

I've known Said for a very long time, before people had begun to hear about him when he was just a young scholar trying to make it. He plays for the audience. And he's full of charm when he wants to turn that on. But he's sort of a late convert. His present political feelings . . . When he was married to his first wife it was very different; his present wife is just a girl from the village. I don't know which came first: his change of heart and then he picked out that new wife; he sent back home for a wife.

Bruce: LeRoi Jones changed wives when he became Baraka.

Absolutely. I don't know whether Said's first wife was Jewish or not, but I expect she might have been.

Diane: She's very rich. I think it was oil money.

She can't be Jewish, then. There's no Jewish oil money. Probably Presbyterian. That's even worse.

Bruce: Or Catholic.

Catholics don't really seem goyim to me.

Diane: Growing up for us, the Others were always the Protestants.

In Sally's town there weren't enough Jews for any anti-Jewish feeling to develop. But the anti-Catholic feeling, anti-Italian Catholic feelings were strong.

Diane: All this othering: Does it come down to the brothers, is that it? You can't learn to love your brother?

I can't learn to love my brother. You pick an unfortunate metaphor. I can't learn to love my brother the Lutheran. He is very religious.

Diane: Was he actually converted? Did he get baptized?

Oh, sure. He's very religious. He really was converted. He ran into some charismatic Lutheran preacher, which seems a contradiction in terms. I have a whole slew of grand-nieces and nephews who I have never seen.

Diane: Did you ever think of converting?

No.

Diane: Kunstler did when he was at Yale. He ran into those high-powered Catholics in the Thomas Moore Society. And of course he wanted to make his family berserk. That was the best part of the idea. Was Christ ever portrayed as some kind of hero to you, or no?

No.

When I was in Hawaii and feeling troubled, I used to slip sometimes into churches. But mostly because they were cool and peaceful. I was de-converted from the very notion of religion so early on in my life.

Diane: It never got therefore made into some kind of taboo that you were attracted to?

No. To know more about it always intrigued me a lot. To see it from the inside. And obviously I married a *shiksa*, so that says something. I married a half-*shiksa* the first time; and a full-fledged one the second time.

Margaret never really knew who or what she was. She had trouble with her name. People would say, "What was your name?" And she never knew whether she was Margaret Shaffner, which was her father's name—he never legally adopted her—or Margaret Shipley. The Shipleys were Quakers. And Joe Shipley—Bud Shipley—was a conscientious objector in World War I on the grounds of being a Quaker. They stayed out of the Civil War, the Shipleys. They stole mules from both sides and sold them to the other.

Diane and Bruce: That sounds like Jews.

It sounds like Quakers to me. Why do you think they're so god-damn rich.

Bruce: "Newton Garver; you've got those mules to answer for."

Newton Garver was the world's most violent pacifist.

Diane: Is he violent?

Oh, god, yes. He flies into great rages and tempers. You've never seen that side of Newton? We used to be pretty close friends of theirs.

Bruce: He was in jail for a while.

Yes, he did.

Diane: For how long?

I don't know how long. He was in jail for a while at least.

Bruce: I heard it was a year. It was during World War II. He was a CO.

Bud never went to jail. They may have decided he was too small to be taken into the armed forces anyhow. Shipleys are very small people. Bud and Buck, as they are known in the family, were as different as two human beings can possibly be. On the one hand, Margaret's mother had been married for a while to this intellectual poet, writer. Her second husband was a gambler. He was the manager of the biggest gambling establishment outside of Cleveland. It's called the Mounds Club, a very elegant place, where in the bad old days Hildegard used to perform. No charge for the entertainment or food, which was very good in its own limited way, but they got you at the gambling table. One of the great thrills of my life was when Buck let me shill one night at the crap table when business was slow.

Buck was associated with the leading gangster in Cleveland who owned the club, a guy named Tommy McGinty. One night Buck was walking down the street with the treasurer of the Mounds Club by his side, who was called (this is like something out of Damon Runyon) Rubber Goldberg—called "Rubber" because he always chewed gum—and Rubber was shot right next to him. It was one of those clean things, where they were careful not to hit any innocent bystander. Buck used to amuse the kids by telling them stories about the first car he had ever stolen, which was a yellow Stutz Bearcat, and about the Purple Gang. He was the calmest, mildest, sweetest man, who I am sure never laid his hands on an instrument of death in his life.

They moved to Vegas and finally were closed down and he retired. He used to run a place in Miami in the wintertime. So Margaret had nobody she thought of as her father. One was a bastard who had betrayed her mother, the other was not her father.

The first person I ever heard use the word "fuzz" was Buck. He used to tell us that when he was a boy and they played crap games, the signal for the cops coming was "fuzz on the Erie."

Bruce: I never heard the word "fuzz" when I was growing up in Brooklyn.

"Fuzz" was purely an underworld term.

Bruce: Did you read [E. L. Doctorow's] Billy Bathgate?

Yes.

Bruce: Did you like it?

No.

Bruce: Why not?

I didn't finally believe it. The language drove me crazy. It was so inflated. The best thing in it was the thing that was lifted right out of the public records, which was the last speech of Dutch Schultz. It's incredible.

Bruce: You can break it into lines and it's a poem.

Yes.

I felt possessive of Dutch Schultz. After all, they killed him in Newark.

We're going to move back to Newark when I retire, Sally.

My mother didn't really want to leave Newark ever, and she insisted on living right across the border in Irvington, where she could look down Springfield Avenue and the still-ravaged shops from the *[1967]* riots. After she came here, she said, "Can't stand this place; too much violence around here, too many *schvartzes*," forgetting that an old woman had been decapitated in a bath tub in the apartment she lived in.

Diane: Oh, my god! How did that happen to happen?

It was kind of a tough place, and the *schvartzes* were moving in.

I think I deeply believed for many years there are only two kinds of people in the world: *schvartzes* and Jews. They were the only people I ever saw.

One who has that deep in his blood is David Ritz. Remember David Ritz?

Bruce: He wrote a book on Marvin Gaye.

He's just done one on Smokey Robinson. He's also written a lot of novels and a lot of them are about interrelations of Jews and Blacks. He always wished he were Black. He's published a lot of stuff. I stay in touch with him all the time, because he was not merely a student of mine here, but his father was my closest friend when I grew up in Newark: Milty Ritz.

Bruce: I didn't know that. Did David come here because of you?

Yes. David will never forget the fact that I was the only person here who ever gave him a B instead of an A.

Milty Ritz was the first Communist I ever knew. He was a second-generation Communist. His father used to give street-corner speeches in Yiddish and take me to see these Yiddish films about Birobidzhan, which was the homeland for Jews set up in the worst land in Central Asia. There was always a soundtrack which said, showing these poor Jews digging up the absolutely nonarable soil: "In Birobidzhan we're building a new life; we're building a Socialist life."

Then Milty and I became Trotskyists, and we began to enter his house with great trepidation. His mother would scream at us for twenty minutes, telling us we were betrayers of the revolution, and then she would say, "But I baked some nice *kuchen* today." His parents were old-timey revolutionaries, who had never been married because this was a bourgeois institution.

Bruce: That was serious business in those days.

You want to know what Milton does now? He's a stockbroker in Dallas, Texas. An unhappily married stockbroker in Dallas, Texas. He went to work in a factory—he never went to college—after we got out of high school. It was a factory where I once worked for the ten most miserable days of my life; midsummer; 120 degrees. Then he became a hat salesman, then he got into business. Then he produced a beautiful daughter who married one of the richest men in America, who said, "I can't have my father-in-law selling hats." So he set him up as a stockbroker.

Bruce: Where did he go wrong?

He's still as brutally emphatic and refuses as much to listen to anybody else's arguments now as when he had completely opposite political views. The rhetoric remains the same, the pitch remains the same.

I was only twelve or thirteen when I ended up in junior high school with Milty Ritz, and Lilly Gecker, and they set me to reading *Kapital*, and *[Lenin's] What Is to Be Done*; peak stuff. I was really educated. I learned to read some texts pretty hard. I was always contemptuous of the kids who said, "FDR is a Fascist; he's attempting to preserve capitalism in America; he's crushing the working class."

Somebody called the riot squad for some reason. We were half-horsing around and half-serious. The cops came and we all ran. I fast enough; Milty not quite fast enough. He ended up in jail overnight. But fortunately, my mother was at that point the Republican County committeewoman in our district, and we reached the proper people and got him sprung.

We took it all very seriously. And there was the agonizing time of the Spanish War, when I kept saying, should I go, should I not go. At that point I was a freshman or sophomore in college. Only one of the people from our Young Communist League group went to the war; he was killed there. I never bothered to ask which side shot him. That can be an embarrassing question.

Bruce: Stephen Spender told me the reason he left Spain was, they had a meeting one night about the decline in contributions from Great Britain. Money had just stopped coming in and they really needed money. He agreed that they really needed money. They said, "Something's got to be done to get the British interested again. The British are very sentimental. They'd really respond to the death of a young poet." He said, "Yes, they would." They said, "So we've decided tomorrow, Stephen, you won't come back with us." He said, "It suddenly occurred to me by 'You won't come back with us.' He would go out, but—"

That shows a certain amount of wisdom on his part.

With all the doubts about it *[the Spanish Civil War]*, that seemed to me the real war, and when World War II came along, it seemed just a fake. A hollow echo. After-the-fact type war. It was strange.

There was a guy who was presumably a student at school with me at NYU at that point, who could arrange passports for you so you could get out of the country. I have decided in the years since that he must have been just a GPU agent or something. I can find his name in no list of my college students from those years.

Diane: Did you see the documentary The Good Fight? *It's about the Spanish Civil War. Basically, it makes the argument that, which some of the old timers in it make, that if people had fought and killed Fascism in Spain, it wouldn't have spread all over. In many ways, it's that ours is the last good fight.*

I guess I had some of that notion in my head. Though, in a way, their revolution was destroyed on both sides. The Russians played games—giving money, then taking it back.

Bruce: If you take exactly the same argument that they make in that film and apply it to Vietnam, it's what we did. In Vietnam we went in and we fought the fight, and, of course, we became the bad guys doing it.

Diane: And lost.

Bruce: The film winds up glorifying war—as long as it's an old war.

Diane: As long as it's ideologically yours.

And as long as it's okay from your point of view.

Bruce: It's like being anti-violence—except for violence I approve of.

Diane: It's one thing to go into a rage. It's another to kill somebody. There is a line.

I'm still in a position to think so.

Diane: "Make mental, not corporeal war," as Blake said.

When I was a kid, in a violent rage I once heaved a large brick at somebody's head, which fortunately enough I was a bad shot enough so that it missed. There are many people I have imagined killing, but that's something else.

But all wars finally get to be the same, whichever side you're on and whatever your ideology is, you're fighting after a while, not quite sure what the hell you're doing there, mostly so it'll be over and you can go home.

Diane: Unless you're professional fighters like Rambo who just like the action.

I suppose there are some people who like it.

Diane: As Adele St. John says in Reds, *"Well, you know, dear, men love that. Why do you think they put on those uniforms and go off and do it?"*

They do it because they want to get away from home. But the price is high.

Bruce: You may not get to come back.

You might as well ask me why I went. I had two kids, and I volunteered. I never would have been taken.

Diane: Did you do it for adventure?

I really don't know why I did it. I give myself all different kinds of different feelings. One is that I felt it was sort of unfair my just sitting there all alone safe, while everyone else was living this experience. I felt that very strongly, because I was already teaching, and my students suddenly—*whoosh!*—were all gone. What was I doing, preaching to a diminishing congregation?

The other reason is I looked around and found I was married, I had a regular job, I was headed for tenure, however slowly. I had a wife and two kids. I hadn't really had a chance to be properly young yet. So it was a chance at renewed youth. The other reason is that somebody came along and sang a siren song about how I would learn a new language, a non-Indo-European language—I was made for learning languages in those days—at government expense. So I went.

But then, it seems after a while that it's more boring than anything else. And I kept thinking, well this isn't the center yet. So I kept volunteering for missions, as they say. I finally was lucky enough to be loaded up and shipped off to Iwo Jima, which satisfied me completely. I landed four days after the initial assault on the island to persuade the Marines not to kill their prisoners but to send them back because they might have valuable information. And as I usually do wherever I go, I went for a swim off the black lava beaches, and I kept pushing aside spars and broken weapons and so forth. When I pushed aside my first body I decided it was *genug [Yiddish: "enough"]*. That day I also saw them take about a thousand assorted dead Japanese and Americans, bulldoze a hole, and shove them all in and bury them to prevent infection. Same hole.

Sailors have a very remote relationship most of the time to that sort of thing. Just working intricate machinery, reading dials. There must be mighty few people who do it because they love it, though I suppose some can get the habit after, so they try it. I don't know.

Bruce: Rambo's a movie. It's not really doing it.
Diane: But there's the appetite.
Bruce: The appetite is not the same as doing it.
But even in *Rambo* the apology is, "They drew first blood."
Diane: That's always the apology. There's a great appetite —
Bruce: That was the name of the novel: First Blood.

The first movie was called *Rambo: First Blood.* That's an interesting movie because it didn't matter—remember, when they find his knife, they ask him who it's for. And he says, "The enemy." The enemy has become the cops instead of the gooks, and it doesn't make much difference. The politics in that movie is really weird.

I once read an account of somebody who had gone to see the leftist guerrilla troops in the Philippines when all hell was breaking loose there. And they were sitting around watching *Rambo*, enjoying it immensely.

We saw *Tales from the Crypt* last night. It's really very faithful to those Gaines comic books—if you've ever read them. They're all very moralistic finally. The bad guys always get what's coming to them in the end. Even gorier than what they had dished out themselves. Weird. Glad I saw it. They lined up all these good directors to do the things.

Bruce: Are you writing fiction?

A little. I have a story which is coming out in *Kenyon Review*. This is a story I wrote quite a while ago, but since I've had to sit on it, I've rewritten it several times. It was originally supposed to have appeared in a hard-bound collection of science fiction called *Last Dangerous Visions* by Harlan Ellison. He stalled off the publication of that book as he wheels and deals. He takes it away from one publisher, then sues them and sells it to another publisher. I finally figured it might never come out and I ran into a guy from *Kenyon Review* who said, "Do you have anything?" And I said, "Yeah, I'd love to see this story come out."

It's a story written out of a deep melancholy pit at the worst point in my life. The title of it is "What Used to Be Called Dead." It begins like a fairy tale and ends like a work of science fiction. In between it goes back to Newark to an imaginary cave under the huge monument of the *Wars of America* built in Military Park in downtown Newark.

Harlan Ellison is one of the maddest human beings that ever lived. He almost always sues.

Bruce: I've seen him interviewed several times. He always seems affronted by someone.

Always. And he almost always sues.

There's a great story about Harlan Ellison, who is obnoxious with everybody but especially with women. He came up to a woman one day and said to her, "What would you say to a little fuck?" And she answered, "Go away, little fuck."

Diane: At one of the Sun Valley conferences—I think it was the one you were there—we were on a bus going up to the Lodge for a cookout. There was a woman, all dressed up in leather with fringes and lots of Navajo silver and turquoise. She said to one of the Indians on the bus, "Oh I just love your culture, it's so blah blah blah." He said, 'Thank you. You're so sympathetic. Do you have any Indian in you?" "No," she said. "Would you like a little?" he said.

I should have done that with you, Sally. "Do you have any Jew in you?"

Oh, "They flee from me who sometime did me seek" *[opening line of Thomas Wyatt's poem "They Flee from Me," mid-sixteenth century].*

Bruce: Leslie, when you did that Today *show, you were talking about the western being the most un-Christian of genres, which is a wonderful point. Have you written about that anywhere?*

I don't know, I may have said something about it. I have never dealt with it head-on. I've talked about it many times, and there may be a little bit of it in *The Return of the Vanishing American*, but I'm not sure. The code of the West is an anti-Christian code, and it's made quite explicit in a lot of films.

Bruce: And even in the fiction.

Yes. It's in Zane Grey right from the start. In *The Virginian* there's an anti-violence attitude. It's women who are identified with Christianity.

Bruce: At the end, he comes around. She says, "If you do that [the final shoot-out] don't come back." He goes out and does it.

One of the great lines is from Zane Grey: "When you buckled on your guns, I knew you were a man."

They still tote guns in Montana.

Bruce: It pulls your pants down.

The silver dollars used to do that.

Diane: Margot Kidder said that Richard Brautigan, Peter Fonda, and Tom McGuane used to hang out in their place in Montana and basically get drunk and shoot.

Bruce: They'd shoot in the kitchen.

Diane: They'd shoot all over the house. They were just a bunch of —

Bruce: Peckinpah, Peter Fonda, Warren Oates, McGuane, and Brautigan—they all had places in this one small area around Livingston.

Right outside of Bozeman.

Bruce: The boys would shoot up the kitchen, she said, and leave it for her to clean up.

The last time I was in Montana I discovered the latest sport of the kids (not the imported Easterners or Californians) was riding down coyotes on motorcycles. At least they weren't riding down the teachers at the state university. I was always sure somebody was going to pull a gun on me. It happened to one of my colleagues there, a kid complaining about a grade. Everybody has guns.

Diane: In class?

Sure. You're allowed to carry a gun in Montana, as long as it's not concealed.

It's a weird place. How I ever got there, I don't know.

Bruce: It really gave you the space you needed.

It gave me a lot. It gave me a chance to live with people who hadn't grown up thinking the same thoughts I was, thinking, reading the same books I was reading.

Diane: It's wonderful, because you never got the least bit dull.

It's possible to do even in Montana. Some of my colleagues did! But it required considerable effort. They were the same dull scholars they all were, except on weekends they would put on cowboy boots and ten-gallon hats and go out fishing in Rattlesnake River.

It's also nice to live in a place which had no history to speak of. When I first went there practically everybody I knew who thought of himself as having roots in Montana meant his grandfather and grandmother had lived there. Period. As I was saying to Sally the other day, I never saw a place where people went from being pioneers to being decadents faster. Three generations, that's all. It was booze that did it mostly. It's the hardest drinking place I ever was, except for Alaska, which is now just what Montana used to be.

My vision of Montana is a woman coming down the street in a mackinaw jacket, her hair in curlers with a kerchief over it.

It's as vile as anyplace else, but the scenery is better. And there are handsome Montanans. Gary Cooper is a real, honest-to-god Montanan. His father was a judge on the Supreme Court in Montana. He grew up in Helena, Montana. Everybody in Montana at a certain point was called Larry or Gary.

Sally: Those who weren't called Laverne?

Laverne is Montana, both male and female. Laverne Hamilton used to run for governor for Montana on the Socialist Workers Party ticket, year after year after year. Maybe Vern is Laverne. Both males and females were called Laverne. Some of them had names that were just like names out of westerns.

The year I taught at Princeton, I used to be driven crazy when I would see names in front of me like Eberhart Faber the Fourth. I would think, "I've heard that someplace before." You go to Montana, you say to some kid, "What's your name?" And he'd say, "Boone Sparrow." Boone Sparrow. That's pretty good.

I was about to say that Montana's the place where I drank the hardest I ever had in my life. But that's not really true. I drank even harder in Princeton. Maybe that was because it was the crisis year of my life. I turned forty, which I took very hard.

Bruce: So you got drunk in Princeton at forty and busted in Buffalo at fifty.

I kept getting drunk and falling in love at age forty. Didn't I tell you this story about when I was absolutely down in the dumps the day I actually turned forty, I was at a party and this fifty- or sixty-year-old woman sitting at the piano looked up and said, "What do you look so sad about?" And I told her why, and she said, "Fucking begins at forty."

Forty's a hard year for men for some reason. Mostly because I had grown up believing I would never live past thirty-five. Here I was five long years past that.

Sally: I thought I'd burn out like a little flower by the time I was twenty-eight.

I really died and was reborn at thirty-five. I was living in Rome and I got hepatitis. I was in a semi-coma for six weeks. I knew I wasn't dead, but I wasn't sure I was alive. I didn't exactly think I wanted to die, but I wouldn't have objected if someone had offered to kill me. I was not cheered up by my Italian doctor, who kept saying to me, "Now laugh at us Italians and our livers." And then I recovered. It was like a second life. I walked down to the street corner to buy a newspaper at the kiosk for the first time, and had to crawl back on my hands and knees. I was weak for a long time after that. It was brutal. When I was getting better, I made up a song, which I would sing.

Diane: How did it go?

I can't remember the tune, but the chorus was: "You can easily tell he's not a lemon, cause the lemon never needs a shave."

I was so thrilled that I was in Italy, exactly *mezzo del cammin*, right? [*Dante: "Nel mezzo del cammin di nostra vita mi ritrovai per una selva oscura"—first line of* Inferno: *"In the middle of life's journey I found myself in a dark forest."*]

I was so thrilled that when I got the letter saying I was going to Italy on the Fulbright Commission that out of sheer high spirits—I was driving and living in a house where the mailbox was up here, and the road was down, with a stone wall beside it—I deliberately swerved the car into the stone wall and smacked it as hard as I could. And there I was in Italy.

It was an important year in my life. It was the first time I ever lectured on American literature.

Diane: What had you taught before that?

Mostly Renaissance, when I wasn't doing freshman composition. If I did Renaissance I did a kind of introduction to criticism, critical theory course.

Diane: Did you teach much Donne?

In the Renaissance poetry course I taught Donne.

[In Italy] they said, "Of course you're going to teach American literature." I thought, "Why?" "Well, you're an American; what else do you know about?" But it turned out to be more than that. They were hungry to know about it. Mussolini had forbidden American literature. An interest in American literature was considered politically suspect, because the two leading nonacademic scholars of American literature were Pavese and Vittorini, who were both Leftists and anti-Fascists. Writing about American literature became a kind of gesture of rebellion against the regime, saying, "Fuck you, Antiquity and the Old Roman way; we're interested in the future." Pavese said, "America has no graveyards to defend."

[Alberto] Moravia I got to know a little. He's proved himself a hero to the end. At age eighty he's just made a connection with a thirty-year-old woman. "They may flee from him, who sometime did him seek." But not quite fast enough to get away. *[A second riff on a line from the poem by Thomas Wyatt (1503–1542): "They flee from me that sometime did me seek."]*

The other nice thing that happened to me in Italy was Ischia. Both summers we were there we would go to the island, which was then absolutely beautiful and unspoiled. No cars were allowed. The only way you could get around was by horse-drawn carriage. There I fell into this strange group of refugee American artists and Italian noblemen down on their luck, all of whom were gay. At the café in town where everybody gathered together, Don Maria, there were two tables at the center of which sat Wystan Auden, and in the center of the other was the Principe of Hessa, the man who would have been the next king of Italy, a guy whose mother had been sent off by his father, turned over to the Nazis, and killed.

Wystan and Chester [Kallman] became our best friends there. Auden was one of the people I liked best to talk to in my whole life. Intelligence is optional for poets, but he was not just intelligent, he was super-intelligent. I would always try to bait him to start him going. I'd say, "Don't you think it's a little strange that two men with the same name were put up on the cross at the same time? Barabbas, after all, means Son of the Father. Maybe the whole story is allegorical." And then he would go. When we got bored with serious conversation, Chester would always amuse everybody by translating Jewish jokes into Neapolitan dialect.

I went back once. There were high-rise hotels, cars. This was a beautiful little beach. There are many little towns on Ischia, which is a pretty big island with a huge volcano—extinct, one hopes—in the center. It's the place where Mussolini himself used to spend his summers and where Donna Rachele, his widow, was still living. The peasants used to stop her in the marketplace and kiss her hand. The language they spoke was absolutely incomprehensible. It sounded more like Chinese than Italian. But they were interested in making money and wine-growing was what they really did. In the summers they would move out of their houses and into the fields and rent the houses to tourists from Rome and Naples. With my family we had to rent two houses. It was just beautiful, with a lemon tree right over the table on the terrace so you could reach up and grab one.

Auden has some beautiful poems about Ischia. One of our neighbors in Rome who followed us down there was a Jewish theologian and scholar, called Theodor Gaster, about whom Auden wrote a poem which I believe is not collected anyplace. It runs as follows,

> Theodor Gaster
> Thinks Judaism a disaster
> But that is not the trade
> For which he gets paid.

Mrs. Gaster was lemon-colored even without hepatitis. She was called by everybody on the island, "La Giallo" *[The Yellow]*. She was the kind of a woman who would say to little children: "Now, children, don't put marbles in your mouth." Kids had never thought of it until that very moment.

I went to teach one summer, the first six weeks while the family stayed there, at the School of Letters, which was then in Indiana. When I came back, they were all of them covered with impetigo.

Diane: How do you get it?

It's an infection which comes if you're not properly cleaned and you don't scrub yourself hard enough. It may be a virus, I'm not sure. But anyhow, you look like you're covered with bark after a while. It's rather disgusting. I myself had nothing but chigger bites. Ever been afflicted with chiggers?

Diane: No, but Bruce has. A warden took him to piss in a chigger patch, not telling him.

A practical joke.

Bruce: He was standing on a stump. I was standing on the ground.

Oh, they're miserable creatures. And everybody has some home remedy for them, but I don't believe in any of them.

Bruce: Like nail polish?

Right.

Bruce: So you rolled in the Indiana grass and got chiggers. I pissed in a Texas cotton field and got them.

Ischia was a very good place for me to write. There was nothing else much to do. I didn't dare touch anybody in my household. Debbie was only two at the time, and she was very much interested in what the neighbors were doing and even when she had to pee she would take a little potty and put it in front of the wall in front of our house so she could sit and watch people moving up and down the road, which was perfectly all right with the locals. It's the only place where we all joined in treading out the wine. Michael, who was real little then, got drunk from the fumes in the pit. But the peasants kept telling us this was very good for any sores you had on your feet, including impetigo.

Figure 13. Leslie and UB colleague Raymond Federman at our house, 1974.

6

June 27, 1989

I think I broke the back of my [Vietnam] piece today. I thought I was just clearing my throat, but it kept going for ten pages. You know, I found myself writing about the difference between the anti-war riots during the Civil War . . . Do you know that hundreds of people were shot down in the streets of New York anti-draft riots? But this was the exact opposite of the ones that happened in Vietnam. It was the working-class people who were rioting against the war, where it was the bourgeois who were favored sons of the middle class who were rioting here; and the cops who were shooting them down were working class with relatives in Vietnam. It was a war fought by the working class and underclasses. It was a weird war, the Vietnam War. Makes it hard.

If you were rich, you could buy your way out of the draft in the Civil War. These rioters were mostly newly arrived ethnics, mostly Irish. They were the wagon drivers, the day laborers. Melville has a poem about it. It's called "From the Roof."

Diane: And they just mowed them down?

They were just mowed down. Nobody knows how many they killed. At the very least scores, maybe hundreds.

Diane: And what was the rationale? That they were rioters?

They were rioters. New York has always been a place of riots. They rioted about everything: pigs in the streets. A law against pigs in the streets caused one riot. I once started to do a thing about the riots of New York, riots against Blacks. Way back. Late eighteenth century.

Diane: Was it "keep them out of our neighborhoods" riots?

Don't let them take our jobs away. There was a trickle of people beginning to come from the South, Black people.

Bruce: How long is this talk to be?

I'm not exactly sure. One of the people in it is going to be a Vietnamese writer, whose work I don't know. They're going to show a lot of films.

Bruce: I'm publishing an article in the next issue of the folklore journal about a festival of Vietnamese films that was in Hawaii last year. It has nothing to do with folklore but it's a really interesting article. I'd like to get the films for Buffalo. There are six of them that are subtitled in English. They have a very different view of the war than anything from here. Their film industry has been operating under incredibly primitive conditions.

I would think. They never had much of a film industry.

When cultural exchanges began with the Vietnamese government, the first two films that the Vietnamese asked for were *Gone with the Wind* and *King Kong*. *King Kong* was Hitler's favorite film. There is a book called *The Table Talk of Hitler*. I don't know how reliable it is, but according to what this guy said that was his favorite film. And his favorite book—you won't believe this—was *The Last of the Mohicans*. The great popular German writer, Karl May, was an imitator. Hitler's favorite song—I scarcely dare tell people this—was "Who's Afraid of the Big Bad Wolf?" He called himself Wolf when he was in hiding once, and his last refuge was called "The Wolf's Den," which is strange, because "Wolf" is a Jewish name in Germany, by and large. There's a lot of Jewish Wolfs in America.

It's just like "Fiedler." You can't tell for sure. The first time I ever met Gershom Scholem, his first question was "Jewish Fiedler or goyish Fiedler"? I saw a lot of Fiedler gravestones in Germany. There are a lot of non-Jewish Fiedlers: the very great German scholar, H. G. Fiedler, Anglo-Saxon.

[The papers from the Vietnam Conference] will probably be published—if I know the guy—probably two years from now. Communicating with him is absolutely maddening. He will write a letter which will arrive on the 15th of June, saying, "I need an answer by June first." He sent it surface mail by mistake. But he's a wonderful fellow; a great host.

Bruce: You leave on Saturday?

Yeah.

Bruce: And you'll be gone how long?

A week. About a week.

I lost my light again, Sally. I'll see if I can light it in the wind. It's the nature of these stogies.

Diane: What was the kind Clint Eastwood smoked in the Leone movies?

The slimmest cigar in the world, which was the favorite cigar—I'm an authority on this subject, because I once tried to write a book on it, which never happened—the favorite cigar of Bertolt Brecht and James Joyce was a cigar called the Virginia. It's smoked in Switzerland, and made in Switzerland or Southern Germany. It's so skinny it has to have straw put in it so it can draw at all.

Diane: Is it elegant looking?

Bertolt Brecht would not have looked elegant with anything. It's not for elegant people. There's a famous poem of Brecht's which ends, "Though the world blow up / I will not let my Virginia go out." It's a marvelous poem. It is the one that begins, "I came out of the Black Woods in my mother's belly." *["Vom armen B." / Of poor B.B.: "Ich, Bertolt Brecht, bin aus den schwarzen Wäldern. / Meine Mutter trug mich in die Städte hinein / Als ich in ihrem Leibe lag. Und die Kälte der Wälder / Wird in mir bis zu meinem Absterben sein."]*

Bruce: So you're writing a book about cigars?

Somebody talked me into it and I talked myself out. So I checked to find out what everybody smoked. Freud smoked Schimmelpennincks, a Dutch cigar, and Mark Twain smoked anything. He smoked a lot of Connecticut cigars.

Bruce: Did he get to Cuba?

I don't think so. He got almost every place in the goddamned world, but I think one of the few places he never was in, as far as I know, is Cuba. He used to go to Bermuda in his old age. That's where he made a pass at a small girl and got into bad trouble. This is one of the weird stories of the end of his life. He either made the pass, or the little girl thought he was making a pass. He had this little troupe of girls he called his Angel Fish.

I wish I had known him. He's the only writer who died before my time that I desperately wish I had known. There was a man who used to come into my father's drugstore who had known him at the end of his life and used to tell stories about him.

They were mostly stories about how he loved to walk on the streets of New York. He pretended he loved privacy but he was miffed if he wasn't noticed by the first person who came along. He liked people pointing, saying, "There goes Mark Twain."

Diane: How long did he live in Buffalo?

A year, sixteen months, maybe. The Cloisters was his old house. It has been much redone, but that was the house he lived in. His father-in-law bought it for him as a surprise. He thought he was going to a hotel. His father-in-law was a big coal merchant in Buffalo and Elmira. Langdon, I think, was his name. When Mark Twain came *[to Buffalo]*, he gave him this house complete with servants, chauffeur, and he bought him a piece of the newspaper. He wanted to make him respectable.

Diane: Did he have money all his life?

From that point on Twain had money. He made at least two fortunes and lost them. At one point he was absolutely bankrupt. That was the point where he turned himself over to his buddy, who was the vice president of Standard Oil, and let him invest his money for him. He died rich. He was the guy who gave Mark Twain the famous advice, which he kept repeating to everybody all his life: "Don't believe this stuff. Put your eggs in one basket, and *watch* that basket!"

Mark Twain was so rich at the end of his life that the only people he really had who could be good friends of his were rich people. Andrew Carnegie was one of his closest buddies. Doesn't that seem strange? They used to write to each other as "St. Andrew" and "St. Mark." They were both self-made men and sort of felt alike. Twain was funny. He was theoretically against high finance but he was in favor of money.

There's scarcely a piece of the world he didn't set his foot on. He traveled through India when nobody was traveling through India. When he took that trip he wrote about in *Following the Equator [1897]*, where he confessed that he really felt at home for the first time in the years seeing all these dark faces around him, he said, "How ugly White people are." He sort of grew up in a world of real Black folks. He was funny on the subject of Black folks. He made all the standard anti-Black jokes in the world. He would say offhand, "I'm the laziest White man in the world." And then there's the famous time when what's-his-name wrote a review of *Innocents Abroad*. He said after the review came out, "I felt like the woman when her baby came White."

Mama came to the city of New York and he took her to a minstrel show—"a nigger show," as he always said.

He loved to lecture. He really needed to see a visible audience in front of him. He loved to be out there talking instead of imagining somebody reading in private. It's a feeling you can get after you've spent a lifetime writing books.

Bruce: You're like that, too.

Yeah, I'm like that.

But the other thing about me is I really have a great necessity to hear something before I write it down. To hear what I want to say. I do it inside my head but that's not so good. So in recent years more and more of what I write I talk out first at least a couple of times before I write it. Maybe that's because I was a performer before I was anything else. It's like my Aunt Matilda's favorite story about me: "Put him on a table and he'll say a poem," she said. That was when I was four years old, or five years old. Poems I used to say were my father's favorite poems: Kipling and Robert Service. I can still do "Gunga Din" from beginning to end. I once discovered that Mary Connolly *[wife of UB English Department colleague Thomas Connolly]* is good at those poems, too.

My father thought he was a poet. He wrote lyrics for popular songs. He wrote poems. He sang the songs. One of his songs got stolen from him. A typical story, right? He sent it off naïvely to somebody, who said, "We can't use it." And then it appeared. Something called "Cross Words." It was punning on crossword puzzles. My father was a very language-obsessed man. He talked differently from anybody I knew. Language was very elegant and he used no malapropisms. Before he would say it, he knew it.

My father's eyes got worse and worse, but he loved to read. In the end he would not read just with his glasses but with a magnifying glass as well. He really believed in reading the newspapers. He read the newspaper from beginning to end. When we were kids, we got quizzed every day at the dinner table about the news of the day. And God forbid if you didn't know what was happening in the world.

Bruce: Was your father religious?

No. My father grew up in a little, tiny town where he was the only Jew in what is West Orange, New Jersey, now. His father was a hatter. He worked in a little hat factory there. The only name my father had for the first ten years of his life was "Sheeny." Which began in malice, but after a while it just became his nickname. It was just what he was called by the other kids. My father had no connection with Jewishness at all.

I don't know how much his father had, but his grandfather was still alive up until the time when I was eight or nine years old. He could speak only Yiddish.

Diane: Do you remember him?

Yes, I do. I remember how impressive looking he was. He had blue, blue eyes and a white, white beard. Many years ago I got the great compliment of my life. I was giving a lecture in Florida and a woman came up from the audience, who was the cousin of my father. She said to me, "You look just like Grandpa." I loved it.

His funeral was one of the traumatic experiences of my life. Because when he died, there was a little graveside sermon delivered by a friend. I couldn't understand a word that was going on because it was all in Yiddish, the parts that weren't in Hebrew. But at one point all the women who were around the grave began screaming and crying and weeping. What the guy had said was, "This man suffered the worst indignity a human being can suffer. He saw his children die before him. And this is because those children abandoned their faith, in America."

My father's family was completely assimilated. The only Jewishness my father had left was anti-Semitism. He used to say at the top of his voice: "One thing I can't stand about Jews is they always talked so damned loud." He was a man who failed at everything he wanted to do. Never made it as a writer. Became a druggist because that just happened. He did it the old way. He went one year to a pharmacy college and then he was an apprentice. He put labels on bottles and he put the corks on the bottle. His store closed down in the Depression.

The store was in a marvelous place. Right across the street from a General Electric factory, where almost all the employees were Black. It was a Black neighborhood. Those guys were the best customers. As soon as they got their paycheck, they would buy large boxes of candy for their wives, hair straightener, skin bleaches, little bags of homeopathics to hang around their necks for "the misery." They were the first guys fired when the Depression came.

Nobody wanted him to close his store. The wholesaler kept saying, "Hang on, hang on. I don't care how much money you owe me." But my father finally couldn't stand it and closed the door.

The years when I was about to go to college he was poor, poor, poor. He couldn't get a job. That was the point in my life when I cried for the first time after I was an adult. I got a scholarship which paid a part of my college tuition, all of which came to only $400. I think I had $200 toward it. One day there was a big family conference as I was about to start out for school. My father said, "You can't go to school. We can't afford it." But I worked for six months, then I did get to go to school.

When my brother and I were both in college, my father was earning—he finally got a job as a kind of salesman for a pharmaceutical company—two thousand dollars a year. It was nothing. My mother hocked her wedding ring at one point. But it was my *[maternal]* grandparents who supported us, really. They had a two-family house, and we moved into one of part of it.

I had very little connection with my father's family. They were a very distant family. They would gather together for big reunions, but I was brought up by my mother's mother and father. It was my grandfather who was sort of my model in life. He was the best human being I've ever known. Truly the best.

My grandfather would drive my grandmother crazy. My grandmother had all the prejudices of the world, deeply rooted. The people she hated worst were Blacks, Irish, and Poles. His three best friends were a Pole and an Irishman and a Black guy.

He also gave me the only piece of advice I ever got from an elder that I believed. He said, "Leslie, I'll tell you the truth. Learn a skill and you can tell the boss, 'Fuck you.'" So I learned a skill.

He was a marvelous man. He grew up more like a peasant than a city person. He lived right on the edge of the city. The kids he played with were all local peasants. He could do all the string games, you know, putting a string around your neck and cutting it. He taught me "cat's cradle." And he told me all the fairy tales, oral versions, never written down, transmitted straight. Kids would come from blocks around to listen to him when he would sit on the porch in the summertime and tell us stories. He drew beautiful little pictures. He had taught himself to read and write, never really gone to school. He came from a poor, poor family. His father sewed the Torah covers, did fancy needle work.

My grandmother was completely analphabetic. The only thing she could write was her name. My grandfather would read to her aloud every evening. He would read her the *roman*, the novel from the *Forward*, which I only realized years later were often stories by Isaac Bashevis Singer. Everybody wanted my grandmother to go to school. My grandmother was a monster. She was a formidable woman, who being of the proper sex in another age would have run the world. All she could run was her family. She never learned to read and write and the family finally persuaded her to go to night school to learn to read and write and three days later the teacher came and begged us to take her out.

She disapproved of everybody in the family, except me. Except my *[daughter]* Debbie, who she only saw when Debbie was a teeny, tiny baby and my grandmother was dying. They looked at each other and their eyes were exactly the same. My grandmother had the bluest eyes that anybody ever had, and as she got older they got paler and paler, liked washed-out jeans. She thought, Debbie's going to be all right. Debbie has those eyes.

My grandmother, when she was a girl, had an affair with the parish priest in her hometown. We found this out only many years later. She was a formidable lady. She always used to say to me, "Your Aunt Matildy wouldn't have been born if I was in Newark, but I was in Buffalo and didn't know a good abortionist." Working-class women have always had abortions. There was always somebody around. There were midwives who would do those things.

My grandfather, in addition to everything else, was the strongest human being I believe I have ever known in my life. Kids would not only listen to his stories, but as a special treat we were allowed to feel his muscles. He worked very hard. He was a shaver of leather, and he would have to push these damn hides. He had enormous shoulder muscles and biceps. He was scared to death of my grandmother, who was a little, tiny woman, who he could have picked up and thrown to the next block. Only once a year, maybe, he would lose his temper. And the only thing he would ever bang on was not my grandmother, but the dining room table, which would collapse under it, and she would run and hide with a neighbor until it blew over.

He would take me sometimes to little street-front *shuls* on the high holidays. Most of the time he was giving me anti-religious propaganda, but when he would take me he would always say the same thing. "Not because I believe, but so you should remember."

Bruce: Did you ever do that with your kids?

Yes. I once danced on Simchat Torah with Eric at the celebration by the Chabbat Hasidim, so they should remember. That was when I had my strange, temporary alliance with those people.

My grandmother, I believe, never entered a *shul* in her life. Certainly not after she left Europe when she was just a young girl. But my grandmother for a long time longed for Europe. She wanted to go back. And when my mother was about four years old, she took her on a trip back to her hometown in Europe. My mother got cholera, and the only way her life was saved is they changed her name officially, to fool the Angel of Death. And it worked. My grandmother decided it wasn't a healthy place for kids. I think she really had a secret notion she was going to stay there and persuade my grandfather to come back. The town was Ternopil, which is now a part of Russia, in the western Ukraine.

My grandfather could speak all the local languages. He could speak Russian, he could speak Polish, he could speak Ukrainian, he could speak Yiddish. Not only that, but he would speak whatever dialect of Yiddish the person he was talking to spoke. So if he talked to a Litvak, he would talk Litvak Yiddish. If he talked to Galitzianer, he would talk Galitzianer Yiddish. My grandmother disapproved. She thought it showed weakness of character.

My grandmother was so formidable that when her oldest son ran off with a *shiksa*, she forbid him to get married, and he wouldn't. He had a baby who was born and got to be a year old, and he wouldn't get married until Grandma said yes, and she finally broke down. Not that she believed in anything at all, as far as I could tell.

One of the last things she told me was, "Listen, Leslie, you're growing up in America. I suppose you'll marry a *shiksa*. But please, not a Polisher *shiksa*." She also told me, "If you marry a *shiksa*, in the end they will call you a Jew bastard." I'm still waiting.

My grandmother's gentile daughter-in-law was one of the sweetest, nicest ladies in the world, who was marvelous to my grandmother. Absolutely marvelous. But that's only another part of her. She had great joy in her too. I would walk back and forth to high school—it must have been about two miles—and I swear for the last half-mile home, I would hear my grandmother and my Aunt Matilda sitting on the front stoop laughing. When they laughed, the whole world quivered. It was she who made Matilda a pianist. She would make her practice four, five, six hours a day. She got to be very good, but she hated it. After my grandmother died, she stopped, cold turkey. Never even touches the keys to amuse herself.

That's my Aunt Matildy, who tells Sally scandalous stories about me when I was a child.

Bruce: All of them true?

All of them true. They're mostly about how ugly I was. These are the stories I grew up with all my life. My grandmother, my Aunt Matilda insists, would take me out and push me in the baby carriage, would put the lid down for fear people would look in. Her family was quite beautiful, most of it, and very vain. A lot of them were actors on the stage in Vienna. One—my cousin Poldy, I guess it was—was a very beautiful young man, who held a huge birthday party to celebrate his thirtieth birthday, and then jumped out of the window because he didn't want to be thirty-one.

Bruce: To his death?

To his death.

All my life long I was told, "Yes, he's ugly, but if you put him on a table he'll say a poem."

My brother, on the other hand, was indeed very handsome. I told you, my brother could have been played by Charlton Heston. I talked to him briefly when my mother died. He agreed to have a strictly business conversation with me. He lives in New Hampshire on a farm. He's retired and he loves to play around and build things. He sees his daughter, though he disapproves completely of her husband, I take it, and of her, because instead of doing something useful in the world, she produced large numbers of children. He would have disapproved if she did anything else, too, I mean he's just into disapproving.

His son, unfortunately, died at age twenty-three of cancer. This was a boy who was trying to reconcile us. He came one day and asked if we had any yard work for him to do when he must have been about sixteen or seventeen. I thought, "There's something awfully familiar about you, kid."

Bruce: Where was this?

Here in Buffalo.

And then he told us who he was. He had a brain tumor. He's the one my brother brought up thinking, "Here was a purebred goy," and sent him off to I guess it was Andover, or one of those fancy schools. His daughter went to Bryn Mawr. She was in a Catholic girls' school right above the Spanish Steps in Rome. The last time I saw her she was about thirteen or fourteen years old, and I was talking someplace in Rome, and she came to see me with a bunch of giggling girlfriends. Carol.

He had two children only. Two children and a mother-in-law, who lived with him all his life long. And she could speak not a word of English. She couldn't speak Yiddish either, though she was Jewish in origin, but she lived outside the Pale, someplace in Georgia. She spoke only Russian, which helped my brother a good deal.

Bruce: He's in the FBI?

He is a Russian specialist *[in the CIA]*. That's his thing. His wife grew up speaking Russian, too. I think she was born in the old country and came when she was five or six. His Russian is flawless. When we still saw him, we tried to make uneasy conversation about how the skiing was in Leningrad and how the ballet was in Moscow. At that point he was going in and out with the diplomatic mail. Until he was declared persona non grata. In fact, he was reported "executed." It turned out to be a mistake. He had dropped three Russians: he briefed them, dropped them into Russia, and they picked them up and killed them. They talked about him, and the garbled story came through in the newspapers that my brother had been killed, too. But fortunately, the people in Washington called my mother beforehand and assured her he was all right.

And at that point they made him American Consul in Istanbul. That was the point where we had our final break. I was living in Athens. I said, "Let's see each other at Christmas time. Do you want to come here or shall I come there?" He wrote me a letter saying, "This may come as a rude shock to you, but I never want to see you again in my life."

Period. That's it. The total contents of the message. This was a conversation my mother and I had many times over. He considers that I stood for many things that he didn't approve of, and that I probably didn't approve of him. But that didn't mean a fuck to me.

He's a rather splendid figure. He was a hero in the war, a commander of a tank company. He did feats like jumping on German tanks and prying the top open and so forth. After the war they put him in charge of maximum security prisoners in an army prison camp, where he had an arsonist fire his furnace and a child-rapist take care of his kids. But with my brother, they wouldn't dare . . . He was tough. He was a football player, a wrestler, a shot-putter.

Diane: Did he stay in touch with your mother?

Barely. He would write her once a month when he remembered. He didn't see her for the last twenty years of her life.

Bruce: Was he embarrassed about being Jewish?

Yes. He was profoundly embarrassed about being Jewish. He was absolutely determined that his kids have no sense of that part of their past and is deeply enraged at me for reasons which are explicable, I believe, in terms of the way brothers get along, which we didn't, mostly by fighting and loving each other. For years he was the closest human being to me in the world. We used to sleep in one bed. He tried to define himself absolutely against me. Whatever I didn't do, he could do. He was just short of two years younger. He was a poet when he was young. But he concealed this part of himself.

He was drafted before we actually entered the war. He was in that first batch of draftees before World War II, and he was an absolute refusenik. He refused to go to officers' candidate school. He hated the Army, and then he became totally converted, and he moved up to commission ranks, and then he was moved in G-2, which is Army Intelligence. And when the war was over he went into the CIA. All this I gather from the story about him in the Russian press, after those guys were killed, which somebody translated for me. The guys told everything about him. I didn't know he was in the CIA. I thought he was American Consul in Istanbul.

My Eric went to see him while he was Consul. Eric was in one of his mad ventures at that point. He must have been sixteen or seventeen, and he decided he was going to hitchhike from Athens to Jerusalem, and Istanbul was on the way. He figured, "I'm an American citizen. An American Consul can't refuse to see me." He went to see him. My brother coldly and politely invited him to dinner, played music which Eric hated from some currently fashionable musical comedy, the whole time to sort of drown out the possibility of conversation. At the end, he shook his hand and said, "We'll never see each other again."

Bruce: What a prick. With a great sense of melodrama.

Diane: Was it that he thought of himself as a high-level person who couldn't afford family ties?

I thought the reason we hadn't seen each other was for that reason, but when he had a public cover position, that wouldn't really work anymore. He may be a good Lutheran, but Christian charity does not operate in him very strongly. He's a Lutheran. But I mean, a really believing, practicing, hardcore Lutheran. [His wife] became a Lutheran too. She was a non- Jew. I mean, a Jewish girl who grew up outside the Jewish tradition. Her culture was Russian.

I sometimes think it was my father's fault. My father always dreamed that one of us would make it into West Point. Really make it into America, right?

Bruce: The ultimate America.

Right. He wanted us to be the first. He would have had no trouble if one of us had to sign a pledge of anti-Semitism.

Diane: There was prejudice against Jews in the Army then?

Yes. Even stronger in the Navy, though that one madman made it to admiral, finally. Rickover, Hyman Rickover. But he was just so goddamn good nobody could stop him. And it took him forever.

The time I was aboard ship for sixty days, I got to know all about Navy politics. All the officers on the ship who were the rank of lieutenant or lieutenant commander were extremely cautious and jealous with each other, because there was great competition about who would get the next promotion. But the one guy they were all very friendly with, they all figured they had nothing to lose, was the one lieutenant who was Jewish. They figured he'd never get promoted. So they had nothing to lose in their dealings with me.

We had one very junior officer who was Jewish, and he was always given the worst assignments. When the bombers came over, they would put him out in the little boats to make smoke, circle the ship, and create smoke. He was in charge of the men *[in the boat]*. But I was absolutely safe in the whole thing, since I was not in the regular chain of command. I was attached directly to the admiral. So nobody bothered me.

Bruce: Were you in the Navy equivalent of Intelligence? Where did the translators fit?

Yes. I was in what the Navy calls Intelligence and also in what the Navy calls Communications. The organizations I belonged to had great names. One was JICPOA *[Joint Intelligence Center Pacific Ocean Area]*. Another had the marvelous name. I got switched to Communications. Communications means breaking codes, and so forth. That organization was called FRUPAC *[Fleet Radio Unit, Pacific]*. For reasons which are beyond me, almost all high-level crypto-analysts are gay. And it was always called FRUITPAC.

Then I was attached to something called RAGFOR—Radio Advance Group Forces. Then I went to the island of Guam, and that's where I was listening to the Japanese radio, Radio Tokyo, on the night the bomb was dropped. That was my duty.

Bruce: Did Radio Tokyo know what had happened?

Absolutely not. The first stories came through, a whole fleet of planes had come over and done a heavy bombing. Then: "No, it was one plane. What the hell is happening? It must be some new kind of weapon," and so on. I didn't know anything about its happening. In the Navy you are always cleared for one particular thing. I had what you would think of as the highest possible clearance in the Navy, above Top Secret, what they call Ultra. But nobody ever said a word to me about the Bomb. We just knew that we had broken the Japanese code and the Japanese didn't know it.

Bruce: Do you remember your serial number?

298383 is my serial number. Leslie Fiedler, j/g 298383. I will say nothing more. I never remember numbers. You were surprised, huh?

I was so secret, I actually have a unit decoration medal, which says, "The reason for giving this award cannot be revealed."

Diane: Did you know what it was?

That was the code business. FRUPAC. I've often wondered why so many of them were gay. They lived these monks' lives. Intelligence, in general, is full of gay people for some reason.

Diane: That Cambridge group in England was, too. Was there a prejudice against gays, or did people just expect it?

There was always the snigger, but what the hell, it was as if they had a handicap of some kind—three eyes or so on. JICPOA, the Intelligence Center, was pretty straight. They were a little scornful of FRUPAC, which was right next door.

[Some people arrive. There's chatter, then there's a pause in the recording during which we seem to have gotten on the subject of torture.]

That's when they put the slivers under your nails.

Bruce: Did you ever hear Lenny Bruce's bit on The Hot Lead Enema? It's "Would you betray your country?" "No, never!" What are they doing to that guy over there. Why are they putting the enema in his ass. HOT LEAD? THEY'RE GIVING HIM A HOT LEAD ENEMA? I'll tell you about my mother. Anything. I'll make up secrets."

Diane: I grew up on all these tales of torture. The Communists were going to torture you and you had to be ready to defend your faith. I lived in mortal fear that they would torture me and that I would fail.

I lived through the opposite side of this fantasy. The prisoners I interrogated were all sure they were going to be tortured by me or one of my underlings. I didn't torture any people.

Diane: Did somebody else do it and then they got to you?

Once they got to the official interrogator they were safe. The problem was the guys who picked them up. Our situation was the interrogation was done on board the ship, which was fifteen hundred yards offshore. The prisoners were taken on the island itself—Iwo Jima—and to persuade the Marines to keep them alive and bring them back was a little difficult. In the heat of combat, you figure, "This is a pain in the ass anyhow, and he's as good as dead."

But the Japanese prisoners didn't have to be tortured in order to speak because their indoctrination was you will never be taken prisoner, you will die first. So once they were taken prisoner, they hadn't been briefed as how to behave and they just sang like little birdies. They were told to commit suicide or to die fighting before they let themselves get shot to death. And the prisoners we did get were by and large, until the very end of things, people who were so badly wounded they couldn't either kill themselves or keep resisting. Almost all of my interrogations were done in the sick bay of the ship, while they were being repaired, sewed up, and so forth.

Catch more flies with honey than with vinegar, right? I kept insisting that the Geneva Conventions be strictly adhered to, which is not only that they not be tortured, but that enlisted men be given half a pack of cigarettes a day and officers a pack of cigarettes a day. Japanese are still great smokers. The whole Orient is full of smokers. That's where tobacco companies still make their money.

Then I would put them on ships to be taken back for permanent detention, and there my heart would sink. The officer would greet me in his hand-tailored uniform with a special gun with his wife's picture embossed on the holster. And I thought, once he gets out of sight, what the hell's going to happen? I'd give a big lecture to some about the Geneva Convention . . .

The only thing we did was allow them to discipline each other when we had groups. We would appoint a *pen cho*, the head of a *pen* was a Japanese, and they would slap people around to keep them in line according to their custom.

The first prisoner who came out I did see, I guess you would call it torture, though it was rather sportivo. They had two Marines who brought him out, and one of them was guiding the little boat that came out and the other had a baseball bat and was swatting the prisoner, not hard, but enough so he'd feel it on one side of the head. It was pretty hard to feel horrified when at the same moment bulldozers were digging huge holes and pushing a thousand bodies of assorted Japanese and Americans into them.

I think prisoners always have a tough time, but not by our interrogators. That was not part of our style.

Diane: You never worried about being tortured?

Me? No. The only thing I worried about was getting bombed. You don't get captured on a ship; you get sunk. We came close one night. Straddled by bombs, one in front and one in back. All my phobias, except for one, disappeared at that point. I have never been afraid of things again. The one is a fear of high places, especially shaky bridges, though I had to conquer that one because during the war I had to climb up the sides of ships a lot. Goddamned rocky sea. You grab for a ladder and you hit the side of the ship. If you grab one minute too soon, the boat will bang into the back of your legs and break them. If you grab too late, you'll miss it.

It's a very selective fear of heights. I don't fear climbing mountains at all, as long as I have something solid under my feet.

Diane: That was one of the interesting things in The Man Who Would Be King. *That rope bridge.*

Bruce: Did you see the Huston thing?

Yeah. They euphemized him a little. The one thing they didn't talk about was his relations with his writers. That was the really stormy part of his life. He drove his writers absolutely crazy. He drove James Agee to drink, who was inclined to drink anyway. It really killed him, some people say. "Come on, have a drink . . . look at me. I've had three." There's a book about him and his relation with writers, called *White Hunter, Black Heart.* It's written by Peter Viertel, who appeared briefly on that clip, which is really about Huston as a bully.

Diane: Clint Eastwood is making a movie in Africa right now. It's supposed to be modeled on Huston.

It probably takes off from Viertel's book.

Somebody did say—one of the actresses—that she would have hated to be a woman in Huston's life. I think it was Betty Bacall.

Bruce: She said something like "He tolerated me because I was Bogey's wife, the mother of Bogey's children. I don't think he really liked women."

Bruce: Can you say what's Jewish about you?

I expect I've already told you about what I really think is Jewish about me. It can be summed up in that little anecdote I told you about my grandfather. "Leslie," he said, "I'm taking you here not because I believe, but so you should remember." I remember.

At one and the same time I don't doubt for a moment that I'm Jewish. But what I mean when I say it is absolutely problematical to me. I'm not very Jewish culturally. Certainly not Jewish in a religious sense. I guess mythologically, I'm Jewish. I believe that I come from an unbroken line of people who go all the way back to Aaron and Abraham. And if my pedigree ends with mythological characters, that's true of all high pedigrees. Right? I am also Jewish in the sense that if Hitler was around, he would have cleared me too. I would have passed the test. I am also Jewish in the sense that if somebody says to me, however friendly or hostile a fashion, "Are you Jewish?" I say, "Yes, I'm Jewish."

I've written a little bit about this whole problem of the strange nature of my Jewishness, in that article which I told you about before for a book on the Holocaust. I have many Jewish vestiges. Every Yom Kippur, I fast. Every Hanukkah, I light the lights of Hanukkah and place them beside the Christmas tree. Every Pesach *[Passover]* I have a seder, which doesn't keep me from dashing out into the yard and shouting, "Christ is Risen!" occasionally too.

That's a past I feel continuous with, however much it may be dissolving. I once wrote a story called "The Last Jew in America." I sometimes feel like the last Jew in America. I really am. You know, Chespa isn't even circumcised. Of my grandsons, three are not circumcised.

Bruce: How can I be a Jew if —

—I have no one to say Kaddish for me? I'm just thinking of the continuity of the thing.

Diane: Did you say Kaddish for your father?

No. It would have annoyed him if I did. Though we had a sort of a Jewish ceremony at his grave. I mean, after all, he was dead and he couldn't object.

Diane: Did you ever find out, at your grandfather's funeral, did they cry out in agreement or that that had been said?

They were crying out because it touched them in a tender place. They felt a little guilty. On the other hand, they didn't change their ways. People remain Jewish in funny ways. I was thinking of a little story when I saw that Izzy Stone had died. Now he's a man who you would think would attack anything and anybody, but I remember once we were sitting in a room together and I had just come back from my first trip to Israel, and I was talking about the way in which so-called Black Jews are discriminated against by White Jews, raving on and on. And suddenly I realized he was motioning at me from across the room, and he said, "Sh, sh." That was his Jewishness talking.

Diane: But he did attack Israel for racism.

I know he did. It took him a little longer.

Diane: But he got there.

The notion of the Jews being destroyed in Israel drives me crazy. If we're going to cease existing, we should do so of our own free will. I'm going back again in January. But most of the people I talk to there are people who have very conflicting notions about the Israeli state. Two of my kids have actually ended up on kibbutzim in Israel. Both Erics. My one absolutely goyish Eric and my one somewhat Jewish Eric. *[His son with Margaret and Sally's son.]* And neither of them liked it very much. My Eric was there at a very bad time, long ago. And he kept saying, "For Christ's sake, the Arabs have to ride in the back of the bus!" On the other hand, I have no doubt that those people are my brothers, cousins, blood-kin.

Diane: Ishmael is the father of the Arabs.

And Abraham is father of the Arabs, is another way to say it.

The only place where there is no anti-Semitism, no native anti-Semitism, is in parts of the world where none of the Jewish-related religions have ever penetrated. In most of the Orient the functions, the feelings that feed into anti-Semitism here get into anti-Chinese feelings. It's certainly true in Vietnam, where almost all the refugees who leave are ethnic Chinese, who they give a hard, hard time on nationalist or racist grounds. But they also say, "They're too smart. They move into all the businesses." On the other hand, we benefited by these super-smart Chinese-Vietnamese, who are now really picking things up in our schools.

I see a face on a street corner in a strange place, and I know when it's a Jewish face and part of me goes out to him.

Diane: Did you ever make a mistake?

The only time I ever almost made a mistake—not quite; I saved myself on the brink—was for many years I wondered about whether Norman Holland was a crypto-Jew or not. I finally decided he can't be, can't be. But his name is suspicious.

Bruce: But he has no irony.

Diane: There are some.

Bruce: Jews without irony?

We kill them as false prophets.

The supreme moment of Jewish irony where I really felt at the same time that I was in some ways sympathetically a Jew, but really not, was my encounter with the money changer in China. I've already told you this story.

Inflation was terrible there, and the local currency was practically valueless. And one day I stopped a guy on a corner, who was a money changer—who was Jewish, of course, as I knew to begin with—and I gave him a buck and he gave me 2,300 yuan, or something. And I said, "Thank you." And he looked up at the heavens—then I was sure he was a Jew. And he said, confirming it absolutely, "Look at him. He gives me good American money. I give him shit paper. And he says thank you?" And I thought, Oh, the Jews will never die.

As if *Gottenyu* is still up there listening. That's the other thing about Jews: everybody calls God "father," but the Jews call him "daddy."

Bruce: I remember my mother saying that all the time; "Ah, Gottenyu! Look what he did!"

My grandmother's only fear about me was someday I would pass her on the street and I would be ashamed of her. As if anybody could be ashamed of my grandmother. Afraid of her, awed by her, yes.

The other thing I realized recently about my grandmother is I can recollect nothing she ever said in her life that wasn't a proverb which was already in existence. She only talked in proverbs. Things I remember her saying: "The apple doesn't fall far from the tree." When I was looking for something I couldn't find, she would say, "Your nose got in the way of your eyes." When somebody was very slow at doing something, she would say, "If I don't get there today, I'll be there tomorrow." And she would even eke this out with Ukrainian or Polish proverbs when she was stuck. Somebody would threaten and not deliver, she would say *[in Polish or Ukrainian]*, "Big wind, little rain."

Bruce: That's the kind of stuff that's absent from my children's lives.

I filled in for my children *[in Missoula]*, because there was this Joe Kramer there, who was an Eastern European Jew. He was one of the strange breed who was never in an American city. He entered the country via Galveston.

He liked to chop wood, and one day he got a little careless and chopped off two of his fingers. He would get up early every morning and walk to the gymnasium, where he would be shooting baskets and running around the track. He was then closing in on seventy. The students in Montana, who had never seen anything like him, loved him. In order to sort of adopt him as a Westerner, they gave him the nickname of Smokey Joe. He would take these kids up the side of the hill, then he would say, "You see the plant on this side? It's thriving because the wind is right. On this side it's not thriving because the wind is wrong. You don't blame the plant because the wind is wrong!"

His sons disappointed him greatly. One became a reporter and actually got bylines for a while in *The New York Times*. And Joe would say, "Why can't he do something socially useful?" He meant it. He despised journalists. He was a menace at all public meetings and lectures because he would get up and ask absolutely endless questions. Sometimes philosophical and sometimes ironic. The first time that we ever had an official speaker from Israel, everybody wondered what he would do. He got up, "Isn't it wonderful that we have a country now all Jews: Jewish soldiers, Jewish cops . . ."

Bruce: I remember, when I was a kid in Brooklyn, a Jewish cop used to come in my father's candy store. Jewish. This was just about the time when Jews were becoming cops—after the Irish. I was very surprised.

You're younger than I am, so you got to see that. They were absolutely unheard of when I was young. In Newark, it was Irish.

Bruce: All the older cops were Irish, all the brass were Irish. This guy was weird. A Jewish cop! It's like the first time I saw a Black cop.

One guy in my college class became a cop. He was Jewish. Ninety-five percent of the kids in my class were Jewish. But he was already a little shaky. His father had been a Jewish butcher. Jewish butchers are famous for being lascivious and obscene.

Diane: Are they?

It's because they hang their meat in the window.

Bruce: Ouch!

7

July 18, 1989

I was in Valencia, a fascinating city. It's the third largest city in Spain but tourists don't go there. So you see a real-live honest-to-god Spanish city, post-Franco: topless bathing on the beaches. In Spain, right? Boxing is not permitted to be shown on television, but they can show bullfights. Figure that out. It's also the best place to eat in Spain and I discovered one thing about Spain hasn't changed since I was first there: the only thing they believe in is eating and drinking. And you work in the intervals.

I got on this weird Spanish schedule, where you live two days every day. Get up in the morning and begin to have lunch about two and you're through at four-thirty. Then you sleep until nine and that's time to go to dinner and that begins at ten or ten-thirty and goes on to two-thirty in the morning. Two-thirty in the morning, life is still swinging on the streets. Walking back to my motel I saw an old woman selling cigars on the street corner and was able to buy cigars at two-thirty in the morning—probably a gypsy woman. These beautiful hand-rolled cigars, and I suddenly remembered, tobacco was a great industry. *Carmen* . . .

You go outside of Valencia and you think you're in Vietnam. There are rice paddies. This is a great rice-raising region of Spain. Since Franco, there's all this ethnic division of Spain. Now it's required by law that the street signs in Valencia be up in two languages, Catalan and Castilian Spanish. And the Valencians are beginning to insist that their language is different from both Catalan and Castilian. They ought to have a third sign up on every street corner!

It was a great session. I saw a lot of movies I hadn't seen before: *Good Morning, Vietnam, Full Metal Jacket,* and *Gardens of Stone,* which is the dullest, most boring movie ever made. I felt as though I had been condemned to sit through it. They were too snooty, but I talked to the organizers and persuaded them to show *Rambo*. They showed *First Blood, Part II*, which is the real Vietnam one, where he goes back to get the POWs. When they showed the thing (I didn't want to see it, since I had recently seen it), I sat in the bar where I discovered they had lots of television monitors showing things from all over the world. One of the things they showed was *Rambo*, and all of the kids from behind the bar climbed over and sat absolutely fascinated through the whole thing—just enthralled.

Getting through to Vietnam is not easy. Getting through to this guy to make the arrangements for him to come (which he finally didn't do) . . . I would have loved to have had a chance to talk to him. There were no Vietnamese there. There were Spaniards, Americans, and British. [The conversation] was pretty good, except from some of the Spaniards you had this old, hardline Stalinism, which they're just discovering and reinventing. What you got was the other side of the Cold War stuff, in which the Evil Empire is America and can do no good. The worst motives are read into everything possible.

But I loved the conference, except it was kind of tragic. My best friend there is a guy named Enrique and it turns out he has cancer. It was really awful. He had a colonoscopy. And he's got spots in his liver now. He's being so goddamned gallant, I couldn't believe it . . . buying a new house. Just got married. He's a young man, thirty-five or thirty-six or something. Got a brand-new wife, Isabel, who was his girl for many years. I discovered this time that you can tell on sight when somebody graduates from being a *potsi* to being a wife. They just move differently. There's just a certain sense of security.

I did the one thing I most wanted to do. I got to swim in the Mediterranean. One day I sneaked off and went swimming. It was beautiful. I just feel like I'm back to the mother of everything.

I don't know if they liked my talk, how well they understood it. It turned out to be a super subtle talk; but all us Americans, from a kid who must have been about twenty-five and been teaching in Spain, to me . . . we were all talking about the myths of the war in terms of there is no history and it has to be constructed now, however you're going to understand it. America may have lost the war in Vietnam, but they sure as hell are winning the war in the area of pop culture. It's the American images of the war in Vietnam which possess the imagination of the whole world.

Let me tell you something of my great etymological discovery. I said to somebody, "What gender is the sea in Spanish?" It's *la mer* in French and *il mare* in Italian. In Spain, it's both. They say in ordinary language, *el mar*, but in poetic language, it's *la mar*, and the sailors say *la mar*. I don't know what to do with this piece of information, but I give it to you free of charge. Spanish is a language I always think I understand; I figure it's a bad dialect of Italian. But I don't quite, because it has the largest vocabulary of any Romance language. It has all those Arabic words, which baffle me completely.

The discussion was pretty good, and I enjoyed the food. All the foods that Sally won't eat, I consume: squid and cuttlefish and octopus. And I had a paella with hare and blood sausage. Paella was invented in Valencia. The beaches are beautiful. Go to Valencia if you go. Nobody goes to Valencia. When the adults are going home at two-thirty in the morning, the kids are just coming out to boogie.

It's still pretty safe. It used to be safe under Franco, because there were three cops on every street corner. The only trouble you run into are Basque nationalists—they decide to blow up some café or something—but there's no street violence to speak of. And they look very prosperous, but I discovered it's a little tricky. I discovered their unemployment has gone up thirteen percent. The other thing that weirded me out in Spain, I kept thinking: "What's wrong with this world? Somehow it looks wrong to me." As I was going home I realized I hadn't seen a Black face. Franco had Moorish troops fighting for him, but he sent them home as soon as he was victorious.

The other thing I discovered was that you say to a lot of those kids who are now spouting Socialist and Communist and Maoist slogans, "Was your father in the war? Was your grandfather in the war?" The answer is "yes," and nine times out of ten, it'll turn out they were on Franco's side. You forget there were a lot of Spaniards who were on that other side. Enrique's father, who is now old and all he talks about is his war experiences, still is a Francista. There's still a wound in that country, but on the other hand, it doesn't feel like . . . there's no touch of Third-Worldishness about it at all. They all have a little touch of Jewish blood and Moorish blood to redeem them, though they deny it.

But anti-Semitism is still strong there. You walk into the johns, and it would say, "Shit on the Jews" and there would be swastikas. Honest to god. Well, they drove them out *[in 1492]*, and they don't want them to come back.

Life is not cheap in Spain. Goods are expensive. The only thing that's cheap are services. The cheapest taxicabs in the world. You can go any place for a buck. Food, I think, was pretty expensive, but I didn't pay for anything. There was big generosity going on. The conference picked up my hotel bill, my breakfasts, and I was taken out to dinner every night I was there, including one night when we had a magnificent feast given by the chancellor of the university, or the Magnificent Rector, whatever they call him.

They do that in Italy. The head of Bologna was called "El Rector Magnifico." When I originally lectured in Bologna many years ago in the early fifties, the Magnificent Rector was called by the students *Felice Battaglia*—"Happy Battle."

The university that set this thing up was very interesting. It only meets in the summer time. It's a big international thing which hosts conferences. Its first meeting was held at one of the great beaches in Spain. This time they held it in Valencia. It was given for credit for students who got little certificates at the end of it. There were fifty-five of them. Great press coverage, with beautiful pictures of all the participants.

The first time I went to Spain was in Franco's time. Everything was tight, tight, tight. I actually went to Santander, which is on the Atlantic coast. It rained almost every day. I went to see my first bullfight there. I was there right at the great time, you know, it was the running of the bulls, Pamplona. In every little town I gather they do this crazy stuff with the bulls. The day before I was there, the matador got it right in the balls. Everybody said he deserved it, he was a show-off.

There's a movement for and against everything. They enjoy being wide open in Spain. They weren't allowed to say anything for so many years. The only thing it's fashionable to be against in almost all quarters, alas, is the Jews. It's weird. I talked to Enrique about it. He would talk to me quite frankly about it. He's a friend. But mostly people are guarded. He said it's there. It's deep. They thought they were the enemy. They cooperated with the goddamn Moors. There are long memories in Spain. It's only five hundred years. It's religion, but now when most Spaniards are not very religious—the church is still there and there are some people who are very religious—but it's a pretty secular society at this point. It's the last remnants of Christianity—anti-Semitism. A disgusting thought. The other thing, the last thing that's left in some Jews is reaction against anti-Semitism. Weird.

I'm supposed to go to Israel in January [1990]. I hope there's something there besides total confusion. One has the sense that there's wheeling and dealing behind the scene now. There's always wheeling and dealing behind the scenes. When people are talking tough . . .

What you get are the extreme fanatics on both sides. The left-wing split-offs and the PLO and the super-orthodox Jews, who really believe God promised them land, Sumer and Judea. How odd of God to choose the Jews. He gave us a lot of trouble. You see, I say "us." There was a big argument about—one of the American speakers kept saying "we" in reference to America, and then the whole thing turned into Spanish and showed you were permeated by American ideology if you said *nos otros* when you meant America, identifying yourself with the monsters who are in control of the government and who napalmed all the innocents. I say *nos otros* for the Jews and for the Americans. I've got the worst of all possible worlds.

I may [publish the Vietnam piece], though I was going to give another version of it at a conference that Bob Newman had organized where the Chinese were coming, and he's now talking about publishing some of those things. I need a vacation from Vietnam and Vietnam films.

I'm baffled by *Apocalypse Now*—because the apocalypse never comes. I do know about the ending, and I've actually seen one version where they show the thing behind the final credits, but in its standard form, it should be called *Apocalypse Interruptus*. It's such a strange film. The people who wrote it are such a weird combination. You know about John Milius, who wrote the original script. He's an extreme right-winger and hawk. He wrote *Conan, the Barbarian*. And *Red Dawn*. On the other hand, he used for his information about it the Michael Herr thing [*Dispatches*]. Herr wrote the narration apparently.

That's the other thing about the film that bothered me this time. It's not a film that trusts its images, its messages. It's words, words, words. They explain everything. That's one thing you can say about *The Deer Hunter*, it really trusts the images to do it. It's a purely mythic film. People say strange things about *Deer Hunter*. Somebody read a huge hunk of some critic's commentary on *Deer Hunter* and it begins with this description of an idyllic working-class community. Idyllic? Where the father is drunk and beats his daughter? Where the girls go to work as checkout girls in supermarkets? Where there's this grimy town in the middle of these beautiful mountains? It's really not so!

I'll tell you the other thing that's bothering me. I have a question. Why are those three films [*Deerhunter, Apocalypse Now, Rambo*] which I picked out all written by Italo-Americans? It suddenly occurred to me. Isn't that odd?

[*Apocalypse Now*] really touches the juvenile in everyone's hearts.

I also realize at this point that [Willard's] quirks come within an inch . . . I mean, he's very much like *Rambo*. If he admired him, he would have been *Rambo*. He learns to fight the enemy with their own tools, adopts the methods of the guerrillas. But he couldn't decide whether he liked Kurtz or he didn't like Kurtz—his Kurtz.

The other thing about that film is he doesn't know what to do about Willard in the end. In one version he was going to have him become Kurtz. Which he almost does. In another version, he was going to have them die together under the bombardment. Instead he gives him this funny cop-out ending, in which he actually carries out his assigned task and thinks he's somehow out of the army at the same time. He has it both ways.

Someday we should bring the real Montanan out, my old Butte buddy, Ed Lahey. The poet—"Blind Horses." He was really thrilled because this summer he was invited to a conference where [Tom] McGuane and company were present. And they celebrated him as the one honest-to-god proletarian poet. Ed Lahey's father was the last independent prospector in Montana. We went to the mine once and Memo *[Leslie's daughter Miriam]* put her finger into the gold dust and started to walk away. She was a little girl then. Very carefully they got all the dust off [her finger]. Ed Lahey keeps calling me and saying, "Come back to Montana—you belong in Montana." And sometimes I think he's right. [Montanans] are so hopelessly drunk all the time.

A film which goes against the grain is *Full Metal Jacket* because it takes place in cities. In everybody's imagination they wanted the wilderness. It's about the Tet Offensive. I hated the whole beginning of it, which is full of clichés about Marine Corps training. That's been done so many times before. Everybody knows it. You want to say, "So what's new?" Kurt has told me some hair-raising stories about [Marine training]. One thing they didn't have in the film: they caught some guy smoking when he wasn't supposed to and they made him eat his pack of cigarettes.

I once had the strange experience of walking down the streets of San Francisco just before I was shipped off for the first time. I was in my brand-new ensign's uniform, and I was with a woman who was a sergeant in the Marine Corps. The hoots and hollers that went on in that street, you wouldn't believe. They were called "BAMs": Broad-assed Marines. The Marine Corps were very proud of their lean buttocks.

How they love their bodies, those guys. I was still with the Marines when I was in China, and every morning as I would walk out, the scene was they would be lying out in the sunlight, all walking naked, rubbing each other down. I was disguised as a Marine. It was ridiculous. Here I was in this Marine uniform, with my buddy who has since become famous. This is Jack Brooks, the congressman. Known as Babbling Brooks in those days. It was clear he was going to become a congressman. The day after we landed in China, in Tientsin, he had a complete set of furniture, a Eurasian girl, and two house boys for us, Number One Boy and Number Two Boy. We knew he was bound to go into politics. He had this beautiful tailor-made uniform. The rule was that if we went out on the streets at all, we were supposed to carry a gun with us. A .45. But it made a bulge in his uniform, which he didn't like. So I was the one who packed the .45. If I ever had to shoot it, I would have shot him or my own foot. I still have that gun. It's my only souvenir. Never been fired in anger, or for that matter, not in anger.

When I was officer of the day once when we were on Guam, there was a scream from the middle of the jungle, and they sent a little group of us out with me at the head of it—and all of us praying it was no goddamn Jap. It turned out to be a wild pig or something. The only thing that threatened me there were the rats. When we went out to pee at night there were these great huge rats looking up at you out of the bushes. The sound would stir them up when we'd tinkle on the leaves.

I liked the second half of *Full Metal Jacket*. It got a little heavy-handed: the sexual symbolism got me down, like the girl clearly in orgasm as she died. It was a good idea, but it didn't work for me. But it was interesting to take it into that factory and into those deserted streets. The beginning of the sniping was good. *Good Morning, Vietnam* disturbed me a little, though it was such a spectacular performance. I kept saying, "What is this movie saying?" If you turned the war over to show biz it would have been better? I don't know what it was saying. The Black guy was very good. God he was great. I don't know who he is. Robin Williams is the triumph of the *tummler*. He has those funny walls around him.

For many years after my own experience, I refused to see any war movie. Just wouldn't go. Because they're all so full of shit. The obvious thing to say about them, which everybody has said, in the first place you think that war is all combat, a climactic moment. They don't give you the sense of the immense boredom of the in-between times. Few of them even give you the sense of exhilaration, which is also part of it. You know, suddenly all the rules are gone. I used to have the feeling that suddenly I was back in the world the way it used to be. This is how all of mankind once smelled. Then you suddenly realize that most of the time we live in a world that's deodorized. The sense of smell you can't get from the movies. That's one problem, the strongest part of my own combat experience . . .

That's one of the reasons I like India—its smells like that. But in India it's the marvelous combination of the smell of drying cow dung, which they're using for fuel; you have the smell of human excrement beside the road; and over the whole thing there's the smell of sandalwood. And suddenly you think, they've taken everything that's sweet in the smell of shit and they've extracted it.

I'm reminded of the line in *The Sun Also Rises*. They're out fishing and he says, "I haven't had so much fun since the war."

It makes my heart break. I really wanted to be an actor.

Which reminds me: Debbie *[Leslie's daughter Deborah]* heard a TV commentator saying, "Gus Gray jumps around in *Great Balls of Fire* like Leslie Fiedler giving a lecture."

[The conference paper] isn't written out yet. They kept asking me for it, and I showed them my notes, which nobody ever believes. But it's in shape to go now. I just have to sit down and do it. It's called "Mythicizing the War," and it says don't be misled by the superficial realism in some of these films, like *The Deerhunter*. You must read them as myths and realize that finally myths are our greater perception. That there is no war that we don't see back through some mythicized version.

I once did a lecture tour in Sicily. Traveled all over the island and my greatest time was I gave a lecture in Caltanissetta to the sulfur miners' union. It sits right in the middle of the island. I was giving a talk on the recent novel in Italy and America. Those guys were the most interesting group I ever talked to. They kept me there until two o'clock in the morning talking. I could still do Italian comfortably then. They were involved with literature and wanted to talk about it. They wanted to talk about Leonardo Sciascia, who is one of the most famous Sicilian writers.

Then another night we arrived in a tiny town—I can't remember what it was—and the honorable society came out to protect us. They knew we were foreigners; they put guards in front of our door—so guests wouldn't be offended by any violence, right?

Sicily is so beautiful. And the Greek ruins there are better than anything in . . . Their politics was very strange. Some of them were extreme left-wingers and others really were dreaming of the day when they could become the Fifty-first State of the Union. All their relatives were here, they said. They were more American than Italian—got more to do with America than with the goddamn North Italians.

In every little town, they would send me off to see the guy who went off to America and lived for a while and came back with his Social Security or whatever. We would talk about the Yankees and the great days.

I toured all over Italy then. I was in Calabria too. This was in '52, maybe. There was strong pro-American feeling. And strong, passionate interest in American literature because Mussolini had forbidden it. *[Elio]* Vittorini was one of the first Italians to write about American literature. He was a Sicilian by birth.

Sally and I have done the other part. Sally went with me once when I was talking in Urbino. In the center of Urbino was the most anti-Semitic painting in Italy: *The Desecration of the Host* by Uccello. It shows the Jew coming in and stabbing the host and the host bleeding. It's sort of a cartoon series of panels, and ends with the Jew being hanged in the last panel. It's right in the Palace. It's a beautiful painting.

Then one of our students loaned us a car. We were surrounded by prosperous Northern Italian students. We did the tour of the whole region. It's so beautiful. Then I took Sally with me down to Fano.

We were the guests of one of the strangest and most interesting men in Italy. His name is Alfredo Rizzardi. Rizzardi is the translator of the *Pisan Cantos* in Italian. He's a first-rate translator. Crazy as a loon. He had a dog whom he'd lost. He claimed his dog committed suicide. "My 'duck' committed suicide." We wondered how a "duck" could commit suicide.

He also translated some of [Sally's] poems. Alfredo Rizzardi came from a long line of translators. His teacher was a man named Carlo Izzo, who taught at a university in Venice. He translated Spenser back, he said, into Italian, returning the debt he owed Spenser. It was a strange group of people.

The chairman of the department then was a man called, believe it or not, Benvenuto Cellini. He happened to be a eunuch who was doing his best to grow a beard and managed to get three hairs to appear, lived with his mother in Rome, and commuted. I used to come up with him. That year I was teaching in Venice and Bologna, and I would go up one day a week to give my lectures. I would always travel with Benvenuto Cellini, who was an ill-tempered fellow. When we got off the train in Venice, the small boys would come and carry our bags. He would always scream the same thing at them: "You're wasting your time, pieces of stupid." Then he would give me a drink before we began.

Cellini once met Alberto Moravia. He said, "Moravia, Moravia, surely I've heard that name some place." And Moravia said, "Benvenuto Cellini, Benvenuto Cellini, surely I've heard that name someplace."

My boss in Rome was the most interesting of all. I don't say his name because he had the evil eye. *[The name Leslie won't say is Mario Praz.]* The first time I went to see him (I can say MP; that's all right), a then-young man named Agustino Lombardo, who is now the senior professor of English literature at the University of Rome: La Sapienza. They had a strange system. If you were an assistant, you were an unpaid assistant to the guy who had the chair. And you hoped that he would stand you in good stead when you took your exams and the time came to be placed. He said to me, "I don't believe in all this stuff," the evil eye . . . "But when you go to see our friend, don't wear your watch." I went to see him, I wore my watch, my watch stopped, I never could have it fixed.

Whenever I go to Italy, I exchange these stories and I get others back. Last time I saw him I was giving a lecture in Rome and he intro-duced me (he was always very nice to me), and afterwards we were driving around with my friend Tekla, who married a whole series of people. Tekla I did tell you about. She's the woman from Oklahoma City who had been driven around by Ralph Ellison when he was a chauffeur for her father, who had the biggest department store in Oklahoma City. Tekla was in the car with us and we drove around, and the car was being driven by somebody from the embassy. It was raining on us, and I swear when I looked out it wasn't raining any place else; just on us. And the car had a minor fender-bender, driven by a woman who was proud she had never had an accident in her life, a woman of fifty or fifty-five. We arrived at Tekla's hotel and let her off, and she said, "Well, he's not such a bad guy: a little rain, a minor accident, at least nobody broke his leg." She went to the desk of the hotel, and there was a telegram saying that her daughter had broken her leg that day back home in Firenze.

He *[Mario Praz]* loved [his reputation]. He fostered it. He had a cast in one eye, which helped. And he played on it all the time. I think he started some of the stories about how he walked into this grand dinner and the chandelier fell down on the table. But he was a man who exploited all his worst sides. Another time Victorio Gassman invited him to come and make some opening remarks after he opened up playing Hamlet. It was the big event of Gassman's life. He said, "Victorio Gassman, who is acting Hamlet tonight, should remember Hamlet's advice to the players." And he sat down.

I would go to see him, and he would say, "What are you up to these days?" I would say I'm trying to write a little article on Moravia, and he would say, "Good. Tear him to pieces; his wife will love it." Elsa Morante *[Moravia's wife]*. She's a novelist herself. His present wife, however—it must be his fourth—is exactly fifty years younger than he is.

I knew Moravia a little. The woman who drove us around Sicily was a girlfriend of his at the time. I once drove with Moravia up into the hills to see his "milk brother," as he said. He had had a nursemaid, and this was her actual child. He came from some place in the north of Italy. He's Jewish. His real name is Alberto Pincherle. He's very smart; very articulate. Essentially icy. He doesn't really give you anything of himself. He likes to tell stories, but they never involve deep feeling. He's like a real writer. He tells anecdotes; has an anecdotal mind.

I liked some of his earlier stuff. I don't know what it would be like going back to it. His reputation is sort of faded as he's grown older. He keeps writing, but I haven't read anything he's written recently. In the fifties and on into the sixties, he was considered the great Italian writer. His only rival was Pavese. Pavese did the smart thing: he died young. Calvino was just starting to come up. He was thought of as a young man who might make it someday. Calvino was thought of as sort of the protégé of Pavese.

It was Pavese who won my heart. Moravia seems so cold for a Jew. I think he leaned hard against all his Jewishness. He was raised as just an upper-bourgeois kid, behind a fence looking out at the people, wearing white gloves when he was sent out to play. Italians are funny.

I finally got to learn how to spot Italian Jews by their names, but at first I didn't recognize them. Anybody who's called after the name of a city or town is likely to be Jewish. If somebody's called "Milano," I'd say he's Jewish. Unless they're like my friend Guido Fink, who still kept the old name.

You know the rumor in Spain is, despite all the anti-Semitism, that Franco came from a Jewish family. Franco is a suspicious name. He's the "Frank."

There's one way I can always open up a conversation when I meet Italians who are being very formal with me. We start telling MP stories.

They realize that I'm not so much of an alien; that I don't believe in the evil eye, and we can talk. As you know, Italians love to gossip anyhow.

The last time I was in Italy, I ran into a woman whom I had known ever since those days, who has the marvelous name of Biancamaria Tedeschini Lalli. She's the professor of English literature now at the Madestero, which is like the teachers' college at the University of Rome. She's a marvelous woman. She's done all this in terms of her career and has six children! The first thing we did was to begin telling MP stories. She knew him in those days. She was a good friend of Agustino. We also told Agustino stories.

When Agustino Lombardo now comes into a group of Italian academics, they practically bow and grovel before him. We knew him when. And we whispered to each other, "He's really a Sicilian." But he's one of those blond, blue-eyed Sicilians, who looks exactly like George Washington. He's called the Lombard. He comes from Catania. It's an Italian joke. When you see a CD license on a plate—it means, of course, Corps Diplomate.

Another Jewish name I discovered was Tedesco. It was a name I used to use over the telephone when I called up to order tickets or something. They would say, "What's the name?" I would say "Fiedler." And they would say, "Huh?" And I would say, "Fi-e-d-ler." No good, I would spell it for them. They still wouldn't get it. So I'd say, "The hell with it. Just put down 'Tedesco.'"

It's funny. There are only thirty thousand Jews in all of Italy; there never were more than fifty thousand. And yet they're in positions of power and influence, from the leadership of the Communist Party to Olivetti. There really is no anti-Semitism in Italy. That's the one place I've been in Europe where there's simply none. When Jennie was born, we had a maid who wanted to take her out and baptize her. So we would say, "But we're Jews!" And she would say, "Yes, but what is your religion?" She did sneak her out and baptize her!

That was Maria. Maria was a marvelous woman. She was sixty years old when she came to work for us. She could pick me up and hold me over her head. She had her hair dyed black—an unbelievable black—with shoe-blacking, I believe. The soldiers would whistle at her in the park when she went out. She used to embarrass me. When I met her on the street, she would kiss my hand. She was from the border region with Yugoslavia, around Trieste. She had a Yugoslav name. Her name was Maria Terschisch, but her only language was Italian. She was completely illiterate. At one point when we were living in our glory we had two maids. When we came home one night, the other who could read was reading to her from the kids' book, a fairy tale about Snow White. Maria was weeping; "What a cruel stepmother," she said. She had grown up in Naples and she was more Neapolitan in her manner. She was absolutely operatic. She would get a letter from home saying her daughter had a slight cold, and she would go into a frenzy. She would say, "Que bruto destino," tearing out handfuls of her hair. Never saw anybody tear her hair before.

I have such complicated feelings about the Italians. Carlo Izzo I mentioned before. I taught with him in Venice. He also taught at Bologna. I would say to him, "When do my lectures begin at Bologna?" And the answer to that is "When would you like to begin?" And I told him when I would like to begin, and he'd say, "I'll post a note on the bulletin board and the students will know to be in such a room." I'd come back to Venice the next day and say, "Did you make arrangements for my class yet?" And he'd open his coat and say, "Stab me! Kill me! Destroy me! I have forgotten. Next week I'll write it on a note and put it inside my watch." And next week, "Stab me!" I couldn't resist—I said, "False thing of Italy!"

He both liked me and was a little jealous. He also was a little politically disturbed because he was a Communist, and I represented American imperialism. But everything's on a human level, bad or good.

One thing we've never talked enough about and we should someday is Newark.

8

August 9, 1989

I've lived in many places, some of them for a long time, like Buffalo and Missoula. But in my deepest imagination, I'm always in Newark. And I don't like it much. But I'm there, for better or worse. As a matter of fact, the last story I wrote, I went back to old Newark memories again. Some of my first stories were about Newark and my very last story. In this story I imagine, for reasons which might be obvious already, Newark burning to the ground. And myself holed up with a bunch of shoe salesmen with whom I used to work in a cave deep under a statue, which is in Military Park. It's called *The Wars of America*: great, monstrous piece of patriotic sculpture.

It's clear to me that the reason Newark stays in my mind is because it's the place where I was—in many different senses and in many different institutions—really educated. I don't just mean I went to school in Newark, but I did go through most of grade school and all of high school in Newark, and even when I went to college, I stayed in Newark four years when I commuted to school in the Bronx every goddamned day, two hours there and two hours back, via streetcar, two trains, subway, all the way up to the Bronx, past the Yankee Stadium, and then I was in sight of the citadel of learning.

The physical parts of all that have somehow by a great conspiracy of fate been eliminated. The college I went to is no longer New York University Heights, but it's been turned into a kind of community college in the Bronx. The high school I went to is now Black and is not called Southside High School anymore, but I'm not sure what, Malcolm X High

School or something of that kind. The house I lived in in Newark is now a super highway; a goddamned slab of concrete runs right through it.

I used to go back and see it because one of the reasons I remember Newark so well is that my mother would never leave it, until the last two or three years of her life when she finally came here to Buffalo. But she insisted on living as close to Newark as possible, across the line in Irvington, on the corner of Grove Street and Springfield where she could look back at the wreck of Springfield Avenue that was burned down and pillaged by the Blacks in the riots in Newark in the sixties. It's never really been repaired. It's just a disaster area, forever. It looks a little like London just after the War.

I come back to Newark because in it were created the images which possess my mind when I write fiction. I think of Newark as a place where I was educated, but it was not the school system which educated me in Newark. That only did me something which I finally think is harmful. I mean it deprived me of something. The main thing that grade school and high school did for me in Newark was to educate me out of my mother tongue. They taught me to speak an artificial standard English, rather than the street language with which I grew up. Black kids always talk about this, but it happens otherwise, too.

All the time I was in school, as I told you, I didn't have a single Jewish teacher, and my classes were ninety to ninety-five percent Jewish. When Yom Kippur came along, the classes were empty. Even the one Gentile kid in the class, who was a Greek and had the marvelous name of Christopholus, but had shortened it to Christy Christ, that's how he's known on the school rolls, he used to stay home, too.

My teachers used to keep me after school and teach me how to pronounce certain vowels, and get rid of certain cadences in my speech, idioms, even basic vocabulary. I remember I got my chief brainwashing by the teacher who prepared me to give the eighth-grade commencement address. Those teachers were brought in from the suburbs. Not only were they Gentiles, but they had nothing to do with urban life either. They must have brought them in in a sealed train. They thought of themselves as missionaries who were saving us. And they had this bunch of kids who were absolutely marvelous.

The class I went through Hawthorne Avenue school with, I would say three-quarters of them have ended up as academics, very distinguished ones, most of them social scientists, most of those sociologists. I had the rare distinction of being in that bunch of bright kids, the brightest boy in Hawthorne Avenue school, which put a lot of pressure on me and also on my teachers. Because in addition to everything else, those teachers, most of whom were dumb beyond belief, were being goyish beyond belief. I would do their grade books for them, and set up when they gave intelligence tests; they couldn't handle the figures. In seventh, eighth, and nineth grade I was doing that for my teachers.

When I went to high school I had one male teacher who happened to be Jewish, and who was really the only real influence on my life in the whole official educational system of Newark, a man whose name was Emanuel Eisenberg. He seemed a tragic figure to us because he had married a Gentile woman, he had come from an Orthodox family, and they had sat *shiva* for him and he was declared officially dead. It was he under whom I wrote my first long critical essay, which turned out to be on a man whom I later studied with and got my PhD under and on whose arm I walked up to get a PhD at the University of Wisconsin. A marvelous man, to whom I dedicated *Love and Death in the American Novel.* His name was William Ellery Leonard.

Leonard gave me the complete wrong notion about what the academic life was like. Leonard was a rebel. He was a pacifist during World War I. He was a person who put himself in front of—in the days of extreme sexual repression and oppression—he once planted himself in front of a student's room where the Dean of Men was wanting to break in to find the guy with a girl, and William Ellery was there was saying, "A man's home is his castle."

He prevented that dean from entering. He was a rather formidable guy, but he was absolutely victimized by the University of Wisconsin because he suffered from severe agoraphobia, and after a while couldn't even leave his apartment. We used to have to go to his rooms to have our classes. The world would come in to see him. He was a poet; he translated *The Cid* into English; he did a translation of *Beowulf.* He knew everything. And whatever courses he taught, I took. That was when I was in graduate school. He gave a course in Robert Burns; I did Robert Burns. He did a course in contemporary successors of Chaucer; I took that. He taught Old Icelandic; I took that. He taught Lucretius; I took that.

I thought that is what a professor really is, a man whose province was the whole world of books and who is completely contemptuous of the standards of the timid people around him. A risk-taker. Well, that turned out to be a mistake.

At any rate, it was Eisenberg, under whom I wrote my fourth-year essay *[on Channing]* in high school. At that point I had discovered what is called now "postmodernism," along with "premodernism." My essay was absolutely incomprehensible and unreadable, but it was very elegant. I have a terrible feeling it exists some place in my files, but I'm afraid to look.

But I was really educated in high school by my fellow students. This is my first Newark education. When I was in junior high school I met my first two Communists, who converted me almost immediately. They were second-generation Communists.

Bruce: You were a Communist in junior high school?

Yes. I was Communist at age thirteen. These two people—Milty Ritz and Lilly Gecker—had parents who were Communists. And they, of course, in order to define their own identity, instead of immediately going to bourgeois values, became Trotskyists. So I was a Communist when I was fourteen; by the time I was nineteen I was a Trotskyist. I was a Communist in the days when you really read everything; not just *Kapital* and *What Is to Be Done?*, but also *Anti-Dühring*, and so forth. We used to quiz each other. And occasionally we would rise and lecture our history professors on the dialectical process in history.

We were unendurable. But at the same moment we were doing this, people would take me aside because all the while I was doing this I was also a very diligent student. They would say, "People are known by the company they keep. Why do you hang out with these mad radicals?" But the mad radicals were also interested in avant-garde literature. So by the time I was fourteen, I was not only reading *Anti-Dühring*, I was reading *Transition*. This was my favorite magazine at the time, where what became *Finnegans Wake* was appearing as a work in progress.

So I started reading *Finnegans Wake* at age fourteen. I may have told you this. The geometry class was once all kept after school because we had been passing a book from hand to hand and whispering to each other. This was the second year of high school geometry class; the book was Louis Aragon's *The Red Front*, translated by e. e. cummings. When we read any American journal it was *Partisan Review*. We respected literature the way we respected revolutionary politics, as something that would blow up the whole world around us. So although we thought of ourselves as extremely literate people, we also despised what we called the "culture vultures" at the "art farts": people who read *New Yorker* and *Harper's, Atlantic Monthly, Saturday Review of Literature,* and so forth.

So I've grown up with this double feeling toward literature: it ought to be in the possession of people who know that it's a weapon to destroy all that's unendurable and tedious in life.

If I spend my life traveling around the world it's because for the first twenty years of it the furthest I can remember going was to New

York, which is ten miles away—a fast trip, right?—where I used to be sent occasionally to bring back shoes when there was a shortage of them, and so forth.

With the hobos I loved in the Park, it was also interesting because the Jesus boys were also there preaching. And various kinds of political agitators. Military Park was sort of Newark's equivalent of Union Square in New York. I learned to heckle. I also learned how to deal with hecklers there. By the time I was fifteen, I was up on soap boxes on street corners. Before I was ever behind the desk, I was on a soap box. I learned all kinds of very neat stunts. When somebody asks a long, long question which is really a speech, the right way to answer is "Yes" or "No." This really deflates them. They would say, "Who's paying you for those remarks, Moscow gold?" and I would say, "Who's paying you to heckle me? McCarter from the Public Service?"—that being a big utility company in Newark, which is also across from the Park. The Park was the center of everything.

One day [in the library] I saw a long line of books with beautiful red covers on them, which turned out to be a translation of *Remembrance of Things Past*. At that point I must have been sixteen. I was taking French. The next time I went to the library I got *À la recherche du temps perdu* in French. I read that book so hard that the first sentence of it continued to ring in my mind forever: "Longtemps, je me suis couché de bonne heure." When I couldn't make it downtown, I went to our branch library, where I also learned something about the world and its relation to books; because there all the books I wanted to read were kept in what was called "the locked room." At age fifteen I remember having a battle with the librarian to be allowed to read *A Portrait of the Artist as a Young Man*, which for some reason was considered a "locked room" book.

But it's a nice way to come to high literature, something forbidden, with a taboo against it. Gave it an extra frisson. After a while she would let me read anything. She was a monstrous lady, with whom I had a strange kind of love-hate relationship. In addition to putting carefully anything that might stimulate you too much away in a locked room, she used to get all the photography magazines, find the nude pictures, and stamp them three times: left tit, right tit, and crotch, left tit, right tit, and crotch. With the date thing.

But the shoe store also educated me. People who work in shoe stores . . . It's a funny kind of world. It was sort of like a demimonde. I was on the edge of the underworld. The most respectable looking guy in the place, who always carried a shiny briefcase under his arm, I finally discovered one day, was a condom peddler; and he kept condoms in his briefcase.

The best shoe salesman is a mythological figure who's haunted me ever since. His name was Morrie Becker. He appears in one of my two early stories, one called "Nobody Ever Died from It." He makes a reappearance in my very last story, whose title is "What Used to Be Called Dead." This is the one about Newark burning to the ground.

Morrie Becker used to entertain us by sitting and shouting at the top of his voice the grossest obscenities at the women who were his customers. And they wouldn't believe that he was saying it. He would take a suede brush for cleaning suede, and he would say, "Lady, this is also good for the hair around the hole." She would look at him and say, "Nobody is saying this to me. I can't believe it." And we would all be lined up behind him.

We only lined up for two things: to hear Morrie Becker work on his customers, and when the word was passed "split vamp, split vamp." That meant a woman had come in who wasn't wearing pants. The salesman would pull her legs apart. So I was into this grossness beyond belief.

He was also queer, Morrie. His code name was "Florence." One of his other favorite routines was to take a shoe and put it in a stretcher and scream at the top of his voice, "Take it out daddy, it hurts." Then he would pull the stretcher out, and the shoe would relax and he would say, "Put it back, daddy, I love it."

The manager would always say he was the best salesman because "he understands their psychology." He was a tragic figure, too. He would walk out and say as he was going home, "Four walls. Diamonds isn't everything." Returning to an obviously lonely life. His sister was a prostitute. His brother was a small-time gangster.

There was also Eddie Seiler in the shoe store. When I was a forty-four boy *[what they called kids with that job in the shoe store]*. I got paid two bucks for a Saturday. Saturday began at eight o'clock. By the time the customers were all gone, we dropped the stock, cleaned the place. It was eleven, eleven-thirty at night, twelve at night. When the NRA *[National Recovery Administration]* came in, Franklin Delano Roosevelt did me a personal favor. My salary was raised from two bucks to two dollars and fifty cents a day.

Eddie Seiler would persuade us to go with him to little local nightclubs because he was a songwriter. He actually wrote two songs which have a kind of small immortality. One of them is called "A Dozen Red Roses for a Blue Lady" and the other is "I Don't Want to Set the World on Fire, I Just Want to Set a Flame in Your Heart." He wrote the lyrics. He died from God knows what, before he was forty.

I got my sexual education—my theoretical sexual education—there. The same guy who peddled condoms, whose name, believe it or not, was Schtupleman *[schtup: Yiddish for "fuck"]*. He was known as Schtupie Schtupleman. He used to tell us long and thrilling stories about his sexual adventures and how you had to do it and so forth.

Diane: Was it against the law to sell condoms?

Yes, it was against the law to sell condoms in those days.

Christmas time came. This is a great Christmas in my life because the other thing I learned to do in the shoe store was drink. We had a Christmas party when I was fifteen. And everybody wanted to pour to the kid. They said to the kid, "Have one more drink." I got drunk out of my mind. That Christmas the hose girls had given Morrie Becker—I get him mixed up: in my stories, I call him Abie Peckerless, the two names are confused in my mind—as a Christmas present a hot dog with two Christmas tree ornaments tied to it.

I nearly blew it all when I tried to organize the shoe salesmen, however. My uncle was the manager of the store. This made it especially difficult. We held union meetings of all kinds, and word would spread to the upper levels of administration in the company and the boss called me in one day and said, "You're a smart boy. You'll succeed in the world. Why are you bothering with this radical stuff? Playing around with unions? Play ball with us, we'll take care of you. We'll help you through college."

That's my Newark basically. It's so ugly.

Bruce: So much of your early literature was autodidact.

Yes.

The first story I ever published and the first poem I ever published were based on something else which belongs to my Newark beginnings. And really belongs to high school. All my friends in the high school, close friends, were (a) radicals and (b) thought they were going to be writers.

None of us thought we were going to be great writers, but we thought we were going to be very good writers who would be totally neglected and would be dead by the age of thirty, preferably in Paris, or Taos would be a second-best bet. And all my life through high school I dreamed of going to Paris, or at least making it into D. H. Lawrence country in New Mexico. And some of the people actually went.

Bruce: Were your parents aware of your peregrinations in the Park and your politics?

Yeah—and they hated them. My father hated my politics. My father was a very political man. He was very anti-Communist. But he was also a liberal Democrat, an anti-Communist liberal Democrat. He claimed that when he was young he had been attracted by such ideas and then decided they were no good. He was very ambitious for us and his main argument was "Communism is going to kill your career. You're destroying yourself."

My father and I would argue about anything. We had a very troubled relationship. When I was fifteen I had a fistfight with my father. Mock fistfight, whose main purpose was that my mother interrupted us. I can't even remember what the occasion was.

He was a poet himself, my father. He wrote lyrics for popular songs. He wrote musical comedies. He was a very defeated and frustrated man. And he also spoke differently from everybody else in the neighborhood. He had an immense vocabulary, no malapropisms. He knew what he was doing. He was a great crossword puzzler and he did cryptograms. He taught me all those things. He died when he was sixty.

Bruce: What terms were you on when he died?

Somewhat better. But his favorite phrase for me was "You're a constant series of shocks and surprises." He must have said that two million times. When he was mad, it was more to the point. Like "Shitheel" or something.

Diane: Did he like your brother?

One of my father's dreams was—I don't know how this got into his head—is that one or another of us would go to West Point.

Bruce: Jews in West Point?

My father grew up in a very funny way. He was born in Newark and lived in Newark finally. But for a while he lived in a suburb of West Orange, which was then completely rural, where there was one factory, which was a hatting factory. His father was a hatter and worked there. My father's friends when he was a kid were all little Gentile boys. The only name he was ever called, he told me, when he was a kid was "Sheeny," which began as an insult and then just became his name, because after a while the kids were friends.

So he lived this funny, semi-rural life. He had a rupture which bothered him all his life which he got. He had been stealing apples from farmers' orchards and got caught on a barbed wire fence in his escape attempt. My father wasn't Jewish at all, except in his anti-Semitism. He would always say in his loudest voice, "I can't stand the Jews. They're so loud."

He never really had the sense that I hadn't quite destroyed my life. My first book was published in 1955 and I think he was already dead. His family didn't live very long. My mother's family, they all live long. He died at sixty. His mother died at fifty-eight. His father died at forty. But there was one long-lived streak in his family. His grandfather, my great-grandfather, whom I knew slightly, slightly, lived to a very old age. I don't think he knew exactly how old he was, but he was quite old. He outlived most of his kids.

Bruce: Do you have any explanation about that high school gang of yours—why it was so literary? Was it just accident? Was there somebody who started the fire?

I don't know what it was; it was partly the Jewish tradition of the book. I mean we came from that generation that wanted to make it, and the skills we had were Gutenberg skills. There was great drive, drive, drive. Up out of that very petit bourgeois life.

Bruce: Making books is more important than making money.

I didn't grow up with anybody who wanted to make money. In my own family, nobody ever really made money. The generation before had been working class.

One in my father's *[family]* was a hatter and another was a leather worker. And then my father was a pharmacist, but he became a pharmacist in a day when it wasn't really an academic profession. It was mostly done as an apprentice. I think he had a year of schooling, and then he went off and put corks in bottles and pasted labels on them and learned to work the scales and bottle the drugs.

Bruce: It's like learning to be a medicine man.

Right. Those kids were all, you know, somebody had fired a gun . . . The two who went into non–social sciences in my class, there was a Kreiger family—Murray Krieger, his father and his uncle were in my class. And they became academics of some sort. One was a historian, I think.

The teachers were baffled by us. For me, writing was power. In the shoe store, I got a load of shit when I first went there. One of the strangest things in the world was for some reason, intended, half-intended, not intended at all, nobody ever learned my name in the shoe store. They called me Lester. When I said, "It's Leslie," they got the "Lee" in their heads, and they called me "Stanley."

Though they gave me a hard time for a while, after a while I made it known all over the store that I was writing a novel about the shoe store and then everybody treated me with immense respect. Power. I had no intention of writing a novel about the shoe store. I was writing stories of the Left Bank.

Bruce: There's a Robert Burns line that I really like, "There's a chile among you and he's taking notes. And, faith, he'll print it."

That's beautiful.

The funny part of it is, it isn't Paris where I went finally. I didn't get to Europe at all until I was thirty-five. And then I went to Italy, and that turned me around completely because I fell in love with Italy for all time. You can put me down anyplace in Rome and I'll walk you to any place else. I spent the first year I was there walking and gawking. I don't usually like cities, but I like Rome.

[A break, during which we got to talking about the Newark library.]

The two good things in Newark were the library and the museum. Which is a very good little museum. Newark itself is strange in some says. I mean, there's nothing left of the old Newark. The town was founded in the seventeenth century. There's no seventeenth-century stuff, no eighteenth-century stuff, damned little nineteenth-century stuff. It's all wiped out.

We used to sit around, those of us who wanted to be writers, and say, "What writer ever came from Newark?" And the answer is only one; Stephen Crane. And then a flood of writers came.

One of the things I did when I was in high school, I belonged to kind of an interschool poetry society, which was presided over, of all things, by Louis Ginsberg—Allen's father. He was a poet. For years he did those little filler poems that appeared on the editorial page of *The New York Times* in the old days. He once gave a reading with Allen. And a third son *[Eugene Brooks Ginsberg]* who writes poetry, I can't think of what he's called. I stayed in lifelong communication with Louis Ginsberg. He was a high school teacher.

I still have a letter of his which I prize very much when Allen was first beginning to become a public figure. "Dear Mr. Fiedler, You may remember me." And so forth and so forth.

"I have this son who I think is a very good poet, but on the other hand, he goes around writing on the wall, 'Fuck the Jews.'"

Diane: He did?

Yeah, he did. At Columbia. "What do you think will become of him?"

So I wrote back, "Dear Louis, These things always work out in the long run. Don't worry about it." About two years later, I had a letter—Allen's picture had appeared in *Time* or *Life*—or something. "Dear Mr. Fiedler, As you see, my boy Allen is doing all right." They got along poorly for a long time but they finally made peace with each other.

Bruce: Allen has such a Talmudic style. He's a classical Jewish kid.

But his Jewishness was somehow identified with his mother. All of his things were identified with his mother, not his father. His father was a very handsome fellow. Big ladies' man.

Bruce: I remember Newark as the ugliest of towns. There's nothing aesthetic about it.

It's not a nice town; nothing beautiful about it. I used to drive through Newark when I used to go see my mother—touch bases—and drive down Bergen Street, which is the place I was nearly arrested for giving a street-corner speech without a license. I got away but my friend Milty got caught.

It was such a weird mixture of things. Another man who was a very good writer and actually published two pretty good novels—another one who published early—before I did, though after Al Eisner, was a guy called Harold Kaplan. H. J. Kaplan he called himself. He used to write a Paris letter for the *Partisan Review* for many years. Kaplan wrote one novel called *The Plenipotentiaries*, a very Jamesian book; I forget what the other one was called *[Paradise Denied]*. He was very gifted in languages; he's absolutely bilingual English and French. His German is also very good. He ended up working for the State Department. He was the PR man on the team of negotiators with the Vietnamese. He was the thirteenth man. And then he went to work for Bernie Cornfeld and various other big businessmen—Bendix Corporation, and so forth—and made a fortune, and gave up writing, by and large.

We all thought of ourselves not merely competing for the prize but competing with each other. It's like Saul Bellow and Isaac Rosenfeld in Chicago. It was through Kaplan that I knew all those people in Chicago. Kappy remained a very literary person for a long time when he lived in Paris before they fell out over various political questions and so forth. He was a good friend of Simone de Beauvoir.

We had a theatrical group, and there were a lot of girls in it who were very gifted. The one woman I remember because I just met her recently was Marion Chaladenko when I knew her. She was quite a gifted actress, and her name is now Toby Cole, and she's ended up writing books on the theory of drama. When I was in Venice recently I met her. She remained a Communist and decided the United States was an unendurable capitalist place and went to live in Venice when it got a Communist mayor. We had a reconciliation.

The best actress in our group was a woman named Diana Merliss. She somehow never made it. The guy who was the leader of the group I once caught doing a comedy act in a sleazy nightclub—not such a great act, but he kept us amused.

Almost all of my high school friends have a lot of money. We were all poor, poor, poor.

Bruce: It's the American dream, Leslie. In two generations.

And the third generation goes back. It's an old saying: "Shirt sleeves to shirt sleeves in three generations."

Eddie Cohen Jurist, who was a successful TV writer and producer, got in bad trouble because he was involved with one of the fixed quiz shows. He was on the Quiz Kids program, which was a little fixed. I happen to know because one day I got a copy of the *Encyclopedia Britannica* for having submitted a question they couldn't answer, and I had not submitted the question; he had just put it in in my name.

We all used to appear in these various Communist productions. Mass recitations: "In Scottsboro murder is going on. In Scottsboro, in Scottsboro, death is threatening."

The people I knew in high school are the best friends I have still. When I was going into graduate school in Madison, I was bored most of the time in class, and especially out of class. I used to hitch to Chicago, and my friend Kappy, whom I've talked to you about a couple of times, he was there at that point. He was doing a degree in French. It was through him that I met that whole group of Chicago writers: Isaac Rosenfeld and Saul Bellow. Lionel Abel was there in those days. Incredible Lionel, who was exactly the same.

Bruce: I can't imagine a young Lionel.

He was NEVER a young Lionel.

Diane: How did he get to Chicago?

He just drifted in those days. He was probably living on some woman. We used to have terrible arguments, Lionel and I, from the first day we ever met.

Bruce: I miss that. I used to enjoy you and Lionel arguing in our department meetings.

Chicago was interesting in those days.

Bruce: Who of those people do you see now?

I still see Milty Ritz, and his son David Ritz has become a writer. And Eddie Jurist, the guy who went into television. When our high school had its fiftieth reunion a while back, we all, of course, refused to go to it, but we gathered ourselves together, just the old groupies. It was a little difficult because politically we were badly divided. There were various subjects that couldn't be mentioned—Israel, most notably. Because a lot of them were red hot Hawks, including Kappy and especially his wife. He's a good friend of that whole [Norman] Podhoretz, Irving Kristol gang. His wife just died recently.

I'm very close to him. His daughter is my goddaughter, in fact. She's called after me, Leslie. She's a good writer. She writes in French. I don't have to consult any books to know the development of French intellectual life. Leslie was in the Sorbonne in '68, and after the events she quit and went off and married a Communist philosophy professor in some provincial lycée. Then she decided he was really a bourgeois in disguise, so she dumped him for a Polish immigrant—Maoist factory worker. At present as you can probably guess, she's living with a Lacanian analyst. She's written a beautiful book, which is called *Luxury Factories*. Very difficult; not quite prose, not quite a poem. The first-person pronoun never appears in it until the very last sentence, though it's an autobiographical account. She went to work in a factory for a while.

Diane: What does she do now?

I'm not sure. She's had various kids along the line. I don't know what she does. Writes. I haven't seen her for a long time. She lives in Paris. Her husband's a Brazilian by birth, but also is a Frenchman. She speaks English with a slight accent. When she and her father get into political arguments, he insists that they conduct them in English. He can speak French as well as she can; but she can't speak English quite as well as he can.

Margaret and I and Celia and Kappy in Chicago in those days used to sleep in one bed. Babies in the bathtub. Everybody was poor, poor, poor. Kappy now has a pension from the government, a pension from Bendix Corporation, some payoff from Bernie Cornfeld. He was involved in some of his shady deals.

Both the people who introduced me to Marxism remain good friends. One was a woman, Lilly, whom I still know and see.

Diane: How does it shake out about Israel?

Most were war hawks. They've all become pretty conservative politically. Milty Ritz, who was the loudest and most vociferous of the Communists, uses exactly the same vocabulary in exactly the same tone of voice now to argue for his new madness.

Diane: Can you say that to him?

To him I can say that, because he really is a good, good friend. Ideas finally don't matter as far as good friends are concerned. I wish my brother knew that.

Figure 14. Leslie, during a lecture at Buffalo State College, 1995.

9

August 20, 1989

Bruce: Last time we talked, I asked about the books that mattered.

I've been thinking about it. It's a large subject. I hardly know how to move in on it. Various approaches suggested themselves to me. I want to see where we get.

Let me talk first about the writers who I wrote about in my life. When I was an undergraduate at NYU, I wrote an honors thesis. And that was on Gerard Manley Hopkins. Would you have guessed that? What occurred to me as I thought back on it is that all my first interests were poets. Because I thought of myself first of all in my whole career as a writer, when I contemplated having a career as a writer, as being a poet. I started out in life as a poet.

I don't know if I told you this, but when I was in the first or second grade, I was permitted to read a poem I had written to the whole school auditorium. I think it was the first grade. The subject of the poem—I was very learned when I was young—was Mercury and the invention of the lyre. It was a little fabulous story I had picked up. At that point I was sunk completely. For the first time, here I was having a public recognition.

My first writing was, by and large, poetry. The first writers I ever wrote about were poets. One of the writers I fell in love with when I was an undergraduate was Gerard Manley Hopkins. A funny story to tell you about Gerard Manly Hopkins. While I was still at NYU, Robert Frost came to visit the campus, and he agreed to talk to one or two people who were interested in poetry. I was one of the people who was picked out. He was already a revered old man. He was professionally old. I mean he was into being old. He was one of the most miserable human beings I have ever met in my entire life. He took this sixteen-year-old kid, which I then was, and decided to put down everything that I believed in.

First of all, it became apparent to him that my politics were leftist politics, and I got a heavy anti-Communist line from him. And then he asked me who my favorite poet was, and I said it was Gerard Manley Hopkins. He looked appalled and said, "We play games sometimes. We ask people what is the opposite of a poet. And some people will say 'grocer,' 'soldier,' or 'dentist.' You know what the real opposite of a poet is?" says Robert Frost to sixteen-year-old me. I said, "No," and he said, "A poetess. And Gerard Manly Hopkins is a poetess."

Diane: Did you attack him in response?

I didn't attack him because, first of all, there was the appalling difference in status. And second of all, for better or worse, if I had to say who my second favorite poet was at that point, it would have been Robert Frost, who has remained a favorite poet of mine all my life long. I love his poetry. My head is full of his poetry. And I thought, "Well, writers are sons of bitches." It was a lesson I had learned early in life. I believed I learned it at that very moment.

When I think back on it, I'm more appalled than I was then. I mean, you don't treat a kid that way.

Diane: It's outrageous at every level. Ugh! Ugh!

When I wrote my master's thesis, I wrote on a poet again. It was on Chaucer. I wrote a Marxist interpretation of Chaucer. Mostly of *Troilus and Cressida*. If you asked me how to do it, I couldn't figure it out. I was working under the supervision of William Ellery Leonard, who I've talked to you about before, who was a great favorite of mine, who at that point had decided that Marxism was nonsense and the whole thing was nonsense, but he was dazzled by what spectacularly brilliant nonsense it was. He gave me an A+. He said, "I don't believe a word of it, but . . ."

In a way, Chaucer is a central figure in my life. At that point I decided I was going to be a medievalist. I took courses in Old Icelandic and Old Provençal, a little High German. It was also at that point that my lifelong love affair with the third poet began: Dante.

When I was sixteen years old, I began to translate *The Divine Comedy*. Got Canto One of *The Inferno* done. I continued playing around with Dante throughout the rest of my life. One of the latest translations I ever did, which I published, in fact, was of Dante's "Sestina." I became especially intrigued with the "stony lady" poem of his.

By the time I came to write my PhD dissertation, I decided that I was going to move on out of the Middle Ages and I put a foot into the seventeenth century. But my dissertation was in fact still being faithful to my first commitment on medieval backgrounds of Donne's songs and sonnets. It was full of learned quotations from Provençal and Gascogne poetry.

In some ways, it was not that I wanted to be a poet and a translator of poetry and a reader of poets, but poets were at the basis of my first interest in literature. And they remain so. The other poet who I picked up an early admiration for—my study was plastered with quotations from him all over—was Blake. "It is better to murder a child in his cradle," and so forth. "The tigers of wrath are wiser than the horses of instruction"; I really believed the crazy son of a bitch, almost every word he said. I'm not much into the longer poems, but shorter Blake poetry I liked. The rhythms of it have much influenced my own poetry a lot. As you know, you press a button, and I'll still say, "The atoms of Democritus / and Newton's particles of light / Are sands upon the Red Sea shore, / Where Israel's tents do shine so bright" *[the final stanza of Blake's "Mock On, Mock On, Voltaire, Rousseau"]*. And "'Twas the Greeks' love of war / Turn'd Love into a boy, / And woman into a statue of stone—/ And away fled every joy" *[final stanza of Blake's "Why Was Cupid a Boy?"]*. This gives my homophobia deep roots.

Even as late as 1946, 1947, when after the war they sent me back to Harvard, the project I was working on was going to be a volume of translations of poetry: twentieth-century poetry from all over the world, Europe, the Far East, and so forth. I finally lost it some place along the line, but I learned a lot doing translations of poems. Italian was one of my favorites. I began playing around after a while with Leopardi. I remember I did a translation of "Sempre caro mi fu quest'ermo colle": "I've always loved this lonely hill" *[Giacomo Leopardi, "L'Infinito"]*.

Diane: And Wyatt. As you said that, it had that rhythm.

He's another poet who was in my head. Haunting me these days, especially. "They flee from me that sometime me seek / With naked foot, stalking in my chamber" *[Once again, the first line of Wyatt's poem "They Flee from Me"]*. It becomes more and more appropriate as time goes by.

But always I had an interest in novels too. I think at some earlier point I told you that when I first went to the library, the first two books I took out on my own—nobody to guide me—were *Tom Sawyer,*

Detective—I don't know why *Tom Sawyer, Detective*; it was just there; anyhow, it was Mark Twain—and Andersen's *Fairy Tales*. The fairy tale interest is something I haven't lost, ever, ever, ever. I still like Andersen better than the Grimms.

Bruce: Andersen was far more a writer than they were.

He just took off in the days of the stories and played with them. He wrote *Kunstmärchen [German: literary fairy tale]*, as the Germans say. My last story is in some ways a combination of science fiction and fairy tale, the one I talked to you about earlier: "What Used to Be Called Dead." It begins with a fairy tale beginning and then it turns into a science fiction story.

I always have pursued those things. In some ways Andersen led me to Novalis and to George MacDonald and on to C. S. Lewis, Charles Williams, and Tolkien finally, which has always remained a favorite of mine. Tolkien was a book which always haunted our house. We all read it aloud to each other, and the big fights in our house used to be to see who would do the reading that day. We have a copy of the first volume of the *Rings* trilogy, which is a present to all of us from Auden. I introduced Auden to Frank Baum, and he introduced me to Tolkien. I'd only known Tolkien as the *Gawain and the Green Knight* man before that.

Mark Twain obviously has always haunted me. I often tell people there are three books which I've read more often than any other, over and over again. People always think they are an odd combination, but somehow they go together: *Huckleberry Finn, Uncle Tom's Cabin*, and James Joyce's *Ulysses*. There are other books I dearly love, but none I return to, to read more often.

I suppose my favorite novel of all, though, which I think of as a favorite novel of novelists (anybody who wants to know how to build a novel has to go to this book where it all started, or as Hemingway would say, "He did first what nobody ever did better"), and that's *Clarissa [Samuel Richardson,* Clarissa; or, The History of a Young Lady: Comprehending the Most Important Concerns of Private Life. And Particularly Shewing, the Distresses That May Attend the Misconduct Both of Parents and Children, in Relation to Marriage, *1748]*. It's a monument of a book. It's built like a brick shithouse. There's not a place in it you can put your hand, and when I get finished with those million words, I wish there were at least a half million more. I've loved epistolary novels ever since. You go one direction out of Richardson and he takes you into demi-porn, soft-core porn, and hard porn.

Liaisons dangereuses [Pierre Choderlos de Laclos, Les Liaisons dangereuses, *1782]* is another favorite book of mine. I refused to go see the
movie. I don't think I could stand it. It's a book I know so well, I'm so
full of built-in responses which would be powerful. No matter how good
the movie was, I would hate it. And then right on to the Marquis de
Sade, right?

And that's another line of writers I love, and it pleases me that
Mark Twain wrote a pornographic novel, too. It's called *1601*. It's written
in pseudo-Elizabethan English. The central theme is an anecdote about
somebody's farts in the court of Queen Elizabeth, and it's the Queen
herself, for which Sir Walter Raleigh gallantly takes the blame. It plays
around and ends with a weird image of impotence. It's the sort of thing
that haunted Mark Twain—about an old man who is attempting to rape
a young girl, and she says, "Piss for me a little bit." And he pisses and his
cock falls and never rose again. They were the last words of the book: "It
would not rise again."

That was a strange book. Mark Twain got it published, I think six
or seven copies only—by the printing press at West Point, where he had
a friend. One of the copies he sent to David Gray, after whom the Gray
Chair is named here *[in the UB English Department]*. He was a poet
in Buffalo. Another was a rabbi in Albany. The third was this unitarian
minister, and I forget who the others were.

Diane: Is it known?

It's known, it's printed, but for some reason, the goddamn Mark
Twain scholars . . . I don't know an official Twain bibliography in which
it appears. But everybody knows it exists and everybody knows it's really,
really Twain's. It's just a little, tiny book.

He was very proud of it. Gray wrote him a letter saying, "When
all the rest of your work is forgotten, you'll be remembered for this."
Half kidding . . . I used to have a dream that I would find Gray's copy
around here, and the correspondence. Twain wrote to Gray. He was the
only friend he made in Buffalo, a real honest-to-god friend. He was the
editor of the other paper. I can never remember which one was the editor of *The Courier* and which was the editor of *The Express*, but one was
the one and one was the other.*[Twain was part-owner and editor of* The
Buffalo Courier *1869–1872; David Gray was editor of the* Buffalo Express.*]*

In his old age, Gray got religion and became a born-again Christian
and decided he was ashamed of his early relationship with Twain, and
his wife apparently destroyed all their correspondence. It was through her

that the Gray Chair was founded. There is *[Gray]* family around, but they don't know about [Gray's relationship with Twain]. The family married into the part of society which hated Twain when he was here—they never accepted him. He didn't make a big try. He wasn't here very long.

In some ways, my relationship early and long continuing with Twain should have indicated something to me—which I was misled about—that what I really like were the kind of books that were available to everybody, and not just a few. But I went astray in my late adolescence and early youth and became a worshipper at other shrines: Henry James, for whom I was absolutely mad for a while, and for whom I have lost my taste. I became a little ashamed of my feeling for Twain. It never went as far as Faulkner. When Faulkner was a young man, he got very hardy and first went off to New Orleans and met all these professional artists. He wrote about Twain. He was on the Mississippi, after all, and he said, "In Europe [Twain] would not be considered even a fourth-rate artist." But he changed his mind. When he bought himself a library later in life when he settled down in Virginia, the first thing he got was a complete Twain. He came to his senses.

Diane: Did he put it on record?

No. But he never spoke straight. He never told the truth about anything. He drives people crazy that way. Some fan would come up to him and say, "You're clearly influenced much by James Joyce's *Ulysses.*" And he'd say, "Never read the book." And then later, he'd give a speech to a bunch of scholars and say, "I was profoundly influenced by modernist literature, especially James Joyce's *Ulysses.*" I don't know whether he was lying the first time or the second time or both times.

Speaking about writers who have influenced me much and who I've loved much, Faulkner has become, as the years go by, more and more an important writer to me. He's a writer I'm tempted to reread too. Though my taste changes a little. I mean, a book which I despised at first, I now consider up among the very best of his books. That's *Sanctuary*, and *Pylon*, which is a miserable book, were Faulkner's two best books.

Bruce: Didn't Camus do a play of Requiem?

Yeah. He translated *Requiem for a Nun.* They had a sort of love affair going for a while. The Faulkner he liked was this kind of tough stuff.

Pylon is the closest thing to a proletarian novel that Faulkner ever wrote. It's got a strike in it, union organizers; it has an urban setting. It's set in New Orleans—pilots attempting to unionize.

The other writer with whom I've had a long, difficult relationship also suffered in my period of elitism. And that was Walt Whitman, who

I loved when I was twelve and thirteen, fourteen, and thought I despised utterly as the worst possible influence on American poetry and world poetry when I was twenty-five, thirty, thirty-five. But I came back to him in 1955. I wrote an essay on the hundredth anniversary of the publication of *Leaves of Grass*, in which I made peace with him. Ever since then I haven't been able to leave him alone. When I teach abroad, I always teach Whitman. That's easy because they've heard of Whitman at least.

I did a selection of his poems and did a preface to it. I've written several times on Whitman; I keep coming back to him over and over again. It was part of the effort that really began in '55, when suddenly I looked back at Whitman through Allen Ginsberg, and he looked different. It just wasn't looking at Whitman through Carl Sandburg, and the sound tracks on the river or something—official United States propaganda, New Deal persuasion. He's a funny writer, and I've wrestled with him for a long time.

Those are some of the writers.

There is another group of writers who are my contemporaries in whom I've been interested and written about a lot. That would be Saul Bellow, for instance, about whom I wrote some of the very first appreciative essays ever written, but whom I ceased writing about after a while for two reasons: one, because I didn't like where he was going as much as I liked where he started out; and after a while I had too much personal involvement with him: I felt as if I were writing on a personal thing. In some ways I think my reaction was kind of ignoble. When he was my personal property (me and ten friends), then I loved him dearly. When he began to belong to the world, then I hated him. But we also drifted apart as the years went by. He became kind of the poet laureate of the neo-orthodox, right-wing *Commentary*-type politicians. And he thought I was "way out in left field," as he said.

Diane: Why?

(a) He didn't like my politics; (b) he didn't like my attempt to come to terms with and at least understand the sixties instead of just condemn it out of hand; and (c), and most important, he's a very paranoid fellow, as most writers indeed are, and he figured, "If Leslie's not writing about my books, it means he hates them, and I can imagine what he would say and that son of a bitch, how does he get away with saying it?" His last recorded remark on me, Saul Bellow's last recorded remark on me, was when an old friend of mine—a guy named Seymour Betsky, who taught for many years in Holland in the Rijksmuseum, who knew both of us—said, "Are you going to be around for a couple of more days?

Leslie's coming in next week." And Bellow said at the top of his voice for the public record, "Leslie Fiedler is the worst fucking thing that ever happened to American literature."

The other writer with whom I retained fairly good relations, though we drifted apart and didn't see each other, was Bernard Malamud. He and I were sort of neighbors, so to speak, for a while. He was teaching in Corvalis, Oregon, while I was in Missoula, and we would go back and forth to see each other from time to time. He was known as "Uncle Bernie" by my kids. He looked like an Uncle Bernie. He's a writer who didn't look like a writer. When he first began, he looked like a high school teacher who was going to get fired any minute, and after a while he looked like that same teacher who'd been made principal of the high school. The high school was in Brooklyn, of course.

One of his books which had disappeared from sight completely, which I sort of rediscovered and therefore have an especially warm feeling for is *The Natural*. It took many years before they made a movie of it, but I sort of brought it back into print. It was kind of ignored. People thought, "What is this nice Jewish boy doing?"

Diane: When did you write that?

About a year or two after it came out, in the fifties—'55, '56, something like that. It's a book I love.

The only book I've loved more in the whole world is a book which I rescued from absolute oblivion, and which now has all-time status, that's Henry Roth's called *Call It Sleep*, which was out of print when I wrote about it. Some magazine, I can't remember which, *American Scholar* maybe, went around asking people, "What's the best forgotten book that you know about?" I said, *Call It Sleep* by Henry Roth, and it happened that in the same issue, responding the same way, Alfred Kazin picked it too. The book was put back into print and the whole history of its reclamation begins after that. That's real *noches [Yiddish: special pleasure]* for a critic.

I was deeply identified with that whole business, and at the same time I was touting these Jewish-American novelists who were my contemporaries: Bellow and Roth and Malamud, especially, who was engaged in recovering the lost Jewish-American novels of the thirties. Roth, Nathanael West, about whom I wrote a lot, too. Both of those have made it very firmly. The writer who I think deserves to be remembered but has slipped out of people's minds again—Fuchs: *Homage to Blenholt, Summer in Williamsburg,* and so forth. Somebody's bringing a batch of thirties novels back into print again, and I'm doing an introduction for one of Daniel Fuchs's novels. Daniel Fuchs wrote his three novels and then went off to Hollywood, where he was very successful, instead of dying young, or killing himself, or disappearing into drunkenness. Nobody's ever forgiven him for that. He wasn't a spectacular success, but he made a good living. I don't think any of his screenplays are as good as, say, Faulkner's at his best.

Bruce: What was the Hemingway script Faulkner worked on?

To Have and Have Not. Very strange, huh? The really good one is *[Raymond Chandler's] The Big Sleep*, but he worked with a really professional woman, Leigh Brackett, on that.

Then there are my pop favorites, the ones I've introduced Sally to when I rescued her from the ghetto of the English Department at the University of Illinois—like Rider Haggard's *She*. There was a great dissertation which could have been written on Rider Haggard's *She* but was abandoned midstream. That's what Margaret Atwood was writing at Harvard when she quit the PhD program. So I've been told, and I do believe it.

It's a strange book, because it's been a favorite book of all kinds of people. Jung was mad for it. Let's put him over there. Margaret Atwood someplace in the middle. And Andrew Lang loved it. It's a very good book.

Then, popular literature of the later nineteenth century in England is fascinating. You've got *Dracula* and *She*. And then a little later I got Sally and everybody in my family to rereading, not so many years ago, all the Tarzan books. They had put them all back into print again in paperback. The politics are so weird, and yet it doesn't matter. It's been translated into Swahili, and it's a great favorite in East Africa. It's always been a favorite book, the Burroughs books, in the Soviet Union.

Bruce: It's the Swahili one that's surprising.

Those books I like, and I have a great taste for the Gothic. *The Monk [Matthew Gregory Lewis: The Monk: A Romance, 1776]* is one of my favorite books in the world. That's another book I reread from time to time. And I swear, my father, who when he was very young read nothing but German philosophy—Nietzsche and Schopenhauer, chiefly—and when he was older read nothing but detective stories and westerns. He turned me on to the detective story and the western. Those I come back to from time to time. I've gone back to reading detective stories again. For a while I went whoring after strange gods; I switched to science fiction. But now I'm back to detective stories.

Bruce: Who do you like in detective stories?

I have two kinds I love. I like the country-house English detective story. I like especially the earlier women writers, from Agatha Christie and Ngaio Marsh, Margery Allingham. I don't like Dorothy Sayers; she's too pretentious. She's always reminding you that this is being written by a literary person and is appealing to you to see if you recognize an illusion or something. I used to be taken in by them, but I don't like them now.

And then I like the hard-boiled American tradition: Dashiell Hammett I really love more and more; Raymond Chandler, somewhat less; and in recent times I like one of the schlockiest of them all, and that's John D. MacDonald—the Travis McGee stories. He just dropped like a fly, didn't he—John D. MacDonald?

I once ended up in a saloon in Sarasota playing liar's poker with a bunch of people, one of whom turned out to be John D. MacDonald. They all had a lot more money than I did then. But I fortunately didn't have my glasses and didn't know what the hell I was looking at. You know how it's played, looking at the serial numbers of the bills. I couldn't see them so I could bluff like hell. I won a lot of money.

Even more I like spy stories. Eric Ambler is classic. I go back to him. And Graham Greene. I like his spy stories. In some ways I feel more comfortable with him when he's writing entertainments than when he's pretending to write great fiction, though I do like the one about the whisky priest, *The Power and the Glory.*

Bruce: Remember Alan Ladd in the film of his This Gun for Hire?

Yes. We saw it recently. The one who could really make movies of Graham Greene is Carol Reed. He did *The Third Man* and *The Idol.*

And then I have a favorite, favorite mad science fiction writer, who is one of my great favorites of all time, one of the few writers I actually made a pilgrimage to see, to Peoria, Illinois. I loved him because he was an eccentric, mid-American type. He tried to make it in LA for a while, and he couldn't stand it and went back to Peoria where he comes from. He writes very great detective stories, especially one called the *Riverworld* series, in which he imagines everybody reconstituted, reanimated, reincorporated, and going down the river in this strange land where they've all been taken, on a river boat which is built by Mark Twain and side by side will be Tom Mix, Jesus Christ, Alice in Wonderland . . .

I took Sally with me once and we went to see him. His name is Philip José Farmer. He's a great favorite of the new writers in France. Philip José

Farmer is a pure Midwestern type. We went to his house, which was a pure Midwestern suburban house in Peoria, where we got fried chicken and strawberry shortcake. The conversation was going on and on, and we were looking around. Sally was thinking, "Who is this guy, and why are we in this boring place?" Suddenly we realized that what he was explaining in this flat, Midwestern voice which makes everything so matter-of-fact and banal, was that there was a ghost which had been haunting him for a while, but he had just located its hideout in one corner of his bathroom, and he was very happy with it now. And his wife looked up and said, "Phil, don't talk that way; they'll think you're crazy." And he looked up with wide eyes and said, "But I am crazy." Indeed he is.

He's the first guy to introduce sex into science fiction. He has a story which is called "Riders of the Purple Wage," the motto of which is the family that blows together grows together. He also writes hardcore porn, a pornographic retelling of the Tarzan stories among others.

He sort of single-handedly opened up science fiction. He's a man of the first generation of science fiction writers. He's a colleague and contemporary of Robert Heinlein. Heinlein actually dedicated *Stranger in a Strange Land* to Philip Farmer, who dedicated one of his books to me. Phil Farmer on Heinlein is marvelous. He said, "The trouble with Bob is he wants to fuck his daughter and he doesn't even have a daughter."

Sally: Tell them about the connection with Vonnegut.

Oh, yes. I have a funny connection with all of this. One of Phil Farmer's books is a book called *Venus on the Half Shell,* and it's written by Kilgore Trout. Kilgore Trout is an imaginary character created by Kurt Vonnegut when he was still writing science fiction. He's his built-in science fiction writer. (By the way, I loved Vonnegut when he was writing science fiction. I liked *The Sirens of Titan,* and *Cat's Cradle. Sirens of Titan* is beautiful.) Vonnegut didn't want the book to appear, and he began writing a series of enraged letters to Phil Farmer, saying, "I'm going to stop you in the courts." And Farmer said, "I'm going to get my name legally changed to Kilgore Trout, and then what are you going to do?" Finally I ended up mediating this conflict between the two of them. I have the correspondence, which is sort of hilarious. They worked it out. The book came out, and some great admirers of Vonnegut I've run into say, "That's one of Vonnegut's best books."

Bruce: The way you describe him, this guy sounds like Kilgore Trout.

Except Kilgore Trout, I think, is supposed to be Theodore Sturgeon. Sturgeon. Trout.

Bruce: I never made that connection!

I never did either, until somebody told me.

I used to go for a while to the conventions of the science fiction writers, so I got to know these guys. They're a weird bunch of people. In the old days, they were so small and so incestuous. They swapped wives, girlfriends, friends, enemies. They all knew each other. And then it all changed, when we passed from the whisky age to the dope age, because they were the last great American alcoholics, the science fiction writers.

Diane: Is Farmer still alive?

Yeah. We hear from him from time to time.

The new generation is very different. Somebody like Phil Farmer as compared with Chip Delany, let's say. I've sort of known him forever, because Kurt went very briefly to the Bronx High School of Science, and Delany and he were contemporaries there.

Bruce: I just thought of something I haven't thought of for forty years when you said that. When I went to Stuyvesant—there were three science high schools in New York: Stuyvesant, Brooklyn Tech, and Bronx Science. When I went to Stuyvesant, that's where I got into science fiction as a kid, because everybody at Stuyvesant was reading science fiction.

Stuyvesant was the school where Bud taught—Margaret's father taught there. According to stories we heard, he didn't teach very hard. He used to sit in the back of his class and read *The New York Times* and he'd let students display initiative on their own.

Diane: What was he supposed to be teaching?

English. He had a perfectly good PhD from Columbia.

Bruce: I used his outline of literature studying for some exams.

He produced all kinds of books like that. He was great for word games. We still play some of his games. He was an absolutely charming fellow. I contributed to his *Encyclopedia of World Literature*. It's one of the first things I ever got printed. But that wasn't because of Margaret. Margaret didn't know him at the time. She got to know him because of me. He was divorced from her mother when she was only seven. Her mother had filled her full of hate and horror of him. She never saw him.

I've lost some book which is absolutely vital in my life. Ah, yes, *Gone with the Wind*. This is a book which I grew up with and quite sure I despised utterly, though I remember with great pleasure seeing the movie when it first came out. I actually saw it in New York when it opened up.

It was a great event of the season. 1939. It was the year of the World Fair; the year I got married; the first year I taught. Thirty-nine's an important year. The year when some of the greatest women in the world were born. *[Sally and Diane were born in 1939.]*

Many years later somebody invited me to a meeting on the thirties; I can't remember when it was—late fifties, early sixties, or something. Various survivors of the thirties were invited, including James T. Farrell and Nelson Algren. And a bunch of politicians and advisors to Roosevelt, who spent half of the whole session arguing about which one of them had really written the second inaugural address. Apparently they'd all had a hand in it someplace.

When I was invited I was feeling a little naughty, as they say. I said, "I'll come and talk if you let me talk about *Gone with the Wind.*" As I said it, it occurred to me most of the books that had been written in the thirties either had disappeared completely or were just read on assignment in class, or had become subjects for PhD dissertations. This was still a book that was being circulated, read, loved. The movie was being shown over and over again. I decided instead of saying all the things that were wrong with *Gone with the Wind,* which a child of two can do, I tried to say what was right with it, which is rather difficult, right? And I did, and since then I've gone back to it again and again and again. I think I've written three separate essays on it at various points. It's a book which absolutely haunts me.

It's one of the books that really, maybe more than anything else, has made me rethink all those distinctions between high and low literature and try to find some common factor which binds together Shakespeare, whose name I haven't even said, though he's obsessed me all my life long, and Sophocles and Edgar Rice Burroughs and Margaret Mitchell and Mark Twain and Dickens.

Dickens is another writer who I've read a lot. There was one point in my life where I read him through every year. I bought a beautiful edition, leather bound, since fallen apart, with nice onionskin paper.

My tastes are always weird, even when I'm in the mainstream. My favorite Dickens novel is *Martin Chuzzlewit.* That's possibly because it's the only novel in which he comes to America. I'm haunted by the coincidence because Martin Chuzzlewit actually reaches Carroll, Illinois, at the very same moment that Huck and Jim were going past it on the raft. And Dickens hated Carroll, Illinois. He thought it represented everything that was worst about America—a stinking, fever-infested swamp, which indeed it is. Those Mississippi towns . . .

We read *Martin Chuzzlewit* when I was a freshman in college, and we also thought we were going to hate it. We loved it. We adapted it to our own ethnic background by changing the name of it. We always referred to it as "Martin Chuzzleberg."

One of the traumatic experiences of my life was in a freshman composition class in college where I got either an A or an F on everything that I turned in.

Diane: What got the Fs?

"Bad taste," written in red ink on the side of the paper. I commuted to school, so I did most of my work riding on the subway. One day we were supposed to write a story instead of the usual "Describe a process." I felt released. This class was full of "don'ts." We had forbidden subjects. We were not allowed to write about sex, the instructor, or a theme on how I couldn't write my theme, which was a very good thing to forbid. But I got carried away this day and I wrote a story about a woman who had an orgasm every time she went through a turnstile in the subway.

Diane: "Bad taste!"

You don't know how bad the taste was! The story ends with her picked up in a subway station, where she fainted away and everybody has abandoned her because New York was the same even then. And as she's dying, she looks up on the wall and there's a crucifix and it seems to be going around and around like the turnstile . . .

Diane: Wonderful!

Bad taste indeed!

I went back many years later and saw some of those people at NYU, and they said, "You used to be a very difficult young man," making me feel (a) I was no longer difficult, (b) I was no longer young, and (c) probably not a man! It was a terrible school, where all the members of the English Department wore sunflowers and "Vote for Landon" buttons. They were all right-wing Republicans. The students were all Communists, Trotskyists, and so forth. They were all goyim; we were all Jews. They had names like Bradford and Adams. I was into not saluting the flag when the ROTC parade went through and everybody stood at attention.

Bruce: Which was duly noted?

It was duly noted and I was kept out of Phi Beta Kappa, though somebody finally rose in protest. I missed it the first time around and was smuggled in belatedly. They tried to civilize us. They used to have "teas" in a beautiful little house. I went to the Heights campus, which is one of the few real honest-to-god campuses in New York. It had Goldmann stadium there in the old days where there were concerts, and the Hall of Fame went around behind it. It had an elegant library which was built by—who was the great architect who was involved in the sex scandal? Stanford White. Insane library—it was round. How do you put books into a round library? But it was beautiful. They used to have Friday afternoon teas to try to teach us to be gentlemen.

Bruce: I was in that library several years ago. It's a beautiful building. It's now Bronx Community College.

It was a nice little school. It was one of the few human-sized schools you could go to. There were only three thousand people there all together. Fifteen hundred arts students and fifteen hundred engineering students. That was it. Just undergraduates. And the teachers were imbeciles.

Diane: All of them?

Almost all of them.

I had one who was very good for me. His name was Mallory. He was not a very bright guy, who worked very hard. He came from New Mexico, I believe, originally, and he had gone on a Rhodes scholarship to Oxford. He came back and he was into those methods. He was the one who ran my honors course. I was relieved from half my course load in my junior and senior year and we read, tutorial style. It was really great.

Diane: What did you read?

We started at the beginning, and finally at the end of two years we were up to the end of the seventeenth century. Meanwhile, I introduced him to Gerard Manley Hopkins and Franz Kafka. We exchanged. He had no notion of what was going on in the living world at all. But he was very good because he could take me through.

Diane: A lot of Rhodes scholars are not very bright. But they're very earnest.

The brightest ones drop out, at least that's been my experience.

The brightest student I ever had in my life, I think, was Mike Fried. Michael Fried. Do you know who he is? He's an art critic these days.

Bruce: He was a Junior Fellow with me at Harvard.

He was at Princeton when I taught there, and he got the prize in the first year and the second year and the third year, and so forth. I had him in a writing class. He was a very interesting kid. He took me home with him one day to explain to his folks out in suburban Long Island that it was okay to be a professor. He thought he was going to be an English professor in those days, that he didn't have to become a doctor or lawyer. He went to Oxford, and he lasted three months. He dropped out and went to Italy, where he educated himself.

Bruce: Are there any of these writers about modern literature that you find interesting? You can take out the adjective.

Geoffrey Hartman I sort of like. Because underneath, I think, someday he's going to throw off all this masking, and he's going to reveal himself for what he really is, which is a mensch. He's got some basic humanity in him, and I like what he has to say.

Who do I like, Sally? There's nobody who really turns me on.

Bruce: If nobody comes to mind, that answers the question.

There's nobody who really turns me on. The last critic who I really learned a lot from was Edmund Wilson, because he was absolutely scrupulous and totally unacademic at the same time. I like sometimes writers—imaginative writers—when they write criticism. One of the last of those was Auden, who was a very good critic. Randall Jarrell was a very good critic.

It's funny that in England and America, as opposed to France, most of the good critics have been creative, imaginative writers, all the way from Dryden on down: Eliot, Pound, John Crowe Ransom, Blackmur. A failed poet, but —

Blackmur was an important person in my life. He's the man who recommended me for the one award I ever got from the National Institute of the Arts people, before they finally decided to take me in. He was the one who invited me to Princeton to take over his creative writing classes, in one of which Mike Fried turned up.

The second best student I ever had—or maybe he's in a tie with Mike Fried—is Jim Cox.

Bruce: The Americanist.

Yes. He was in the best class I ever had in my life. That was at the School of Letters, which at that point had moved to Indiana from Kenyon College. In that class was Jim Cox. The paper he did for that class was published. It was his first published thing. It was called "The Sad Initiation of Huckleberry Finn." Mark Spilka was in that class. And then there's the one the students thought was the brightest of all—oh, what's the name of that prick who's become more right-wing than Norman Podhoretz? He edits *New Criterion* or one of those right-wing newspapers. He still owes me a paper. What is his name? You'd know it. *[Leslie mentioned in the April 22 session that it was Hilton Kramer.]*

We gave him his master's exam. He walked into the master's exam, and the faculty was pretty good that year. It consisted of John Crowe Ransom, Blackmur, Francis Fergusson. Either that year or the next year, William Empson was there. And then there were the three of us who were called "The Boys" in those days: Robert Fitzgerald, Randall Jarrell, and me. This guy—I hope to god his name comes to me—thought the jury was going to ask something about the New Criticism or something and Ransom leaned back and he quoted two lines of poetry to him, which rhymed at the end. It happened to come from Shelley. He said "Pope." He was dead. He was dead!

There was a very bright woman in that class, who's only written one book since. Her name was Sally Sears. She wrote a book on Henry James. She's been teaching for many years at Stony Brook. They were an incredible class. Jim Cox was one of the brightest and nicest human beings I've ever known.

Bruce: Remember Stalky? [Newton Stallknect.]

Sure. I remember Mrs. Stalky, who was an impossible woman. They were divorced.

Bruce: I remember her looking at everybody disapprovingly. He brought in some people in The History and Logic of Science. And then they fucked him. They forced him out of [the Department of] Philosophy. He had cats. Big cats, I don't know what they were. And after all this happened, I was at his house in Bloomington. He had a house with a stone wall around it at the top of the campus. A cat jumped on his lap and he said, "Cats are very naïve. They think people were created by the Great Cat entirely for their pleasure."

There were a whole bunch of people in that English Department who despised, feared, and hated the people in the School of Letters.

Bruce: My first summer in the School of Letters, I had classes with John Berryman and Robert Fitzgerald.

Robert Fitzgerald and Randall and I used to go swimming in the quarries.

Bruce: The H-Hole.

Yeah. Which got immortalized in film [Breaking Away, *1979*]. I say swimming—Randall couldn't swim. He clung to a log and kicked his feet. He and I discovered certain things we had in common, which was our love of fairy tales and of another writer I should mention, and that's Kipling—something which bound us together. He could quote Kipling endlessly, and I could match him part of the way.

The first long poem I ever memorized in my life was my show-off poem when I was seven or eight. The family would trot me out to say it. It was "Gunga Din":

You may talk o' gin and beer
When you're quartered safe out 'ere,
An' you're sent to penny-fights an' Aldershot it;
But when it comes to slaughter
You will do your work on water,
An' you'll lick the bloomin' boots of 'im that's got it.
Now in Injia's sunny clime,
Where I used to spend my time
A-servin' of 'Er Majesty the Queen,
Of all them blackfaced crew
The finest man I knew
Was our regimental bhisti, Gunga Din.

The only other person I ever met who could recite that beside Randall was Mary Connolly. My father taught me that and Robert Service. I told you, my father was a frustrated literary man, poet . . .

Bruce: My mother told me the other day that my father used to read western novels in bed and it got her furious. She thoroughly disapproved of western novels. She said, "He really liked *those things."*

I met all the great western writers through my father. Like Louis L'Amour. Later—I think this came up at some point—I discovered the one great woman writer of westerns. She taught with me in Montana. Her name is Dorothy Johnson. She wrote *The Hanging Tree* and *The Man Who Shot Liberty Valance*, and *A Man Called Horse*. She taught in the School of Journalism.

Diane: What was she like?

She stood about so high. She was the same in all her dimensions. She was a little, round woman; came from a real Western family. It used to be a great source of delight for everybody to watch her get up on a horse. Her rear view was tremendous. But she was a good rider. She had gone East and worked for *Ladies' Home Journal* or something for many years and then came back home again.

There were only two local writers that were celebrated, she and Bud Guthrie—A. B. Guthrie. Guthrie and I had a stormy relation, but a friendly one. It was like all relationships in Montana. All the hostility got dissolved in alcohol. There was a very good writer, a writer I much admired, whose reputation has almost disappeared, who taught with me for a while in Montana: Walter van Tilburg Clark. Does that mean anything to you?

Bruce: Ox-Bow Incident.

Yes. Another one of his books was made into a movie, *The Track of the Cat*, but that wasn't much good. He was a writer who blocked absolutely about age forty and spent twenty-five years drinking himself to death without producing anything to show. He believed in living in nature, but even more he believed in sitting at a bar and talking about how he believed in living in nature. But even more, he believed in living at a bar and talking about how he believed in living in nature. He was a charming fellow.

Bruce: Did you ever read any of Jim Crumley's novels, James Crumley? The Last Good Kiss?

I have a Crumley book around here someplace. I haven't read it. That's why the name is familiar to me.

Bruce: The Last Good Kiss is a detective novel set in Missoula. He's a big burly guy. You'd like him. We met Crumley at a conference at Sun Valley where Bill Kittredge was giving a paper that he plagiarized from me.

Oh, shame on Bill Kittredge.

Bruce: He'd heard me give it the year before. After he gave it, I said, "That was a fascinating paper." He said, "I thought you'd like it." I said, "It's the one you heard me give here last year." Then he said, "I've been trying to remember where I got some of it." He was so sweet about it.

Talking about great critics, one came to Montana when I was still there because he loved Montana so. He and his wife had helped map Glacier Park when they were very young: that's I. A. Richards. He was very ancient when he came to Montana, which was a long time ago, and absolutely charming and loving. A great couple.

The only other one I saw like that was Upton Sinclair. I heard him give one of his last talks. His wife was in the audience. When he would wander away from the topic she would rise in the audience and say, "You already said that, Upton." And he would say, "Most beautiful woman in the world."

The year I was chairman of the department in Montana we decided we would bring culture to Montana. So our two visitors were Faulkner and Auden. Auden was an immense success for some reason. People came and camped in the fields to hear him from little towns in Montana.

Diane: How about Faulkner?

Faulkner everybody turned out to hear, but nobody could hear him. He was so miserable. In the first place, we weren't prepared for one thing, which was how small he was. He was quite miniature, so the microphone had to be set low down so he could talk into it properly. But he was one of those miserable people who backed away from the mic when he talked. And besides, he had a very small voice and he talked fast, fast, fast. So you had to read the account of the speech in the paper the next day to know what he said.

But he was absolutely great when he came to class. He actually came to some of the classes, and I had instructions from his editors as to how to treat him. Two sets of instructions: one was give him two drinks before lunch and one before dinner, and after dinner it doesn't matter what happens; the other was to keep him from sitting next to inquisitive ladies.

But we did sit him next to an inquisitive lady, which caused one of the great remarks I've heard, which is not recorded anyplace and should be. She turned to him and said, "How come no writer whose written about Montana has ever succeeded in obtaining the national or international fame that you have writing about the South?" She probably said, "A. B. Guthrie, he loves Montana." And Faulkner said, "To write about a place, you've got to hate it." And then he stopped . . . "the way a man hates his own wife."

The great remark of Wystan, however, was quite different. We took him out to dinner to the only local place where you could get an edible steak, and two girls came in in homemade formals, obviously for the function, I think they called it, of the night. He was at that point feeling naughty, and at the top of his voice he said, "My dears, I know exactly how they feel. I used to be a mad queen myself."

I remember Margaret made him put on shoes before he gave his talk. He wanted to go in slippers.

Diane: I always thought he was more formal than that.

He would be formal or informal, depending.

Diane: On how much he'd drunk?

He always drank a lot, but he drank mostly wine. Depending on whether he was feeling naughty or not. We knew him quite well, so he was relaxed with us. Poets don't have to be smart, but he was smart.

We paid each of those guys two hundred dollars to come and talk for us, which I begged from door to door, going to the local Episcopal priest. We had no money. We were poor, poor, poor. The one we missed getting, the third one, was supposed to be Dylan Thomas, but he got drunk in Seattle, which was his stop before. So my only conversation with Dylan Thomas was his voice over the phone saying, "Things have got frightfully mucked up." He had to give the money back!

Faulkner was so great with students. He really taught me something. I didn't understand it at first, but it gradually sunk in. Kids would ask him a question, and he would answer presumably way off there someplace, as if he hadn't heard. And then I realized that what he was doing was answering the question they wanted to ask but couldn't quite manage to ask.

Bruce: So he was really listening.

He was listening deep. But he had such a little, tiny voice.

Diane: What year would that have been?

It had to be before I went off to Princeton, '54, '55. I pulled out in the midst of a big hassle when I went off to Princeton. I didn't do the third year of my chairmanship.

Bruce: So you've been a university administrator twice. [Leslie was chair of the UB English Department 1971–1974.]

I got into bad trouble the first time. I tried to hire a Black guy, and the thing got stymied. I got up at a meeting of students and called on the president of the university to resign . . . So the president did resign, and I stayed and went away for a year and came back.

When I finally did leave, they decided their hearts were broken. Have I told you about the old Indian-fighting general in Miles City, who looked up when he heard I was leaving? He was one of the guys who had screamed at me, as a Communist, an Easterner, and Jew. And he said, "I always knew that son of a bitch would desert us in the end." Montana people are so great.

I saw the best part of it in the midst of the fight when it wasn't clear whether he was going to go or stay, and everybody was screaming at me. I got an invitation from a family called White, who ran one of the largest ranches in Montana. It was in Two Dot, Montana. Called Two Dot after the brand of their ranch. Absolutely beautiful house. The man was a kind of tough guy with a lot of money, who branded and castrated his own cattle, and who drove around the ranch in a Cadillac because he said it was higher off the ground than most of the other cars and he'd miss a bump.

I woke up in the morning and there next to my bed were a pile of *Partisan Reviews*. These were families—you've read "The Diamond as Big as the Ritz"? This was a diamond as big as the Ritz. The daughter was sent to Wellesley, the son was sent to Princeton. They married the next ranch. They were baronial families.

Bruce: And they subscribed to Partisan Review.

They subscribed to *Partisan Review*, and they wanted to show me I wasn't surrounded by yahoos. But on the other hand, they were all for Goldwater. We got in a big argument after lots of drinks. We were screaming at each other.

Figure 15. Leslie while taping one of these recordings at his house, 1989.

Hubbell Medal Acceptance Speech
(MLA, 1994)

Leslie A. Fiedler

Churlish as it may seem, I propose today—before thanking you properly—to reflect a little on the ironies implicit in your giving me this award. Let me begin by making it clear that, unlike most of you and those you have thus honored before, I am not a professional scholar, specializing in American literature, but an unreconstructed amateur, a dilettante who stumbled accidentally into your area of expertise. I have, as you are surely aware, never been a member of the American Literature Section of the MLA. Indeed, if my failing flesh had permitted me to attend this luncheon, it would have been the first time I have ever attended one.

This is not, let me assure you, out of mere snobbishness, but because I would have felt an interloper, an uninvited guest. After all, in graduate school I took no courses and wrote no papers on American literature, concentrating instead on the poetry of the Middle Ages and the English seventeenth century under mentors who believed and sought to persuade me that only second-rate minds wasted their time in studying American books. I did not even then, however, share their elitist beliefs, convinced indeed that the canon should be opened even wider than the pioneers of American studies were then proposing.

In fact, in a review of *The Literary History of the United States*, which I wrote shortly after getting my final degree, I scolded its editors for having sought to canonize only those classic American authors already dead and sanctified by the passage of time, while ignoring still living and problematical modernists like T. S. Eliot and Ezra Pound. Nonetheless, I was not sure (indeed, I have doubts to this very day) that any writers, living or dead, who embody in our own tongue our own deepest nightmares and dreams ought to be taught in American classrooms. Would it not be better, I wondered, to keep them sources of private delight rather than turning them into required reading for students in quest of good grades and teachers seeking promotion and tenure.

In any case, for nearly a decade after I had myself become an instructor, I taught no courses in American writers nor did I publish anything about them; though, of course, I did continue to read them secretly and in silence, not breaking that silence until one day in 1947 when quite inadvertently I found myself writing my infamous little essay, "Come Back to the Raft, Ag'in, Huck Honey."

I had been reading to my two sons (then seven and nine), as I was accustomed to do at bedtime, a passage from *The Adventures of Huckleberry Finn* about Huck and Jim on the raft; and afterward between sleeping and waking, I found myself redreaming Twain's idyllic dream of interethnic male bonding and the flight from civilization. Then, I awoke fully to realize how central that erotic myth was not just to our literature but to our whole culture and rushed to my desk to get the insight down before it vanished forever. The little prose lyric which it insisted on becoming I sent off immediately to the *Partisan Review*—the kind of little magazine, publication in which, in those benighted times, was still more of a hindrance than a help to academic advancement.

To my surprise, however, it was widely read (or more often misread) and responded to in the academy as well as out. Not that it was generally admired. On the contrary, it was either dismissed as a boutade, a joke in bad taste, or condemned as a calumny of the tradition it purported to explore and a travesty of scholarship. Needless to say, among those condemning it on the latter grounds were the sort of scholars who had at that point been awarded the honor you bestow on me today.

A half century later, however, that much-maligned essay has refused to die. I myself reprinted it in my first book, *An End to Innocence*, where it was flanked by a dozen or so other pieces, some literary, some autobiographical or political—but all more like what academics of the old school would have called "mere journalism," rather than "true scholarship." Yet it has appeared since in many languages; and, in another ironic turn of the screw, has become assigned reading in university classes on literature. In addition, it was this volume, that persuaded those with no sense of where

I was really coming from or heading to, that I was—however misguided and perverse I might be—a would-be scholar of American letters.

Certainly, it was that misapprehension which led to my being granted a Fulbright Fellowship to Italy, where, I discovered I was expected to lecture (as I had never yet done at home) on the literature of my native land. Though I thought of myself as a comparatist, a mythographer, a literary anthropologist, anything but an "Americanist," I felt disconcertingly at ease in that new role. This was, I have come to realize, because as a stranger in a strange land, I was able to teach our books as a literature in a foreign tongue. Indeed, at the University of Bologna my own language was so unfamiliar to the students I addressed that I had to lecture in theirs. In any case, what I ended up trying to do was to translate the parochial insights I had sketched out in "Come Back to the Raft" into more university terms; which is to say, treating our literature not in isolation but in relation to Western culture as a whole—specifically, to deal with it as the first post-colonial literature of the modern world.

To do so properly, it soon became clear to me, would require more than a handful of irregularly scheduled lectures; and so, on my return home, I began to plan what turned out to be a rather formidable series of books, four in all, which together constituted a critical history of our literature from the end of the eighteenth century to the last decades of the twentieth. It took me nearly three decades to complete that project, and, indeed, I did not start *Love and Death in the American Novel*, the first of those books, until seven or eight years after I had conceived it. Though that volume has turned out to be finally the best known and most highly respected of all my works, initially it baffled and dismayed many of its readers—mostly, perhaps, because of its generic ambiguity. Librarians have classified it either as literary history or criticism, but I have always considered it a work of art rather than scholarship, since it seeks not to prove its most outrageous theses but to charm the skeptical into a willing suspension of disbelief. More specifically, I think of it as a gothic novel in scholarly disguise: haunted like the dark novels so central to our tradition, by ghosts out of the European past which our White founding fathers fled, along with vengeful specters of the Native Americans they displaced and menacing shadows cast by the Africans they enslaved to work the soil. But as its title indicates, its themes are erotic as well as thanatic, though, to be sure, its eros is as dark as Thanatos, eventuating not in happy heterosexual unions, but in foredoomed male bonding, brother-sister incest, and necrophilia.

Moreover, to make clear that the tale it seeks to tell is mythic rather than factual, poetic rather than prosaic, I eschewed such conventional academic trappings as footnotes and bibliographies. So, too, I spoke not just in the solemn and magisterial third person, but also in the informal first; thus permitting myself to indulge in high rhetoric and low humor. For this reason, the reaction of more conventional scholars was overwhelmingly negative, as it was to the three succeeding volumes, *Waiting for the End*, *The Return of the Vanishing American*, and *What Was Literature?* So that for while it seemed as if I were to be doomed forever to be labeled a disturber of the peace, an *enfant terrible*, the "wild man of American Letters."

But nothing is forever, of course. As I approach my eightieth year, I am made aware by occasions like this that I have come to be thought of as a perfectly respectable scholar, an Americanist par excellence. I must confess to being pleased a little, but even more I am dismayed—wanting to cry out against such misapprehensions, to protest that I have remained a jack-of-all-fields and master of none, continuing to write and speak as I have from the first, about whatever moves me at the moment. And this has turned out to be not just the literature of many nations and eras beside my own: ancient Greek tragedy, the classic Chinese novel, Old Provençal poetry, the English Victorian novel, Kafka and James Joyce, Jaroslav Hašek and Chrétien de Troyes, and especially Shakespeare and Dante.

I have also dealt with subjects as remote from my presumable field of expertise as theology and psychology, voting studies and the war in Vietnam, Japanese woodblock engravings, pornography and comic books, sideshows and circuses, bioethics and organ transplants. I have talked about them, moreover, not just in the classroom and at gatherings of my fellow academics, but to trade unionists, nurses and dermatologists, as well as on talk shows presided over by Dick Cavett and William Buckley, Merv Griffin and Phil Donahue—earning myself a listing in *Who's Who in Entertainment*.

Similarly, I have less and less often published in academic journals (never in the *PMLA*), preferring to appear in magazines aimed at a nonprofessional audience, like *The Nation*, *The New Republic*, *Psychology Today*, *Esquire*, and (most scandalous of all) *Playboy*. Despite all this, I am presently praised by the sort of scholars who first ignored me, then vilified me (sometimes while stealing my ideas without acknowledgment)—though, to be sure, it is only for what I have written about American literature.

Even more disturbingly, I am now routinely quoted in jargon-ridden, reader-unfriendly works I cannot bring myself to read, and am listed honorifically in the kind of footnotes and bibliographies I have always eschewed. But most disturbingly of all, as a result (in a culture where nothing fails like success) some younger, future-oriented critics have begun to speak of me as old-fashioned, a member of a moribund establishment. I was, however, heartened when Camille Paglia, the most future-oriented of them all, the enfant terrible, in fact, of her generation as I was of mine, was moved by a new edition of *Love and Death in the American Novel* to write, "Fiedler created an American intellectual style that was truncated by the invasion of faddish French theory in the 70's and 80's. Let's turn back to Fiedler and begin again."

Her words not merely reassure me that I am still not PC. They also make me aware that whatever I have written about it has always been from an essentially American point of view and in an essentially American voice; and that therefore I am in the deepest sense an "Americanist"—a true colleague (despite their original doubts and my own continuing ones) of all those who have earlier received this award and you who so graciously bestow it on me now. As such a colleague, I feel free to say in conclusion—straight out and without irony—what I hope you realize I have been—in my customary perverse and ambivalent way—trying to say throughout these remarks, *thank you, thank you very much.*

Leslie A. Fiedler
Buffalo, New York
December 19, 1994

Blackballing the Fiedlers
(*The New Republic, September 9, 1967*)

Bruce Jackson

Originally published in *The New Republic*, September 9, 1967

Shortly after his arrest on a misdemeanor narcotics charge (the rarely enforced statute against anyone who "opens or maintains a place or places where any narcotic drug is unlawfully used"), Leslie A. Fiedler, who doesn't use, sell, or donate marijuana, was notified by the Traveler's Indemnity Company that his homeowner's policy was being canceled. There was no explanation, just the simple statement that his account was not wanted, along with another statement informing him that should he fail to get another policy within ten days, the Manufacturers and Traders Trust Company might foreclose his mortgage. Fiedler reinsured the house with the United States Fidelity and Guaranty Company, which, a few weeks later, also canceled out without explanation.

The Fiedlers realized the first cancellation was perhaps not so gratuitous as they had thought, so they went to an independent insurance agent and requested that he get them a policy with a company that knew the facts—that Fiedler, professor of English at the State University of New York at Buffalo, had been accused of a misdemeanor—and that would insure. The agent was encouraging and the Fiedlers relaxed a bit. On the ninth day of the ten-day period, Margaret Fiedler tried to find out what the agent had accomplished, but each time she called, the agent's secretary told her he had just stepped out and would call back in a few minutes. He never called and, in desperation, Margaret phoned the mortgage department at the bank to explain. The bank did the explaining: the agent had called the *bank* the day *before* and said he hadn't obtained the policy, so the next move was up to the bank. Late in the tenth day Margaret was given a binder by Allstate, the insurance firm owned by Sears. Two weeks later (August 16), the Fiedlers received a refund from the Rochester regional Allstate office, and a note that said,

> All insurance companies have certain qualifying standards which, together with our judgment and experience, tell us whether we can provide insurance in each individual case. Risks that can be insured by one company might not meet the standards of another company.
>
> Sometimes, because of these standards, we must give up business we would otherwise like to have. This happens only after thorough consideration is given each case.
>
> We're sorry we won't be able to accept your application for insurance protection. . . .
>
> As you see, a period of time remains before your protection stops. This will allow you time to apply for similar insurance elsewhere. We urge you to do so. Then you won't run the risk of being without protection.
>
> Thank you for your friendly interest in Allstate.

The Allstate agent knew quite well the Fiedlers did not want to "run the risk of being without protection" (which is why they applied in the first place) and that without such insurance they would lose their house (Congress has guaranteed most veterans the right to a home loan, but it has left the veto power in the hands of the insurance companies); he knew also that they had been blackballed and no regular American insurance company would handle their account. This is like Boston's Louise Day Hicks telling Roxbury Negroes that education will solve their problems while her school committee maintains in Roxbury the worst schools in the state.

Who rolled the blackball? Conversation around the university focused on three possibilities: (1) the Buffalo Police Department resorted to extralegal pressures in the hope of running Fiedler out of town; (2)

Fiedler's bank, perhaps pressured by some outraged local Brahmin, requested each insurance company in turn to reject Fiedler's policy; or (3) some of Fiedler's neighbors in Buffalo's comfortable Central Park section ($25,000–$50,000 homes, only recently invaded by professors) complained to their own insurance companies, and through them effected the blackball. Investigation by friends of the university has pretty much ruled out the second possibility: the bank seems sincerely interested in getting the Fiedlers insured and the problem settled; the first and third possibilities, neither mutually exclusive, are both still talked about.

There did not, until very recently, seem to be any recourse. Household insurance agreements are terminable at the will of either party and, as with moving companies, there is little government protection for the consumer except in cases of demonstrable fraud. It has been reported that a few days ago the home office of Allstate, when queried about its acceptance of the blackball, agreed to instruct its local agents to reinstate the policy.

But even if the insurance problem is resolved there are other, continuing aspects to the campaign that is being waged against the Fiedlers. The arrest has broad connotations for a town that still cannot accept the major university that now occupies the buildings and land which only a few years ago housed a homey, familiar, socially and intellectually innocuous diploma mill, and also cannot accept the strange clothes, the occasional beards, the iconoclastic entertainments (the San Francisco Mime Troupe, Ginsberg, *MacBird*, etc.), the out-of-town accents.

The puzzlement and outrage manifest themselves most directly in hate mail. Last year, university president Martin Meyerson was the object of much of it; this year Fiedler is the target. Like the following:

> Having read the expansive article concerning you and your activities, "On Being Busted at Fifty," which appeared first in the *New York Review of Books* and was reprinted by the *Buffalo Evening News* there seems one logical avenue—*Return to the land of your ancestors*, taking Dr. Myerson for moral support, as well as Leary. Our taxes might then be diverted into *sounder areas of need*.
>
> —Concerned Tax-Payer, Logical Parent,
> Clear minded individual able to "get along"
> without hallucinations in a busy world.

Or this one (printed in block letters and unsigned):

> . . . You [i.e., the UB faculty] are a bunch of the hated Jewish and commie rat nest. Its the 2nd best in the US after the Red nest—U of Cal at Berkeley. And its hero Meyerson when he was thrown out there. Who in hell got him here? . . . How come that leftie rats and poisoners of young minds remain at UB. Why don't you all go to stinking Russia. Or the damned hated Israel?

A few of Fiedler's respectable middle-class neighbors have joined the assault. A friend of mine was walking by the Fiedler house and noticed a group of neighborhood children, who ranged in age from about eight to ten, standing before the house shouting and throwing papers and bottles on the lawn. She was at first surprised (she lives in the neighborhood and knew the children to be generally well behaved), then shocked when she realized the parents of the children were standing across the street, calmly watching. "Those kids don't read newspapers," she said to me, "and I know they didn't think up that lawn littering by themselves." A few neighbors have remained friendly, or at least civil (one became friendly for the first time only after the harassment began), but others now refuse to say hello or even nod when they pass the Fiedlers on the street.

It isn't only the police, the cranks, the neighbors, and the insurance cartel. Someone persuaded the University of Amsterdam, where Fiedler was supposed to go next month on a Fulbright, to withdraw its previously confirmed invitation. Fiedler was not even accorded the courtesy of a direct letter from that university, but instead was informed thirdhand by an official in the American Fulbright Commission (which disagreed with the Dutch action and has tried, without success, to set things aright). Fiedler wrote the rector of the University of Amsterdam, inquiring about the report he received and asking why they reneged on his appointment. In his reply the rector vaguely alluded to proceedings "in progress" and said, "Personally I may add that I read one of your articles on the narcotic problem and personal freedom, which impressed me very much and which I thought straight-forward. I certainly will welcome an opportunity to meet you personally." He knows that it is now probably too late for the Fulbright Commission to get Fiedler an appointment elsewhere in Europe for this fall, and, the academic world working the way it does, this means Fiedler may have several months without a position. The rector never communicated with any official of this university about Fiedler's status (which is unchanged, since he is not convicted of any crime). There is a movement beginning to boycott the Netherlands as a Fulbright location.

The financial burden on the Fiedlers is considerable (some contributions have arrived for the defense fund, but not nearly enough), but at least there is a mechanism for defense against the legal charge. But against the other attacks there is no defense. Neighbors and strangers, bigots and xenophobes, a Dutch university and several of the unassailable American insurance companies have proclaimed Fiedler guilty, whether he is guilty or not.

Personae

Leslie mentions a lot of names in these conversations. Here are brief notes on most of them, mainly compiled by Ryan Bell from public domain sources. They'll give you some idea of who they were or what they did and enough information to chase them down if you want to know more.

Abel, Lionel (1910–2001): playwright, essayist, theater critic. Author of *Metatheatre: A New View of Dramatic Form* (1963). Obie for his play *Absalom* (1956). Member of UB English Department 1967–1979.

Agee, James (1909–1955): American novelist, screenwriter, and journalist. His book *Let Us Now Praise Famous Men* (1941) arose from his experiences observing Alabama sharecroppers with photographer Walker Evans. His best-known screenplays include those for *The African Queen* (1951) and *The Night of the Hunter* (1955). He posthumously won the 1958 Pulitzer Prize for fiction for his autobiographical novel *A Death in the Family* (1957).

Alvarez, Alfred (1929–2019): English writer who published under the name A. Alvarez or Al Alvarez. Poetry editor and critic for *The Observer*. Author of *The Savage God* (1972), a study of suicide partly based on his relationship with Sylvia Plath, and a classic book about poker, *The Biggest Game in Town* (1983). Editor of the influential *The New Poetry* (1962).

Aragon, Louis (1897–1982): French poet and writer best known for his association with the avant-garde movements Dada and Surrealism, the latter of which he helped formally theorize with André Breton and Philippe Soupault as an editor of the journal *Littérature* from 1919 to 1921. He was active in the French Communist Party and the French Resistance, frequently writing and editing for anti-Fascist and party-affiliated publications from the early 1930s onward.

Baldwin, James (1924–1987): African-American writer and civil rights and gay liberation activist, best known for the semi-autobiographical novel *Go Tell It on the Mountain* (1953) and a collection of essays, *Notes of Native Son* (1955). Some other works are *Giovanni's Room* (1956), *Blues for Mr. Charlie* (play, 1964), *Another Country* (1962), and *The Fire Next Time* (1963).

Baraka, Amiri (Everett Leroy Jones, 1934–2014): Highly influential and often controversial writer of poetry, fiction, plays, essays, and music criticism. Born in Newark. Involved with Black Mountain and Beat poets. He published under the name LeRoi Jones until the assassination of Malcom X (1965), after which he changed his name to Amiri Baraka, left his wife and two children, moved to Harlem, and founded the Black Arts Repertory/Theater School (BARTS). Some of his books of poetry: *Preface to a Twenty Volume Suicide Note* (1961), *Transbluesency: The Selected Poems of Amiri Baraka/LeRoy Jones* (1995), *Funk Lore: New Poems* (1996), *Somebody Blew Up America & Other Poems* (2003); plays: *Dutchman* (1964), *A Black Mass* 1966), *Slave Ship* (1970), *Most Dangerous Man in America (W.E.B. Du Bois)* (2013); fiction: *The System of Dante's Hell* (1965), *Un Poco Low Coup* (2004), *Tales of the Out & the Gone* (2006); and non-fiction: *Blues People* (1963), *Black Music* (1968), *Kawaida Studies: The New Nationalism* (1972), *The Autobiography of LeRoi Jones/Amiri Baraka* (1984), and *The Essence of Reparations* (2003).

Bashō, Matsuo (1644–1694): Edo-era Japanese poet. Hailed as a master of the haiku—then called "hokku"—which originated from the collaborative haikai no renga form that he also practiced.

Baum, L. Frank (1856–1919): author of *The Wonderful Wizard of Oz* (1900), thirteen other Oz novels, and forty-one other novels.

Beauvoir, Simone de (1908–1986): French philosopher and writer who was influential to both existentialism and feminist thought. From 1929 to 1980, she was in a romantic and collaborative relationship with Jean-Paul Sartre. Some of her key works include philosophical texts such as *The*

Second Sex (1949) and *The Ethics of Ambiguity* (1947), in addition to the novels *She Came to Stay* (1943) and *The Mandarins* (1954).

Bellow, Saul (1915–2005): Canadian-American novelist whose work often explored the dissonances of contemporary society and Jewish-American identity. He won the 1975 Nobel Prize in literature and the 1976 Pulitzer Prize for Fiction (for *Humboldt's Gift*). Some of his other works include *The Adventures of Augie March* (1953), *Seize the Day* (1956), *Henderson the Rain King* (1959), *Herzog* (1964), *Mr. Sammler's Planet* (1970), and *Ravelstein* (2000).

Bernstein, Carl (1944–): American investigative journalist and author. Best known for his Watergate reporting with Bob Woodward for *The Washington Post*, which resulted in *All the President's Men* (book 1974, film 1976). Some of his other books: *Loyalties: A Son's Memoir* (1989), *A Woman in Charge: The Life of Hillary Rodham Clinton* (2007), and *Chasing History: A Kid in the Newsroom* (2022).

Berryman, John (1914–1972): American poet and scholar, born in McAlester, Oklahoma, died (suicide), Minneapolis. Pulitzer Prize for *77 Dream Songs* (1964). Some of his other books: *Poems* (1942), *The Dispossessed* (1948), *Stephen Crane* (1950), *Homage to Mistress Bradstreet* (1956), *His Toy, His Dream, His Rest* (1968), *Love & Fame* (1970), *Delusions Etc.* (1972), and the posthumous *Recovery* (1973).

Blackmur, Richard P. (1904–1965): American literary critic, poet, high school expellee, and autodidact who obtained a literary education through working at a bookstore and sneaking into lectures at Harvard University. His formalist criticism, best represented in early books *The Double Agent* (1935) and *Language as Gesture* (1952), made him a major figure of New Criticism. He taught creative writing and English literature for nearly twenty-five years at Princeton University, where he also founded and directed the Christian Gauss Seminars in Criticism.

Borglum, Gutzon (1867–1941): American sculptor best known for his public works—most notably Mount Rushmore, which he worked on from 1927 until his death. He was close to Theodore Roosevelt, who originally exhibited the sculptor's bust of Abraham Lincoln in the White House. He is controversial for his extensive relationships with the Ku Klux Klan and

United Daughters of the Confederacy. He also did a sculpture of Lincoln in Newark that Leslie recalls.

Brecht, Bertholt (1898–1956): German playwright, theater theorist, and poet. Best known for *Threepenny Opera* (1928, written with Elisabeth Hauptmann and Kurt Weill), with music by Hanns Eisler, with whom he would collaborate through much of his career. Fled Nazi Germany in 1933, moved to Southern California in 1941. Cowrote the screenplay for Fritz Lang's *Hangmen Also Die!* (1943). After the War, he was black-listed in Hollywood (he was a lifelong Marxist, though never a member of the Communist Party). After his encounter with HUAC in 1947, he returned to Europe, eventually settling in East Berlin. Some of his other plays are: *The Rise and Fall of the City of Mahagonny* (1927–1929), *The Mother* (1930–1931), *Life of Galileo* (1937–1939), *Mother Courage and Her Children* (1938–1939), *The Good Person of Szechwan* (1939–1943), *The Dutchess of Malfi* (1943), *The Caucasian Chalk Circle* (1943–1945), and *The Trial of Joan of Arc at Rouen, 1431* (1952).

Brooks, Jack (1922–2012): Democratic-Party politician who served as a congressman for Texas from 1953 to 1995. His influential Brooks Act (1972) required competitive bidding for federal computing contracts and subsequently aided in the development of the computer industry. A member of the House Judiciary Committee, he participated in the impeachment process against Richard Nixon. As chair of the committee, he sponsored the Americans with Disabilities Act (1990), the Omnibus Crime Control Act (1991), and the Civil Rights Act of 1991. Pal of Leslie's in Tientsin.

Brown, Norman Oliver (1913–2002): American writer and scholar whose works touched on literature, history, psychoanalysis, and culture. He worked at Wesleyan University, the University of Rochester, and the University of California, Santa Cruz. Some of his notable books include *Life Against Death: The Psychoanalytical Meaning of History* (1959), *Love's Body* (1966), *Closing Time* (1973), *Apocalypse and/or Metamorphosis* (1991), and the posthumously published *The Challenge of Islam* (2009).

Buckley, William F., Jr. (1925–2008): American conservative writer. Founder of the highly influential conservative journal *National Review* (1955). First came to attention for *God and Man at Yale* (1951). That was followed by more than fifty other books, some of which are *McCarthy and His Enemies: The Record and Its Meaning* (1954), *Up from Liberalism* (1959), *The Committee and Its Critics: A Calm Review of the House Committee on Un-American Activities* (1962), *On the Firing Line: The Public Life of Our Public Figures* (1989), *Nearer, My God: An Autobiography of Faith* (1997), *Miles Gone By: A Literary Autobiography* (2004), *Flying High: Remembering Barry Goldwater* (2008), and *Buckley vs. Vidal: The Historic 1968 ABC News Debates* (2015). Longtime host of PBS *Firing Line* (1966–1999).

Burke, Kenneth (1897–1993): literary critic, poet, and novelist. Early in his career, he was an editor for the influential modernist literary magazine *The Dial*. He is best known for his theoretical work, which largely examines the relationships between language, symbols, rhetoric, and ideology.

Burnham, James (1905–1987): American philosopher, political theorist, and professor. He is best known for his 1941 book *The Managerial Revolution*, in which he theorizes and predicts the development of a managerial class whose technical knowledge would allow it, rather than the working class, to overpower capitalist hegemony. Though he was initially a prominent activist of the American left, befriending Leon Trotsky early in his career, he turned to the political right and American conservatism in the 1940s, espousing anti-Soviet and anti-Communist views that led to extensive employment with the Office of Strategic Services (OSS) and its successor, the Central Intelligence Agency (CIA). Through the support of the latter organization, he helped found the liberal anti-Communist propaganda group the Congress for Cultural Freedom. He was instrumental in the founding and development of William F. Buckley's influential conservative magazine, *National Review*.

Cal, *see* Lowell, Robert

Calvino, Italo (1923–1985): Italian writer who authored conceptually labyrinthine and structurally innovative novels such as *Difficult Loves* (1970), *Invisible Cities* (1972), *If On a Winter's Night a Traveler* (1979), and *Mr. Palomar* (1983). From 1968 onward, he was a member of Oulipo, a mostly French group of experimental writers interested in formal constraints and developing a "workshop of potential literature."

Capote, Truman (1924–1984): American writer who published novels, stories, screenplays, and plays. Much of his work, like his famous true-crime novel *In Cold Blood* (1966), is associated with the New Journalism movement. As a novelist, he wrote *Breakfast at Tiffany's* (1958), *Other Voices, Other Rooms* (1948), and *The Grass Harp* (1951).

Carver, Catharine DeFrance (1921–1997): American publisher. In New York, she was employed by Viking Press, Harcourt Brace, J. B. Lippincott & Co., and others, working with writers such as Lionel Trilling, Hannah Arendt, Saul Bellow, and Flannery O'Connor. She relocated to London in the 1960s, working for Chatto & Windus, Oxford University Press, and Yale University Press.

Chambers, Whittaker (1901–1961): began his career as a Marxist writer, contributing to publications such as *New Masses* and editing the *Daily Worker* in the late 1920s. Throughout the 1930s, he worked as a spy for the Soviet GRU (Main Intelligence Directorate), but when Stalinism eventually weakened his faith in Communism, he alleged the existence of a network of Communist spies within the American government, speaking to officials in 1939; by 1945, the FBI began to take his case seriously, and in 1948, he testified before the House Un-American Activities Committee, leading to the public trial of US State Department and UN official Alger Hiss, who was found guilty of two counts of perjury in 1950. Chambers, who spent the 1940s as writer-editor for *Time* magazine, wrote for the *National Review* in the 1950s and the bestselling anti-Communist memoir *Witness* (1952).

Chopin, Kate (1850–1904): American writer whose short stories and novels, often set in Louisiana, were highly influential to early twentieth-century feminist fiction, particularly for writers of Southern and/or Catholic backgrounds. She died of a brain hemorrhage in 1904, five years after the publication of her then-controversial masterpiece *The Awakening* (1899).

Clark, Walter van Tilburg (1909–1971): American novelist, short story writer, and educator. With novels such as his debut, *The Ox-Bow Incident* (1940), he presented a startlingly modern take on the American western, stripping the genre of its usual tropes and utilizing it as a forum for philosophical and psychological inquiry. Beginning in the 1950s, he primarily focused on teaching creative writing at universities such as the University of Montana, San Francisco State University, and eventually the University of Nevada, Reno—his alma mater.

Cocks, John C. "Jay," Jr. (1944–): American film critic and screenwriter. Collaborated with Martin Scorsese on *The Age of Innocence* (1993), *Gangs of New York* (2002), and other films. In 2025, he was nominated for an Academy Award for Best Adapted Screenplay, with James Mangold, for the film *A Complete Unknown*.

Cole, Toby (1916–2008): American theater agent best known for running New York's Actors and Authors Agency from 1957 to 1973. She worked extensively as a labor organizer during her teenage years and was barred from entering college; subsequently, she became active in New York's left-wing New Theatre League. She began her work as an agent by attempting to resurrect the careers of actors affected by McCarthy-era blacklisting, such as actor-comedian Zero Mostel. Throughout her career—which would follow her from New York to Venice and, eventually, the San Francisco Bay area—she was a champion of not only progressive political causes, but also aesthetically radical writers and playwrights such as Luigi Pirandello, Peter Handke, Bertolt Brecht, and Saul Bellow. She authored and edited several books, most notably the collections *Actors on Acting* (1949), *Directors on Directing* (1953), and *Playwrights on Playwriting* (1960).

Cook, Albert S. (1853–1927): American academic and scholar who was active in various fields; after teaching mathematics as a teenager and studying the sciences in college, he went on to become one of the leading literary critics and philologists of his time, specializing in Old English and poetics. He published prolifically, authoring or editing over three hundred books in his lifetime. He created what came to be the legendary University at Buffalo English Department of the late 1960s.

Cowley, Malcolm (1898–1989): American writer and editor best known for his influential work at Viking Press, where he instigated critical reappraisals of writers such as F. Scott Fitzgerald and William Faulkner while also helping launch the careers of Jack Kerouac and Ken Kesey, among others. Throughout the 1920s, he lived in Paris, where he was immersed in a community of cosmopolitan literary expatriates that included Ernest

Hemingway and Gertrude Stein. In the early 1940s, his political past attracted negative attention when he was hired as an analyst by poet Archibald MacLeish, then the head of the War Department's Office of Facts and Figures; as a result, Cowley resigned and retired from all political publishing. As a writer, he is best known for his first book of poetry, *Blue Juniata* (1929), and his memoir, *Exile's Return* (1934, revised in 1951).

Cox, James (1925–2012): student of Leslie's at the School of Letters, Indiana University Faculty there 1957–1963, then Dartmouth faculty 1963–1990. Author of *Mark Twain: The Fate of Humor*.

Cunliffe, Marcus Falkner (1922–1990): British professor of American studies and history whose work often explored the perceptions Americans and Europeans hold of each other. He wrote or edited approximately fifteen books in his lifetime, including *The Literature of the United States* (1954), *George Washington: Man and Monument* (1958), and *Soldiers and Civilians: The Martial Spirit in America, 1775–1865* (1969).

Dana, John Cotton (1856–1929): founder and director of the Newark Public Library and the Newark Museum (both 1902–1929).

Davis, Charles Twitchell (1918–1981): first Black professor to teach at Princeton (which also denied him tenure because he was Black). First Black master of Yale's John C. Calhoun College, chair of Yale's Afro-American studies program. Best known for *Black Is the Color of the Cosmos* (1982) and *The Slave's Narrative* (1982).

Decter, Midge (1927–2022): American journalist and editor who, along with her husband Norman Podhoretz, was an early exponent of the American neoconservatism movement. As an editor, she worked for publications such as *Midstream, Commentary*, and *Harper's Magazine*. She was associated with organizations such as the Committee of the Free World, an anti-Communist think tank, for which she served as cochair alongside Donald Rumsfeld.

Delany, Samuel R. "Chip" (1942–): prolific writer of fiction (particularly science fiction), memoirs, and essays. Some of his works are *Babel-17* (1966), *Hogg* (1969–1995), *Nova* (1968), *Dahlgren* (1975), *The Motion of Light in Water: Sex and Science Fiction Writing in the East Village* (1988), and *Dark Reflections* (2007). Recipient of four Nebula Awards and two Hugo Awards. Member of UB English Department 1975–2015.

DeMott, Benjamin Haile (1924–2005): American writer and English professor who taught at Amherst College for more than forty years while carving out a parallel career as a cultural critic, often writing about the mythologies of American culture and ideology. He is particularly known for a trilogy of books he published in his final decades: *The Imperial Middle: Why Americans Can't Think Straight About Class* (1990), *The Trouble with Friendship: Why Americans Can't Think Straight About Race* (1995), and *Killer Woman Blues: Why Americans Can't Think Straight About Gender* (2000).

Didion, Joan (1934–2021): journalist, novelist, and essayist. Associated with New Journalism, she is best known for her coverage of American and Californian culture in collections such as *Slouching Towards Bethlehem* (1968) and *The White Album* (1979), as well as for her novels *Play It as It Lays* (1970) and *A Book of Common Prayer* (1977).

Douglas, Ann (1942–): American literary historian and the Parr Professor Emerita of English and Comparative Literature at Columbia University. Her books include *The Feminization of American Culture* (1977) and *Terrible Honesty: Mongrel Manhattan in the 1920s* (1995).

Ellison, Harlan (1934–2018): American writer. He is best known for his sci-fi and speculative fiction, as well as for his film and television screenplays. He published his first novel, *Web of the City*, in 1958 before moving to California to write for Hollywood. In addition to his numerous short stories and novellas, he wrote for programs such as *Star Trek* and edited the influential science fiction anthologies *Dangerous Visions* (1967) and *Again, Dangerous Visions* (1972).

Ellison, Ralph (Waldo) (1913–1994): American writer best known for the novel *Invisible Man* (1953) and a collection of essays, *Shadow and Act* (1964). After graduating from Tuskegee Institute (which he found as class conscious as White colleges) he went to New York, where he met Langston Hughes and Richard Wright. He was a friend and sometime collaborator of photographer Gordon Parks. He was, for a time, involved with the Communist Party; his sense during World War II that the party had betrayed African Americans was part of the inspiration for *Invisible Man*. A 1965 *Book Week* poll of two hundred writers and editors named *Invisible Man* the most important novel since World War II.

Empson, William (1906–1984): English literary critic and poet whose method of close reading analysis, typically applied to early and premodernist works, was influential to the development of New Criticism. Some of his key critical works include *Seven Types of Ambiguity* (1930), *Some Versions of Pastoral* (1935), *Milton's God* (1961), and *Using Biography* (1985).

Farmer, Philip José (1918–2009): American writer and novelist. He is primarily known for his science fiction and fantasy works, many of which are pastiches that utilize others' fictional characters; notably, he published *Venus on the Half-Shell* (1975) under the name "Kilgore Trout"—a recurring character in Kurt Vonnegut's novels—to minor controversy. Some of his other works include the *World of Tiers* series (1965–1993), the *Riverworld* series (1971–1983), *The Other Log of Phileas Fogg* (1973), and *Doc Savage: His Apocalyptic Life* (1973).

Farrell, James Thomas (1904–1979): American novelist and poet. He is best known for his *Studs Lonigan* trilogy (1932–1935); informed by his Irish-American upbringing in Chicago, the trilogy depicts the slow destruction of its protagonist at the hands of capitalism, the Catholic Church, and life in the city. Though active in Trotskyist politics early in his career, he drifted toward neoconservatism in his final decades, helping found the second Committee on the Present Danger in 1976.

Faulkner, William (1897–1962): American novelist from Lafayette County, Mississippi. He is celebrated for his contributions to literary modernism and his highly stylized, stream-of-conscious prose. Some of his most notable works include *The Sound and the Fury* (1929), *As I Lay Dying* (1930), *Sanctuary* (1931), *Light in August* (1932), *Absalom, Absalom!* (1936), and *A Fable* (1952). He won the Nobel Prize in Literature (1949), the National Book Award (1951, 1955), and the Pulitzer Prize for Fiction (1955, 1963).

Ferber, Edna (1885–1968): American novelist, short story writer, and playwright whose work often explored the social prejudices of Midwestern American life. She is best known for her Pulitzer Prize–winning novel *So*

Big (1924), her 1926 novel-turned-Broadway hit *Show Boat*, and 1930's *Cimarron*, which was adapted into an Academy Award–winning film a year after its publication. She was associated with the Algonquin Round Table, a circle of intellectuals and artists who took lunch together at Manhattan's Algonquin Hotel throughout the 1920s.

Fergusson, Francis (1904–1986): American literary critic and professor who specialized in drama and mythology. His best-known work, *The Idea of a Theater* (1949), examines a handful of plays across traditions and centuries, from Sophocles to Pirandello, to argue that drama's universal feature is its imperative to reflect the nature of its time and place.

Fiedler, Harold I. (1919–2011). Leslie's estranged brother. Served in a tank battalion in World War II. Received the Purple Heart and Bronze Star for military operations in Germany in 1945. Became a lieutenant colonel in military intelligence and then served twenty-four years in the CIA, where, according to the Peterborough (NH) *Union Leader* obituary (November 9, 2011), "his duties included chief of base in southeastern Europe, deputy chief for area operations and the division level in headquarters and as chief of operations training at a domestic training facility . . . (he) obtained coveted super-grade ranks."

Fiedler, Margaret (née Margaret Ann Shipley, 1909–2005): Leslie's wife, 1939–1972. Mother of Kurt (1941), Eric (1943), Michael (1947), Deborah (1949), Jenny (1952), and Miriam (Memo, 1955).

Fiedler, Sally Andersen (1939–2016): Leslie's wife, 1973 until his death. Mother of Eric and Soren Andersen. Author of *Eleanor Mooseheart* (1992) and *A Trick of Seeing: Poems Selected and New* (2007).

Fitzgerald, Robert Stuart (1910–1985): American poet, critic, translator, and professor. He is best known for his translations of Greek classics, particularly those of Homer, Euripides, Sophocles, and Virgil. His volumes of poetry include *Poems* (1935), *A Wreath for the Sea* (1943), *In the Rose of Time: Poems, 1939–1956* (1956), and *Spring Shade: Poems, 1931–1970* (1971).

Ford, John (1894–1973): influential and Academy Award–winning film director who was active during the Golden Age of Hollywood. Noted for his westerns, he also directed films in other genres. He is remembered for classic films such as *The Informer* (1935), *Stagecoach* (1939), *The Grapes of Wrath* (1940), *How Green Was My Valley* (1941), *My Darling Clementine* (1946), *Fort Apache* (1948), *The Quiet Man* (1952), *The Searchers* (1956), and *The Man Who Shot Liberty Valance* (1962).

Foss, Lukas (1922–2009): German-American composer, pianist, and conductor. Though his early work is noted for its neoclassicism, his later work is decidedly avant-garde. He is particularly remembered for his experiments with chance and probability, which he developed through the Improvisation Chamber Ensemble, a group he founded in 1957 while teaching at UCLA. He later taught at the University at Buffalo, where he founded the Center for Creative and Performing Arts.

Franco, Franciso (1892–1975): Spanish Nationalist general who served as dictator of Spain, under the title of "Caudillo," from 1939 to 1975. Hundreds of thousands of Spaniards were killed by his regime.

Fried, Michael Martin (1939–): art historian, critic, and poet. He is best known for his 1967 essay "Art and Objecthood," in which he critiques minimalist art for its self-conscious theatricality. He is also noted for his concept of absorption, which he developed as an alternative to theatricality in 1980's *Absorption and Theatricality: Painting and Beholder in the Age of Diderot*. In recent decades, he has written extensively on art history and literature, including books on photography, Caravaggio, Flaubert, literary impressionism, and Manet.

Frost, Robert (1874–1963): influential American poet whose work often utilized plain, colloquial language to depict life in rural America. He received the Pulitzer Prize for Poetry five times and was appointed as the Poet Laureate of the United States in 1958.

Fuchs, Daniel (1909–1993): screenwriter, novelist, and essayist. He was raised in Brooklyn, which provided inspiration for his three novels, *Summer in Williamsburg* (1934), *Homage to Blenholt* (1936), and *Low Company* (1937). At the age of twenty-six, he moved to California to work as a screenwriter; he is well known for his scripts for noir films such as *Criss Cross* (1949) and *Panic in the Streets* (1950).

Garver, Newton (1928–2014): American philosopher, peace activist, and professor. He is best known for his readings of Ludwig Wittgenstein, as well as his related concept of transcendental naturalism. He taught at the University at Buffalo from 1961 to 1995.

Gassman, Vittorio (1922–2000): Italian actor, director, and screenwriter renowned for his work in both theater and cinema. He was popularly known as *Il Mattatore*, a title he earned due to his starring role in Dino Risi's 1960 film of the same name.

Gaster, Theodor Herzl (1906–1992): British-American scholar who wrote about comparative religion and mythology in books such as *Thespis: Ritual, Myth, and Drama in the Ancient Near East* (1950), *Holy and the Profane: Evolution of Jewish Folkways* (1955), and *Myth, Legend, and Custom in the Old Testament* (1969). He is also noted for his translations of the Dead Sea Scrolls, which he published with added introductions and notes as *The Dead Sea Scriptures* (1956).

Ginsberg, Allen (1926–1997): American poet, writer, and social activist. A core figure in both the Beat Generation and the San Francisco Renaissance, he links the modernist verse of his idols—such as his early mentor, William Carlos Williams—to the American counterculture of the 1960s and 1970s. He is best known for his epic poem *Howl* (1956), whose descriptions of homosexuality and trenchant critiques of American culture garnered considerable controversy and led to the arrest of City Lights publisher Lawrence Ferlinghetti.

Goodman, Paul (1911–1972): American writer whose work spanned social criticism, psychoanalysis, and experimental literature. Much of his output, such as *Growing Up Absurd* (1960), was influential to the New Left and the counterculture of the 1960s. Additionally, with Fritz and Laura Perls, he was responsible for theorizing Gestalt therapy.

Grey, Zane (1872–1939): American writer and dentist. Of his many novels, he is most celebrated for his westerns, such as *The Lone Star Ranger* (1914), *The Rainbow Trail* (1915), *The Border Legion* (1916), *To the Last Man* (1921), *The Call of the Canyon* (1924), *Under the Tonto Rim* (1926), and his bestselling work *Riders of the Purple Sage* (1912). There have been over one hundred film adaptations of his works.

Guthrie, A. B., Jr. (1901–1991): American writer, screenwriter, and scholar best known for his westerns, such as his Pulitzer Prize–winning novel *The*

Way West (1950). That novel, *The Big Sky* (1947), and *These Thousand Hills* (1956) spawned film adaptations shortly after their publications. He also wrote the screenplays for *Shane* (1953) and *The Kentuckian* (1955), receiving an Academy Award nomination for the former.

Habib, Philip (1920–1992): US career diplomat from 1949 to 1987. Instrumental in a negotiating cease-fire in the long-running Lebanese Civil War (1975–1990). Chief of staff for the US delegation to the Paris Peace Talks (1968–1971). Helped negotiate the Camp David Accords (1978).

Hagman, Larry (1931–2012): American film and television actor, director, and producer. He is best known for his roles in the television series *Dallas* (1978–1991) and *I Dream of Jeannie* (1965–1970), in addition to films such as *Fail-Safe* (1964), *Harry and Tonto* (1974), *S.O.B.* (1981), *Nixon* (1995), and *Primary Colors* (1998).

Haldeman-Julius, Emanuel (1889–1951): American writer, publisher, and social reformer noted for his dedication to Socialist and atheist thought. He was an editor of the Socialist newspaper *Appeal to Reason*, eventually purchasing their printing presses to get into the publishing business. With his wife, Marcet Haldeman, he is best known for publishing the enormously popular and famously affordable *Little Blue Books* series, which featured works of literature, philosophy, and social commentary printed in staple-bound pulp pamphlets.

Haley, Alex (1921–1992): American writer whose first published book was written with Malcolm X: *The Autobiography of Malcolm X* (1965). Other than that book, he is best known for *Roots: The Saga of an American Family* (1976), which details his own family's history as slaves in America. That book won him a special Pulitzer Prize and spawned multiple successful television miniseries adaptations.

Hamako Watanabe (b. Hamako Kato, 1910–1999): popular singer and actress during Japan's Shōwa period. She began her career in entertainment after working as a music instructor, releasing a number of hit songs by the mid-1930s. During the Second Sino-Japanese War, she was sent to Japanese-occupied China to raise morale among troops, and many of her songs from this era emphasized patriotic sentiments. She was held as a prisoner of war for over a year following the surrender of Japan, but her career resumed following her repatriation.

Hartman, Geoffrey (1929–2016): literary theorist who spent most of his academic career in Yale's Comparative Literature Department. Some of his books are *The Unmediated Vision: An Interpretation of Wordsworth* (1954), *André Malraux* (1960), *The Fate of Reading and Other Essays* (1975), *Criticism in the Wilderness: The Study of Literature Today* (1980), *Saving the Text: Literature/Derrida/Philosophy* (1981), *The Unremarkable Wordsworth* (1987), *The Longest Shadow: In the Aftermath of the Holocaust* (1996), and *Scars of the Spirit: The Struggle Against Inauthenticity* (2004).

Hassan, Ihab Habib (1925–2015): Egyptian-American literary critic and writer whose work focuses on twentieth-century avant-garde and experimental writing. He was an early and important theorist of postmodernism, articulating its key features and distinctions from modernism in his 1971 monograph *The Dismemberment of Orpheus: Toward a Postmodern Literature*. Throughout his career, he taught at several institutions, most notably the University of Wisconsin–Milwaukee, where he remained for nearly three decades.

Hathaway, Baxter (1909–1984): American critic, novelist, poet, and professor. He is best known for developing Cornell's creative writing program. While at Cornell, he also launched the influential and ongoing literary journal *Epoch* with other faculty members, including his wife, Sherry Hathaway. He and Sherry would later found Ithaca House, a small press dedicated primarily to poetry and visual art.

Hearst, Fanny (1889–1968): popular American novelist whose sentimental, romantic works touched on key social issues, such as women's rights, economic conditions, and race relations. One of the most widely read and highest-paid twentieth-century writers. At least thirty films are based on her works. Some of her books are: *Star-Dust: The Story of an American Girl* (1921), *Back Street* (1931), *Imitation of Life* (1933), and *Hallelujah* (1944). Her 1918 short story, "Humoresque," was a film (1920) and stage play (1923). Her novel *Imitation of Life* was made into two feature films: 1934 and 1939.

Herr, Michael (1940–2016): American writer, journalist, and screenwriter. He is perhaps best known for his coverage of the Vietnam War in *Esquire* and in his 1977 memoir *Dispatches*. He also assisted in the writing of Vietnam War films *Apocalypse Now* (1979) and *Full Metal Jacket* (1987), serving as associate producer for the latter.

Hildegard (Loretta Sell) (1906–2005): American cabaret singer popular in the 1930s and 1940s.

Hoffman, Abbie (1936–1989): American political and social activist in the civil rights and anti–Vietnam War movements. Cofounder of the Youth International Party (the "Yippies") and a member of the Chicago Seven—a group of activists tried for various charges during the 1968 Democratic Convention. Hoffman and four others were convicted, but the charges were thrown out on appeal. Author of *Steal This Book* (1971) and, with Jonathan Silvers, *Steal This Urine Test: Fighting Drug Hysteria in America* (1987). His death was ruled a suicide (he'd taken about 150 phenobarbital tablets).

Holland, Norman (1927–2017): American literary critic and professor. After beginning his career as a New Critic in the 1950s, he later became a major figure in psychoanalytic theory, reader-response theory, and cognitive poetics. His numerous books include *Psychoanalysis and Shakespeare* (1966), *Poems in Persons* (1973), *5 Readers Reading* (1975), *Laughing* (1982), and *The Critical I* (1992). In 1993, he founded the PSYART online discussion group, launching its accompanying journal, *PsyArt: A Hyperlink Journal for the Psychology of the Arts*, four years later. Member of the UB English Department 1966–1983.

Hook, Sidney (1902–1989): American pragmatist philosopher whose work concerned history, education, politics, and more. Though he was a Marxist during his youth, he went on to become a staunch critic of Communism and, later, the New Left. He helped found CIA-funded agencies such as the Congress for Cultural Freedom and the American Committee for Cultural Freedom. Some of his published books include *Reason, Social Myths, and Democracy* (1940), *The Hero in History: A Study in Limitation and Possibility* (1943), and *Common Sense and the Fifth Amendment* (1957).

Hopkins, Gerard Manley (1844–1889): English poet and Jesuit priest. Known for his "sprung rhythm" and vivid imagery, his poetry was influential to the work of later poets such as T. S. Eliot, W. H. Auden, and Dylan Thomas.

Howe, Irving (1920–1993): American literary critic and political activist. Associated with leftist politics throughout his career, he helped found the

Democratic Socialist Organizing Committee, which would later transform into the Democratic Socialists of America. In addition to writing for publications such as the *Partisan Review* and *The New Republic*, he authored several books on literature, politics, and culture, including his National Book Award–winning analysis of Eastern European Jewish culture in America, *World of Our Fathers* (1976).

Hugo, Richard (1923–1982): American poet and novelist whose work is noted for its resonances with Northwestern American life, particularly Montana and his native Seattle. He taught at the University of Montana for eighteen years (he was hired as Leslie Fiedler's replacement), directing their creative writing program. His many poetry collections include *A Run of Jacks* (1961), *Good Luck in Cracked Italian* (1969), and *31 Letters and 13 Dreams* (1977).

Hurst, Fannie (1889–1968): American writer of novels and short stories. Popular following the First World War, she published novels such as *Lummox* (1923), *Back Street* (1931), and *Imitation of Life* (1933), in addition to over three hundred short stories.

Huston, John (1906–1987): American director, screenwriter, and actor. After studying painting, he pursued writing in Mexico, primarily focusing on plays and short stories before turning to screenplays and moving to Hollywood. After writing for several films in the late 1930s and early 1940s—including his screenplays for *Dr. Ehrlich's Magic Bullet* (1940), *Sergeant York* (1941), and *High Sierra* (1941), starring Humphrey Bogart—he made his directorial debut with another Bogart-leading film, *The Maltese Falcon* (1941), based on Dashiell Hammett's detective novel. Additional films with Bogart following the war would cement his reputation as a leading director, namely *The Treasure of the Sierra Madre* (1948) and *Key Largo* (1948). He also directed films such as *The Asphalt Jungle* (1950), *The African Queen* (1951), *Heaven Knows, Mr. Allison* (1957), *The Man Who Would Be King* (1975), and *Under the Volcano* (1984). He is known for his many literary adaptations, including Stephen Crane's *The Red Badge of Courage* (1951), Herman Melville's *Moby Dick* (1956), Ernest Hemingway's *A Farewell to Arms* (1957, uncredited), Flannery O'Connor's *Wise Blood* (1979, as Jhon Huston), and James Joyce's *The Dead* (1987).

Ingersoll, Robert Green (1833–1899): American lawyer, writer, politician, and orator who was nicknamed "The Great Agnostic." Though he served as Illinois Attorney General, many believe that his unapologetic agnosticism prevented him from holding higher political office.

Irvine, Reed (1922–2004): American conservative economist. He is best known for founding Accuracy in Media, a conservative media watchdog led by his conviction that mainstream American media holds Socialist biases.

Izzo, Carlo (1901–1979): Italian translator, teacher, and literary critic. Some of his books are: *Poesia americana contemporanea e poesia negra* (1949), *Autobiografismo di Charles Dickens* (1954), *Un metafisico della narrazione: Nathaniel Hawthorne* (1955), *Blues e spirituals: Poesie anonime e d'autore dei negri d'America* (1963), and *Poesia negro-americana* (1963).

Jarrell, Randall (1914–1965): American poet, critic, novelist, and author of children's books. His poetry is noted for its attention to the rich details of American speech and vernacular, as represented in collections including *Little Friend, Little Friend* (1945) and *The Woman at the Washington Zoo* (1960). He was the recipient of a Guggenheim Fellowship, the National Book Award, and a grant from the National Institute of Arts and Letters. He was the 11th Consultant in Poetry for the Library of Congress.

Johnson, Dorothy Marie (1905–1984): American writer who was best known for her westerns. In addition to her novels *The Hanging Tree* (1957), *Buffalo Woman* (1977), and *All the Buffalo Returning* (1979), she wrote short stories and nonfiction. In addition to *The Hanging Tree*, her stories "A Man Called Horse" (1950) and "The Man Who Shot Liberty Valance" (1953) were adapted into successful films.

Joyce, James (1882–1941): Irish writer considered one of the most influential writers of the twentieth century. He published four works of fiction—a short story collection, *Dubliners* (1914), and the novels *A Portrait of the Artist as a Young Man* (1916), *Ulysses* (1922), and *Finnegans Wake* (1939)—as well as three books of poetry and a play. *Ulysses* was long the target of censors: it was banned in the US until 1934 and England until 1936.

Jurist, Ed (1916–1993): Hollywood writer and producer. Some of the shows on which he worked were *The Aldrich Family*, *Hawaiian Eye*, *77 Sunset Strip*, *Bewitched*, and *The Flying Nun*.

Kallman, Chester (1921–1075): American poet and translator. Collaborator with W. H. Auden on several librettos. The sole beneficiary of Auden's estate.

Kaplan, Harold J. (1916–2015): American writer. Author of the novels *The Plenipotentiaries* (1950) and *Anywhere Else* (1951).

Kazin, Alfred (1915–1998): American writer and literary critic. He is best known for his analyses of American literature in books such as *On Native Grounds: An Interpretation of Modern American Prose Literature* (1942) and *A Writer's America: Landscape in Literature* (1988), as well as for his exploration of Jewish-American life and the immigrant experience in memoir-novels such as *A Walker in the City* (1951), *Starting Out in the '30s* (1965), and *New York Jew* (1978). In contrast to the New Critical method of his milieu, his criticism deemphasized form and style in favor of historically informed readings of literary works. In 1996, he became the first recipient of the Truman Capote Lifetime Achievement Award in Literary Criticism.

Kelley, William Melvin (1937–2017): American novelist and writer whose satirical work examined American race relations. He is known for novels such as *A Different Drummer* (1962) and *dem* (1967). Today, he is often cited as the originator of the word "woke," which appears in his 1962 *New York Times* op-ed examining the African-American roots of Beatnik slang, "If You're Woke, You Dig It."

Kendall, Willmoore, Jr. (1909–1967): American conservative writer and political philosopher. After working for multiple agencies within the United States federal government, including the CIA precursor the Central Intelligence Group, he became a professor of political science at Yale, where his staunch anti-Communism influenced the conservatism of students such as William F. Buckley Jr., with whom he helped found *National Review*, and L. Brent Bozell Jr. Due to his controversial political views and notoriously cantankerous demeanor, he was dismissed from the university in 1961, following fourteen years of teaching. In his political philosophy, he is known for his opposition to liberal democracy and moral relativism, represented in books such as *The Conservative Affirmation* (1963).

Kidder, Margot (1948–2018): Canadian-American actress and environmental and political activist, She played Lois Lane in four Superman films (1978–1987). Some of her other films: *Quackser Fortune Has a*

Cousin in the Bronx (1970), *Black Christmas* (1974), *The Great Waldo Pepper* (1975), *92 in the Shade* (1975), and *The Amityville Horror* (1978). She was briefly married to Thomas McGuane (1976–1977), John Heard (1979–1980—they were together just six days), and Philippe de Broca (1983–1984). Her death was ruled a suicide.

King, Edward (1612–1637): poet friend of John Milton who died by drowning at twenty-five. Subject of Milton's poem "Lycidas."

Kittredge, George Lyman (1860–1941): literary critic and scholar of the philological school. During his time, he was a leading scholar of Shakespeare, Chaucer, folklore, and folk song. He taught extensively at Harvard University and Radcliffe College. Some of his key works include *Observations on the Language of Chaucer's Troilus* (1894), *The Mother Tongue* (1902, with Sarah Louise Arnold), *The Old Farmer and His Almanack* (1920), *Witchcraft in Old and New England* (1929), and *The Complete Works of Shakespeare* (1936).

Koch, Edward (1924–2013): American politician who served in the United States House of Representatives from 1969 to 1977, and later as mayor of New York City from 1978 to 1989. Though a lifelong Democrat, he primarily supported Republican candidates after leaving office.

Kramer, Hilton (1928–2012): art critic and essayist. Cofounder and coeditor of conservative *The New Criterion*. Chief art critic for *The New York Times* from 1965 to 1982. Later, critic of the *Times* and other publications for what he considered their leftist bias. Scorned pop art, conceptual art, postmodern art, and action painting. Some of his books are *The Revenge of the Philistines* (1985), *The Twilight of the Intellectuals: Culture and Politics in the Era of the Cold War* (1999), and *The Triumph of Modernism: The Art World 1985–2005* (2006).

Krieger, Murray (1923–2000): born in Newark. One of the most influential New Critics. Some of his books are *The New Apologists for Poetry* (1956), *The Tragic Vision* (1960), *A Window to Criticism* (1964), *Theory of Criticism: A Tradition and Its System* (1976), and *The Institution of Theory* (1994).

Kristol, Irving (1920–2009): American journalist, editor, and public intellectual who is sometimes regarded as "the godfather of neoconservatism."

Throughout his life, he contributed to publications such as *Commentary*, *Encounter*, *The Reporter*, and *The Wall Street Journal*. He founded the Institute for Education Affairs, as well as the publications *The Public Interest* and *The National Interest*. Some of his books include *On the Democratic Idea in America* (1972), *Two Cheers for Capitalism: A Penetrating Assessment of Free Enterprise and the Corporate System* (1978), *Reflections of a Neo-conservative: Looking Back, Looking Ahead* (1983), and *Neoconservatism: The Autobiography of an Idea* (1995).

L'Amour, Louis (1908–1988): prolific American writer, primarily westerns (100 novels, more than 250 short stories). All of his books are still in print; more than 320 million copies have been sold.

Lalli, Bianamaria Tedeschini (1928–2022): Italian scholar of American studies. Joined faculty of l'Università deli Studi di Roma "La Sapienza" in 1958. Some of her books are *Henry David Thoreau* (1954), *Emily Dickinson Prospettive critiche* (1963), *I puritani* (1965), and *Gertrude Stein, l'sperimento dello scrivere* (1976).

Langdon, Jervis (1809–1870): New York coal company magnate and the father of Mark Twain's wife, Olivia.

Lawrence, D. H. (1885–1930): English writer whose major works, often critical of modern society and risqué in theme, were highly influential to modernist literature. Though he also wrote poetry, drama, criticism, and more, he is best remembered for his novels, which include *Sons and Lovers* (1913), *The Rainbow* (1915), *Women in Love* (1920), and *Lady Chatterley's Lover* (1928).

Leary, Timothy (1920–1996): psychologist and advocate for LSD and other psychedelic drugs. Arrested thirty-six times in the 1960s and 1970s. In the early 1960s, he ran the Harvard Psilocybin Project, at first experimenting with the mushroom extract, then moving on to LSD. Harvard fired him and his colleague Richard Alpert in 1963. His drug disciples included Allen Ginsberg, Jack Kerouac, and Charles Olson. In 1963, as his work became more and more suspect in ordinary research circles, three heirs of the Mellon fortune gave him access to a sixty-four-room mansion in Millbrook, New York, where, for five years, he continued his psychedelic sessions. Famous for the slogan "Turn on, tune in, drop out." He gradually morphed from psychological researcher to quasi-religious guru. His extensive legal troubles in the 1960s resulted in long prison sentences, a prison escape, and finally to his turning FBI informant and entering witness protection. He later became an advocate for space travel and life extension.

Leavis, F. R. (Frank Raymond Leavis, 1895–1978): prominent English literary critic. Though he is often associated with New Criticism, he was not actually affiliated with the movement, rejecting their imperative that a text must be viewed as a self-contained formal object. Some of his key works include *New Bearings in English Poetry* (1932), *For Continuity* (1933), *Education and the University* (1943), *The Great Tradition* (1948), and *The Common Pursuit* (1952).

Legman, Gershon (1917–1999): American folklorist and culture critic. He moved to Valbonne, France, in 1953 after the US Post Office went after him for his 1949 book, *Love and Death*, an attack on sexual censorship and comic books. With the exception of a one-year visiting professorship at UC San Diego, 1964–1965, he spent the rest of his life there, publishing prolifically, without any institutional support. He is the person, more than any other, who made research into erotic folklore and erotic verbal behavior academically respectable and who made accessible to other scholars material that scholarly journals had long been afraid to publish. He claimed authorship of the slogan "Make love, not war," and credit for making origami known in the West. Some of his books: *Love and Death: A Study in Censorship* (1949), *The Limerick: 1,700 Examples with Notes, Variants, and Index* (1953), *The Horn Book: Studies in Erotic Folklore and Bibliography* (1954), *The Fake Revolt: The Naked Truth About the Hippy Revolt* (1967), *Rationale of the Dirty Joke: An Analysis of Sexual Humor, First Series* (1968), *No Laughing Matter: Rationale of the Dirty Joke, Second Series* (1975), and *The New Limerick: 2,750 Unpublished Examples, American and British* (1977). Six volumes of his autobiography, *The Peregrine Penis*, were published posthumously under various titles 2016–2018.

Leopardi, Giacomo (1798–1837): Italian philosopher, poet and essayist, the greatest Italian poet of the nineteenth century, and a major figure in literary Romanticism.

Levin, Harry Tuchman (1912–1994): American literary scholar of modernism and comparative literature. Spent his entire academic career at

Harvard: as a student (BA summa cum laude 1933), Junior Fellow in the Society of Fellows (1933–1939), and then faculty member until his retirement in 1983. Some of his books: *James Joyce: A Critical Introduction*, *Toward Stendhal*, *The Overreacher: A Study of Christopher Marlowe* (1952), *Symbolism and Fiction* (1956), *The Power of Blackness: Hawthorne, Poe, Melville* (1958), *The Question of Hamlet* (1959), *The Gates of Horn: A Study of Five French Realists* (1963), and *Playboys and Killjoys: An Essay on the Theory and Practice of Comedy* (1988).

Levitas, Sol (1894–1960): Russian-American editor and journalist. After working as business manager for the American political publication *The New Leader*, he served as the magazine's managing editor from 1936 to 1960, steering it toward a liberal anti-Communist orientation.

Lewis, R. W. B. (Richard Warrington Baldwin Lewis, 1917–2002): American literary critic and scholar. He is notable for being an influential and early contributor to the field of American studies, and is perhaps best known for his *Edith Wharton: A Biography* (1975), for which he was awarded the Pulitzer Prize for Biography or Autobiography, the National Book Critics Circle Award for nonfiction, and a Bancroft Prize. Some of his other books: *The American Adam: Innocence, Tragedy, and Tradition in the Nineteenth Century* (1955), *The Picaresque Saint: Representative Figures in Contemporary Fiction* (1959), *Herman Melville* (1962), *The Poetry of Hart Crane: A Critical Study* (1967), and *The Jameses: A Family Narrative* (1991).

Lombardo, Agostino (1927–2005): Italian literary critic, scholar, and translator who is noted for his studies of American literature, Henry James, and Shakespeare. He founded *StudiAmericani*, the first Italian journal devoted to criticism and analysis of American literature.

Lovestone, Jay (originally Jacob Liebstein, 1897–1990): General Secretary of the Communist Party USA (CPUSA), the leader of an oppositionist Communist movement of the 1930s (the Lovestoneites), AFL-CIO official, and, for many years, CIA informant.

Lowell, Robert "Cal" (1917–1977): influential American confessional poet. *Mayflower* descendant. Pulitzer Prize in poetry 1947 and 1974. Left Harvard after two years and went to study with Allen Tate and John Crowe

Ransom first at Vanderbilt, then at Kenyon College. Long relationships with John Berryman, Randall Jarrell, Elizabeth Bishop, and other major poets. Struggled with bipolar disorder much of his adult life, often resulting in admission to McLean Hospital. Some of his books: *Land of Unlikeliness* (1944), *Lord Weary's Castle* (1945), *The Mills of the Kavanaughs* (1951), *For the Union Dead* (1964), *The Dolphin* (1973), and the posthumous *Collected Prose* (1987) and *Collected Poems* (2003).

Macdonald, Dwight (1906–1982): American writer, editor, critic, and activist best known for his criticism of mass culture and media. He was associated with the New York Intellectuals early in his career, editing for the *Partisan Review* from 1937 to 1943; in 1944, he founded *politics*, a pacifist journal intended to rival the journal of his previous employer. Throughout the 1950s and 1960s, he was a prominent film critic—first for *Esquire*, and later for the *Today* show. Some of his books include *Fascism and the American Scene* (1938), *The Root Is Man: Two Essays in Politics* (1953), and *Against the American Grain: Essays on the Effects of Mass Culture* (1962). UB English faculty in the late 1960s and early 1970s.

MacDonald, John D. (1916–1986): American novelist and short story writer best known for his thrillers and crime novels, which were often set in Florida. He began publishing short stories in 1936, eventually writing novels such as *The Brass Cupcake* (1950), *The Executioners* (1957), and *The Girl, the Gold Watch & Everything* (1962). Beginning in 1964 with *The Deep Blue Good-by*, he published twenty-one novels featuring his character Travis McGee, a "salvage consultant." Several of his works have been adapted for film and television; most notably, *The Executioners*, which was adapted twice (in 1962 and 1991) under the title *Cape Fear*.

Magoon, Francis Peabody (1895–1979): Harvard medievalist and English literature scholar, before which he was a World War I RAF ace (though from a prominent American family, he pretended he was Canadian, claiming his birth records had been lost in a fire). Long interest in folklore: with Alexander Krappe, he did the first scholarly translation of the Grimms' *Kinder und Hausmärchen*. He was Albert Lord's thesis advisor (*The Singer of Tales*) and did a prose translation of the Finnish *Kalevala* (1963).

Mailer, Norman (1923–2007): American writer, filmmaker, essayist, and occasional political activist. First came to prominence with his World

War II novel, *The Naked and the Dead* (1948). Pulitzer prizes for his accounts of the October 1967 anti-war demonstration at the Pentagon, *The Armies of the Night: History as a Novel / The Novel as History* (1968), and the criminal career and execution of Gary Gilmore, *The Executioner's Song* (1979). One of the founders of *The Village Voice* (1955). Some of his other books: *Barbary Shore* (1951), *The Deer Park* (1955), *Advertisements for Myself* (1959), *An American Dream* (1965), *Why Are We in Vietnam?* (1967), *Miami and the Siege of Chicago: An Informal History of the Republican and Democratic Conventions of 1968* (1968), *The Prisoner of Sex* (1971), *Of a Fire on the Moon* (1971), *Marilyn: A Biography* (1973), *Ancient Evenings* (1983), *Harlot's Ghost* (1991), *Oswald's Tale: An American Mystery* (1985), and *The Castle in the Forest* (2007).

Malamud, Bernard (1914–1986): American novelist and short story writer whose work grappled with the social issues of midcentury American and Jewish life. His serious writing career began during his time as a freshman composition instructor at Oregon State University, during which he devoted three days per week to his fiction. His best-known novels include *The Natural* (1952) and the Pulitzer Prize and National Book Award–winning *The Fixer* (1966), both of which were adapted into successful films.

Manheim, Ralph (1907–1992): primarily translated German and French works into English. He is known for his translations of Bertolt Brecht, Louis-Ferdinand Céline, Peter Handke, Martin Heidegger, Hermann Hesse, and Adolf Hitler.

Mansfield, Mike (1903–2001): Democratic congressman for the state of Montana from 1943 to 1953 before serving as a senator from 1953 to 1977 (Senate Majority Leader beginning in 1961). He was uncommonly critical of the Vietnam War for a US politician, and the so-called "Mansfield Mandates" of 1969 and 1973, passed as amendments in Congress, limited military research funding. After retiring from Congress, he served as the US Ambassador to Japan from 1977 to 1988.

Marcus, Steven (1928–2018): American psychoanalytic literary critic known for his work on Dickens and Victorian pornography. Did his graduate work and spent most of his academic career at Columbia. Some of his books: *Dickens: From Pickwick to Dombey* (1961), *The Other Victorians: A Study of Sexuality and Pornography in Mid-Nineteenth Century England*

(1966), *Engels, Manchester and the Working Class* (1974), *Freud and the Culture of Psychoanalysis* (1984).

Matthiessen, F. O. (Francis Otto Matthiessen, 1902–1950): American scholar, critic, and educator. As a scholar, he published work on American writers such as Ralph Waldo Emerson, William James, Henry James, Sinclair Lewis, Herman Melville, Henry David Thoreau, Walt Whitman, and Nathaniel Hawthorne. He was also known for his advocacy for labor and left-wing politics, having worked as president of the Harvard Teachers Union. Some of his books include *The Achievement of T. S. Eliot: An Essay on the Nature of Poetry* (1935), *American Renaissance: Art and Expression in the Age of Emerson and Whitman* (1941), *Henry James: The Major Phase* (1944), and *From the Heart of Europe* (1948).

May, Karl (1842–1912): popular and prolific German author best known for novels and travel stories set in exotic locales: the American Old West, the Orient, the Middle East, and so forth. An estimated two hundred million copies of his books were published. Albert Einstein was a fan. So was Adolf Hitler.

McCarthy, Mary (1912–1989): American novelist, critic, and political activist known for novels such as *The Group* (1963), *The Groves of Academe* (1952), and *The Company She Keeps* (1942), featuring her celebrated short story "The Man in the Brooks Brothers Shirt," which appeared in the *Partisan Review* a year prior. She is also notable for her opposition to the Vietnam War and her highly publicized feud with Lillian Hellman, whom she critiqued for her support of Joseph Stalin.

MacLaine, Shirley (1934–): an American actress and author who began her career as a teenager during the Golden Age of Hollywood. She is best known for films such as *The Trouble with Harry* (1955), *Around the World in 80 Days* (1956), *Some Came Running* (1958), *Ask Any Girl* (1959), *The Apartment* (1960), *The Children's Hour* (1961), *Irma la Douce* (1963), *Sweet Charity* (1969), *Terms of Endearment* (1983), *The Turning Point* (1977), *Being There* (1979), *Madame Sousatzka* (1988), *Steel Magnolias* (1989), and *Postcards from the Edge* (1990).

McGuane, Tom (1939–): American writer of novels, short fiction, and screenplays. Some of his novels are *The Sporting Club* (1969), *Ninety-Two in the Shade* (1973), *The Missouri Breaks* (1976—screenplay and paperback), *Panama* (1978), *Nobody's Angel* (1981), *Nothing but Blue Skies* (1992), and *Driving on the Rim* (2010). His screenplays are *Rancho Deluxe* (1975), *92 in the Shade* (1975), *The Missouri Breaks* (1976; also paperback novel), *Tom Horn* (1981), and *Cold Feet* (1981).

Meredith, Burgess (1907–1997): American actor and director. In the Golden Age of Hollywood, he appeared in films such as *Winterset* (1936), *Of Mice and Men* (1939), and *The Story of G.I. Joe* (1945). Later on, he continued to act in popular television shows in addition to films such as *The Day of the Locust* (1975), *Rocky* (1976), *Foul Play* (1978), and *Clash of the Titans* (1981). He also found success in the theater as both a performer and director, sharing a Special Tony Award with James Thurber for *A Thurber Carnival* (1960).

Merriam, H. G. (Harold Guy Merriam, 1883–1980): American professor of literature. From 1919 to 1964, he taught at the University of Montana; there, he founded and edited a literary magazine of student works (*Frontier*, eventually to become *Frontier to Midland*), introduced creative writing to the English curriculum, initiated a series of writing conferences, served as chair of the English Department and the Division of the New Humanities, and was pivotal in the development of the Montana Institute of the Arts, for which he served as its first president and edited the *Montana Institute of the Arts Quarterly*. He is credited for championing the works of American writers in a time when US-based literary studies still predominantly focused on British literature.

Meyer, Russ (1922–2004): American filmmaker known for his campy exploitation films, often casting large-breasted women—his signature—and featuring titles such as *Faster, Pussycat! Kill! Kill!* (1965), *Vixen!* (1968), *Supervixens* (1975), *Beneath the Valley of the Ultra-Vixens* (1979), and *Beyond the Valley of the Dolls* (1970). Though he briefly worked with 20th Century Fox, his output was largely independent; he wrote, directed, distributed, and even financed most of his films.

Milius, John (1944–): an American screenwriter and director who wrote for films such as *Evel Knievel* (1971), *Dirty Harry* (1971), *Jeremiah Johnson* (1972), *Jaws* (1975), *Indiana Jones and the Temple of Doom* (1984), *The Hunt for Red October* (1990), *Saving Private Ryan* (1998), and *Behind*

Enemy Lines (2001). He also wrote nearly every film that he directed, including *Dillinger* (1973), *The Wind and the Lion* (1975), *Big Wednesday* (1978), *Conan the Barbarian* (1982), *Red Dawn* (1984), and *Farewell to the King* (1989).

Miller, Arthur (1915–2005): American playwright and screenwriter whose notable early plays include *All My Sons* (1948), *Death of a Salesman* (1949), *The Crucible* (1953), and *A View from the Bridge* (1955). After he testified before the House Un-American Activities Committee but refused to name names, he was found guilty of contempt of Congress in 1957; the charge was overruled the following year. From 1951 to 1961, he was married to Marilyn Monroe, who appeared in Miller-penned films such as *Let's Make Love* (1960) and John Huston's *The Misfits* (1961). He remained prolific in the following decades, authoring over thirty stage plays in his career.

Millett, Kate (1934–2017): American feminist, educator, writer, artist, and activist. Some of her books: *Sexual Politics* (1970), *Going to Iran* (1982), *The Politics of Cruelty: An Essay on the Literature of Political Imprisonment* (1994).

Mishima, Yukio (1925–1970): Japanese novelist, playwright, and poet whose far-right political beliefs would famously lead him to attempt a coup d'état and to commit suicide by *seppuku*. Some of his works include the novels *Confessions of a Mask* (1949), *The Temple of the Golden Pavilion* (1959), and *The Sea of Fertility* tetralogy (1969–1971).

Mitchell, Margaret (1900–1949): American writer whose only novel, *Gone with the Wind* (1936), won both the National Book Award for Fiction and the Pulitzer Prize for Fiction. From 1922 to 1926, she was a journalist for *The Atlanta Journal*.

Moravia, Alberto (1907–1990): Italian novelist and journalist whose fiction is noted for its minimalist and stark style as well as its exploration of bourgeois ennui, sexuality, and existential themes. Several of his works have been adapted into well-known films, including Bernardo Bertolucci's *The Conformist* (1970, based on Moravia's 1947 novel of the same name) and Jean-Luc Godard's *Contempt* (1963, based on Moravia's 1954 novel *A Ghost at Noon* or *Contempt*). He famously remarked that the two most important facts of his life were Fascism and his childhood tubercular infection.

Moynahan, Julian Lane (1925–2014): American academic, literary critic, book reviewer, novelist, and poet. He was particularly prolific in the 1960s and 1970s, predominantly writing on the works of D. H. Lawrence and Vladimir Nabokov.

Nathan, John (1940–): American writer, filmmaker, translator, and Japanologist who is perhaps best known for his English translations of Japanese writers such as Yukio Mishima, Kenzaburō Ōe, and Kōbō Abe. He has published a number of books on Japanese culture, including 1974's *Mishima: A Biography*, 1999's *Sony: The Private Life*, and 2004's *Japan Unbound: A Volatile Nation's Quest for Pride and Purpose*. He won an Emmy in 1982 for his documentary film on Japanese KFC, *The Colonel Comes to Japan*.

Novalis (Georg Friedrich Philipp von Hardenberg, 1772–1801): German aristocrat, Romantic poet, novelist, philosopher, and mystic. Friend of Friedrich Schiller and Friedrich Schlegel. Known for his notion of "magical idealism," an attempt to integrate the natural and imaginative worlds. Influenced Richard Wagner, Walter Pater, Martin Heidegger, Hermann Hesse, Jorge Luis Borges, and André Breton and the Surrealists.

Nye, Lee (1926–1999): American photographer. His best-known photographs, collectively known as the Eddie's Club Collection, document the working-class patrons of the Missoula bar he worked at in the late 1960s and early 1970s.

O'Connor, Carroll (1924–2001): American actor. He is best known for his role as Archie Bunker on the sitcoms *All in the Family* (1971–1979) and *Archie Bunker's Place* (1979–1983). He also appeared in the program *In the Heat of the Night* (1988–1995).

Odets, Clifford (1906–1963): American playwright, screenwriter, director, and actor whose successful Broadway dramas were highly influential from the 1930s onward, becoming important touchstones for playwrights such as Arthur Miller and David Mamet. Starting in 1936 and continuing throughout the 1940s, he focused on film, writing screenplays for films such as *The General Died at Dawn* (1936), *None but the Lonely Heart* (1944; also directed), *Sweet Smell of Success* (1957), and *The Story on Page One* (1959; also directed). Some of his other plays are *Till the Day I Die*

(1935), *Golden Boy* (1937), *Clash by Night* (1941), *The Big Knife* (1949), and *The Country Girl* (1950).

Oz, Amos (1939–2018): Israeli writer, veteran of the 1967 and 1973 wars, and peace advocate. Author of fourteen novels, two children's books, five short story collections, and twelve collections of essays. One of the first Israelis to advocate a two-state solution. An opponent of the Settlement movement. In 2013, he told *The New York Times*, "The Israeli-Palestinian conflict is a clash of right and right. Tragedies are resolved in one of two ways: The Shakespearean way or the Anton Chekhov way. In a tragedy by Shakespeare, the stage at the end is littered with dead bodies. In a tragedy by Chekhov, everyone is unhappy, bitter, disillusioned and melancholy, but they are alive. My colleagues in the peace movement and I are working for a Chekhovian, not a Shakespearean conclusion."

Paine, Thomas (1737–1809): born in England and moved to North America in 1774. His pamphlets *Common Sense* (1776) and *The American Crisis* (1776–1783) were influential documents of the American Revolution. He returned to Europe in 1787 and spent much of his time in France, where he again became embroiled in revolution; for his *Rights of Man* (1791), a defense of the French Revolution, he was found guilty of seditious libel in England. In his philosophy, espoused in texts like *The Age of Reason* (1794–1807), Paine promoted Deism and free thought.

Parrington, Vernon Louis (1871–1929): American literary historian and scholar best known for his Pulitzer Prize–winning history of American letters, *Main Currents in American Thought*, which is widely considered to be a founding text of American studies. His reputation suffered a steep decline in the 1950s, coinciding with the rise of New Criticism.

Pavese, Cesare (1908–1950): one of the most influential Italian writers of the twentieth century, best known for his work as a novelist, poet, critic, and translator. An anti-Fascist and eventual Communist, he was sent to prison in 1935 for political dissent when he was discovered with the letters of another political prisoner. His fiction often examines the complex political, social, and ideological commitments of its characters.

Praz, Mario (1896–1982): Italian art and literature critic. Known for his writings on English literature and on interior design and decoration. Some of his books: *The Romantic Agony* (1933), first published in Italian as *La carne, la morte, e il diavolo nella letteratura romantica*, 1930; *Studies in Seventeenth-Century Imagery* (1939); *The Hero in Eclipse in Victorian Fiction* (1956); and *An Illustrated History of Interior Decoration from Pompeii to Art Nouveau* (1964).

Rachele, Donna (Rachele Guidi, 1890–1979): second wife of Italian dictator Benito Mussolini.

Rankin, Jeanette (1880–1973): suffragist and civil rights advocate, born near Missoula nine years before Montana became a state. She was the first woman elected to federal office in the US. She was elected to the House in 1916 and again in 1940. She was one of fifty members of the House to vote against the US declaration of war against Germany in 1917 and the only member of the House to vote against the declaration of war on Japan in 1941. In Congress, she introduced what eventually became the Nineteenth Amendment to the US Constitution, which gave women the right to vote. A founder of the ACLU.

Ransom, John Crowe (1888–1974): an American literary critic, poet, and educator best known as an important early figure of New Criticism. Though not particularly prolific as a poet, he was the recipient of both the Bollingen Prize for Poetry (1951) and the National Book Award (1964) for the previous year's *Selected Poems*. He worked at Kenyon College from 1937 to 1959 and was the founding editor of the *Kenyon Review.*

Richards, I. A. (1893–1979): English literary critic, poet, and editor who is best known as an early and important contributor to New Criticism. Initially trained in philosophy, he believed that literary criticism should only be pursued in conjunction with a cognate field. He is notable for his multiple collaborations with linguist, philosopher, and writer Charles Kay Ogden, such as 1922's *The Meaning of Meaning: A Study of the Influence of Language upon Thought and of the Science of Symbolism*, which was influential to the fields of semiotics and structuralism.

Rickover, Hyman (1900–1986): US admiral who first directed development of nuclear naval propulsion. On active duty for sixty-three years, making him the longest-serving naval officer and longest-serving member of US Armed Forces. Known as "the father of the Nuclear Navy."

Ritz, David (1943–): American writer, novelist, and music critic. He is best known for coauthoring the autobiographies of several musicians, including Ray Charles, Marvin Gaye, Etta James, Janet Jackson, and R. Kelly. He has also contributed the liner notes to over a hundred albums, including the Aretha Franklin box set *Queen of Soul: The Atlantic Recordings*, for which he won a Grammy for Best Album Notes.

Rizzardi, Alfredo (1927–2004): Italian writer, poet, professor of English and North American Literature at Universities of Bologna and Urbino. Translator of poetry by American and Canadian writers, among them Ezra Pound, William Carlos Williams, Herman Melville, and Joe Rosenblatt.

Rosenberg, Julius (1918–1953), and Ethel Rosenberg (1915–1953): American married couple who were executed in 1953, two years after being convicted of spying for the Soviet Union. Numerous intellectuals, artists, and leaders—including Jean-Pale Sartre, Albert Einstein, Bertolt Brecht, Pablo Picasso, and Pope Pius XII—openly protested and advocated against the executions.

Rosenfeld, Isaac (1918–1956): American writer widely associated with the New York intellectual circles. After dropping out of New York University following a year in their philosophy program, he made a name for himself through his short stories and book reviews in publications such as the *Partisan Review* and *The New Republic*, as well as his sole novel, *Passage from Home* (1946). Scholar and critic Mark Shechner has noted that Rosenfeld's work "helped fashion a uniquely American voice by marrying the incisiveness of Mark Twain to the Russian melancholy of Dostoevsky."

Roth, Philip (1933–2018): American novelist and short story writer known for his experimental and metafictional novels, which were often narrated by his literary alter ego, Nathan Zuckerman. A good portion of his work is based on growing up Jewish in Newark. Among other honors, he received the National Book Award for Fiction for *Goodbye, Columbus* (1959); two National Book Critics Circle Awards for *The Counterlife* (1986) and *Sabbath's Theater* (1995); three PEN/Faulkner Awards for *Operation Shylock* (1993), *The Human Stain* (2000), and *Everyman* (2006); and a Pulitzer Prize for *American Pastoral* (1997). Some of his other novels include *Portnoy's Complaint* (1969), *Our Gang* (1971), *The Breast* (1972), *The Dying*

Animal (2001), *The Plot Against America* (2004), *Exit Ghost* (2007), *The Humbling* (2009), and *Nemesis* (2010).

Rubin, Jerry (1938–1994): American anti-war activist best known as one of the cofounders of the Youth International Party (the Yippies), his participation in the demonstrations at the 1968 Democratic Convention in Chicago, and his being a defendant in the Chicago Seven cases resulting from those demonstrations. He appeared before the House Un-American Activities Committee in Viet Cong pajamas, wearing war paint and carrying a toy M-16 rifle. With Abbie Hoffman and others he disrupted the New York Stock Exchange by tossing money—most of it play money—from the balcony to the Exchange floor. Introduced a pig named Pigasus as the Yippies' candidate for president and demanded Secret Service protection for it. Helped organize the October 1967 March on the pentagon. Along with Abbie Hoffman, showed up for one day of the Chicago Seven trial wearing judges' robes, under which they were wearing Chicago police shirts. Author of *DO IT! Scenarios of the Revolution* (1970), *Growing (Up) at Thirty-Seven* (1976).

Sacco and Vanzetti (Nicola Sacco, 1891–1927; Bartolomeo Vanzetti, 1888–1927): Italian-American immigrants and anarchists who were sentenced to death for the 1920 murder of Alessandro Berardelli and Frederick Parmenter. Though the case prompted international controversy—with many calling for their release—they were executed in 1927.

Said, Edward (1935–2003): Palestinian-American critic, theorist, scholar, and political activist. He was a foundational early contributor to postcolonial studies and, in his work and life, an ardent advocate for Palestinian self-determination. Some of his most important works include *Orientalism* (1978), *The Question of Palestine* (1979), *Covering Islam: How the Media and the Experts Determine How We See the Rest of the World* (1981), *The World, the Text, and the Critic* (1983), *Nationalism, Colonialism, and Literature: Yeats and Decolonization* (1988), *Culture and Imperialism* (1993), *The Politics of Dispossession* (1994), and *The End of the Peace Process* (2000). He taught at Columbia University from 1963 to 2003.

Scholem, Gershom (1897–1982): influential Israeli philosopher and historian, most significant leader in modern academic study of the Kabbala, first professor of Jewish mysticism at Hebrew University of Jerusalem. Close to Walter Benjamin, Martin Buber, and Leo Strauss. Some books in English: *Major Trends in Jewish Mysticism* (1941), *On the Kabbalah and Its Symbolism* (1965), *Kabbalah* (1974), *Walter Benjamin: The Story of a Friendship* (1981), and *On the Possibility of Jewish Mysticism in Our Time* (1994).

School of Letters: a summer institute focusing on literary criticism that began at Kenyon College and moved to Indiana University in 1951. The original senior fellows were John Crowe Ransom, Lionel Trilling, Philip Rahv, Austin Warren, and Allen Tate. For most of its time in Bloomington, the School was directed by Newton Stallknecht. The visiting academics, poets, and critics who taught in the School included Northrop Frye, William Empson, John Berryman, Leslie Fiedler, and R. P. Blackmur. Its students included James M. Cox, Geoffrey H. Hartman, and Bruce Jackson. The School was dissolved in 1972.

Schüfftan, Eugen (1893–1977): German cinematographer known for inventing the "Schüfftan process," a filming technique that used mirrors to insert actors into miniature sets. The technique was widely used until it was displaced in the mid-twentieth century by traveling matte and bluescreen techniques. He won the 1962 Best Cinematography, Black and White, Oscar for *The Hustler*. Some of his other films were *Metropolis* (1927), *L'Atlantide* (1932), *Children of the Fog* (1935), *Eyes Without a Face* (1958), *Something Wild* (1961), and *Lilith* (1964).

Sciascia, Leonardo (1921–1989): Italian novelist, essayist, playwright, and politician. He is best known for his novels, many of which explore the complex links between power, sociality, the Mafia, and political life in twentieth-century Sicily. Several of his novels have been adapted by Italian filmmakers, including *Equal Danger*, which was the basis for Francesco Rosi's 1976 film *Cadaveri Eccellenti / Illustrious Corpses*.

Service, Robert W. (1874–1958): British-born Canadian poet sometimes called "The Poet of the Yukon" and "The Canadian Kipling." Best known for two Yukon Gold Rush poems: "The Shooting of Dan McGrew" and "The Cremation of Sam McGee." He moved to Paris in 1913. After ambulance service in the war, he wrote more poems and began writing thriller novels. He fled the Nazis (who wanted to arrest him because he'd written a satirical poem about Hitler), spent the war years in California, then the rest of his life back in France. Much of the literary establishment scorned him, in part because he was the most commercially successful poet of the century. Some of his books of poetry: *Songs of a Sourdough* (1907), *Rhymes of a Rolling Stone* (1912), *Rhymes of a Red-Cross Man* (1916), *Ballads of a Bohemian* (1921), *Rhymes of a Roughneck: A Book of Verse* (1950), *Lyrics of a Lowbrow: A Book of Verse* (1951), and *Carols of an Old Codger* (1955).

Shactman, Max (1904–1972): Polish-American Marxist theorist who, throughout the 1930s, was closely associated with Trotskyism. After helping to found the Communist League of America, which would later merge with the American Workers Party to become the US Workers Party, he founded *The New International*, editing the journal from 1934 to 1941. His criticism of the Soviet Union and insistence that Stalinism marked the emergence of a new "bureaucratic collectivist" ruling class has defined a school of thought now known as Shachtmanism.

Shipley, Joseph "Bud" (1893–1988): father of Leslie's first wife, Margaret. American literary critic, author, and editor. In 1918, he became the theater critic for the Socialist daily newspaper *The Call*, which later became *The New Leader*; Shipley would remain with the paper until 1962. He wrote and edited a total of twenty books, including the first major volume devoted to the work of Eugene O'Neill.

Simon, John (1925–2019): Serbian-American author and literary, theater, and film critic. He moved to the United States in 1941 before serving in the US Air Force, earning a PhD in comparative literature at Harvard, and eventually launching a career as a theater critic for *New York Magazine*, where he would remain for thirty-six years. He is controversial for his scathing and mordant style, which often critiqued the physical appearance of actors.

Sinclair, John (1941–2024): American poet, writer, and political activist best known for his jazz-influenced performance poetry and his stint as manager for Detroit proto-punk rockers MC5. In 1969, he was sentenced to ten years in prison on marijuana-related charges; this led to a number of high-profile protests and demonstrations of solidarity, including the star-studded "John Sinclair Freedom Rally" of 1971 (featuring John

Lennon, Yoko Ono, Stevie Wonder, Phil Ochs, Archie Shepp, Allen Ginsberg, Bobby Seale, and others) and the 1972 release of John Lennon's song "John Sinclair."

Sinclair, Upton (1878–1968): American writer, muckraker journalist, and political activist. Unsuccessful candidate for governor in California in 1934. Author of almost one hundred books of fiction and nonfiction. Some of his novels are: *Courtmartialed* (1898), *The Jungle* (1906—which led to the Pure Food and Drug Act), *The Metropolis* (1908), *King Coal* (1917), *Oil!* (1927—filmed as *There Will Be Blood*, 2007), *Little Steel* (1938), *Dragon's Teeth* (1942, Pulitzer Prize), *A World to Win* (1946), *The Return of Lanny Budd* (1953), and *The Coal War* (1976).

Singer, I. B. (Isaac Bashevis Singer, 1903–1991): Polish-born Jewish-American writer of novels, plays, and essays who often published in Yiddish before translating his own work into English. He won the Nobel Prize for Literature in 1978—the same year that the English translation of his novel *Shosha* was published—as well as two US National Book Awards, for *A Day of Pleasure: Stories of a Boy Growing Up in Warsaw* (1970; Children's Literature) and *A Crown of Feathers and Other Stories* (1974, Fiction).

Smith, Al (1873–1944): governor of New York 1919–1920 and 1923–1928. Democratic Party candidate in 1928 presidential election, which he lost in a landslide. Smith was the first Roman Catholic to be the nominee of either major party in a US presidential election. After failing to get the Democratic nomination again in 1932, he became a strong opponent of FDR's New Deal.

Snow, C. P. (1905–1980): English novelist, physical chemist, and politician. After earning his PhD in physics from Christ's College, he served several positions in the British Civil Service. He is perhaps best remembered for his 1959 lecture-turned-book *The Two Cultures and the Scientific Revolution*, in which he argues that the widening gulf between the humanities and modern science impedes communication and productive change. Eleven of his seventeen novels make up the *Strangers and Brothers* series, which follows the life of narrator-protagonist Lewis Eliot.

Spender, Stephen (1909–1995): English poet, novelist, essayist, and translator. Early in his career, he was associated with both the Auden Group and the Bloomsbury Group. His works tended to focus on social protest and class struggle, though he would abandon left-wing politics by the late 1940s. He coedited *Encounter* magazine from 1953 to 1966, resigning after the CIA was revealed to be the publication's funding source.

Spilka, Mark (1925–2001): literary critic and professor of English literature. He published studies of D. H. Lawrence, Ernest Hemingway, and Charles Dickens. He taught at Brown University, the University of Michigan, the University of Tulsa, Indiana University, and Jerusalem's Hebrew University.

Stallknecht, Newton "Stalky" (1906–1981): American philosopher and professor of comparative literature at Indiana University, where he was also longtime director of the School of Letters.

Stein, Gertrude (1874–1946): American poet, writer, and art collector. Strongly influenced by the historic avant-garde and influential to subsequent generations of experimental writing. Much of her writing is characterized by its innovative form, repetition, fragmentation, and attention to sound. She spent over thirty years in Paris, from 1903 to 1934, where she hosted a now-legendary salon frequented by artists and writers such as Ernest Hemingway, Ezra Pound, F. Scott Fitzgerald, Pablo Picasso, Henri Matisse, and more. Some of her works include *Three Lives* (1909), *Tender Buttons* (1914), *The Making of Americans* (1925), *The Autobiography of Alice B. Toklas* (1933), and *Stanzas in Meditation* (1956).

Stein, Sol (1926–2019): American novelist, playwright, publisher, and editor best known for his time as editor in chief at Stein & Day publishers, which he founded with his then-wife, Patricia Day, in 1962. In the early 1950s, he worked as a scriptwriter for the Voice of America, which translated his scripts into forty-six languages before broadcasting them around the world. Stein & Day closed its doors in 1989—the same year Sol Stein and Patricia Day worked with their youngest son, David Day Stein, to develop WritePro, a software program that teaches its users how to write fiction.

Steinbeck, John (1902–1968): American writer and novelist. Mostly set in the American West Coast, his fiction often reflected his ongoing engagement with leftist politics. His 1939 novel *The Grapes of Wrath* won the Pulitzer Prize for Literature; in 1962, he won the Nobel Prize for

Literature. Some of his other major works include *Tortilla Flat* (1935), *The Red Pony* (1933), *Of Mice and Men* (1937), *Cannery Row* (1945), and *East of Eden* (1952).

Steiner, George (1929–2020): Franco-American literary critic, much of it exploring the relationships between language, literature, and society. He is perhaps best known for 1975's *After Babel: Aspects of Language and Translation*. He was a professor of English and comparative literature at the University of Geneva for twenty years, teaching in four languages.

Stone, I. F. (1907–1989): American investigative journalist who is remembered for his progressive politics and his newsletter, *I. F. Stone's Weekly* (1953–1971), in addition to his earlier work for publications such as *The Nation* and *The New York Post*. Since his death, he has been accused of Soviet espionage. Some of his books: *Underground to Palestine* (1946), *This Is Israel* (1948), *The Killings at Kent State* (1971), *The Trial of Socrates* (1988), and *A Nonconformist History of Our Times* (1989).

Tolkien, J. R. R. (1892–1973): Oxford-educated English philologist and fiction writer best known for *The Hobbit* (1937) and *The Lord of the Rings* (three volumes, 1954–1955). In the Battle of the Somme in 1916 he contracted trench fever from lice; he also survived several bombings and a gas attack. While teaching at Leeds in the early 1920s, he did translations of *Sir Gawain and the Green Knight*, *Pearl*, and *Orfeo* (these would not be published until 1975). Returned to Oxford in 1925 and remained there until his retirement in 1959.

Trilling, Lionel (1905–1975): writer and educator who was known as one of the leading American literary critics of his time. Long associated with the *Partisan Review*. His work investigated the links between literature, culture, and history. For thirty years, he cotaught Columbia's Colloquium on Important Books. Many of his students—such as Sol Stein, David Lehman, Cynthia Ozick, and Beatniks Jack Kerouac, Allen Ginsberg, and Lucien Carr—went on to become prominent novelists, poets, and scholars.

Trotsky, Leon (1870–1940): Russian Revolutionary, Soviet politician, and political theorist. A key figure in the 1905 and October 1917 Russian Revolutions, he helped form the Soviet Union before being forced into exile, and eventually murdered, by Joseph Stalin's regime. Sharply critical of Stalinism, his Marxist and Leninist-influenced ideas, known as Trotsky-ism, called for an international and permanent Socialist revolution.

Tumin, Melvin (1919–1994): American sociologist best known for his work on race relations and desegregation, some of which was published by the Anti-Defamation League in 1957. Much of his work challenged the inevitability of social stratification implied by the Davis-Moore hypothesis. In 1967, he published *Social Stratification: The Forms and Functions of Inequality*. He taught at Princeton University from 1947 until his retirement in 1989.

Utamaro, Kitagawa (1753–1806): Japanese artist renowned for his ukiyo-e woodblock prints and portraits. By the mid-nineteenth century, his work reached Europe, where it influenced subsequent Impressionist painting.

Viertel, Peter (1920–2007): German-born novelist and screenwriter who spent much of his life in the United States. By the time he was hired by the US Office of Strategic Services, a CIA predecessor, he had already published an acclaimed novel, 1940's *The Canyon*, and penned screen-plays and scripts for Hollywood, including one that would become Alfred Hitchcock's *Saboteur* (1942). He was perhaps best known for his novel *White Hunter, Black Heart* (1953), a fictionalized account of his experiences working with John Huston on *The African Queen* (1951); in 1990, the book was adapted into a film by Clint Eastwood.

Vittorini, Elio (1908–1966): Italian writer and editor who was an important figure in Italian modernism. His anti-Fascist sentiments and leftist politics significantly delayed the publication of much of his work and resulted in his arrest and incarceration in the early 1940s. He is best known for his novel *Conversations in Sicily* (1941). After the war, he primarily worked as an editor, publishing works by young Italians such as Italo Calvino.

Vonnegut, Kurt (1922–2007): American novelist and humorist. Some of his books: *Cat's Cradle* (1963), *Slaughterhouse-Five* (1969), *Breakfast of Champions* (1973), *Galápagos* (1985), and *Timequake* (1997). During World War II, he was captured by the Germans in the Battle of the Bulge and imprisoned in Dresden, where he experienced and survived the Allied firebombing of the city; this experience would influence the confluence of empathetic humanism and bitter cynicism that would grow to characterize his subsequent writing.

Watanabe, Hamako (1910–1999): popular singer and actress during Japan's Shōwa period. She began her career in entertainment after working as a music instructor, releasing a number of hit songs by the mid-1930s. During the Second Sino-Japanese War, she was sent to Japanese-occupied China to raise morale among the troops. Many of her songs from this era stressed patriotic sentiments. She was held as a prisoner of war for over a year following the surrender of Japan, but her career resumed following her repatriation.

West, Nathanael (1903–1940): American novelist and screenwriter best known for his two satirical novels: *Miss Lonelyhearts* (1933) and *The Day of the Locust* (1939). He made little money from his novels. He supported himself the last few years of his life writing in Hollywood for such B movies as *Five Came Back* (1939), *Stranger on the Third Floor* (1940), and *The Spirit of Culver* (1940).

White, Stanford (1853–1906): American architect known for his commercial and residential projects in New York City and throughout the US Northeast. His architectural work is overshadowed in popular memory by his 1906 murder at the hands of Harry Kendall Thaw, a wealthy railroad tycoon, which resulted in what was dubbed the "Trial of the Century" by journalists. Thaw publicly murdered White at the Madison Square Theater, alleging that White had previously drugged and raped his wife, Evelyn Nesbit Thaw. The murder and trial were the basis of Richard Fleischer's film *The Girl in the Red Velvet Swing* (1955).

Wilbur, Richard (1921–2017): American poet and translator of French literature known for his restrained and formalist verse that continued the tradition of Robert Frost and W. H. Auden. He received the Pulitzer Prize for Poetry twice, in 1957 and 1989, and was named US Poet Laureate in 1987.

Williams, Charles (1886–1945): prolific English novelist, poet, playwright, theologian, and literary critic. Some of his novels are *War in Heaven* (1930), *Descent into Hell* (1937), and *All Hallows' Eve* (1945). W. H. Auden is said to have reread his unconventional history of the church, *The Descent of the Dove* (1939), every year.

Wilson, Edmund, Jr. (1895–1972): American literary critic and journalist whose highly regarded work fostered widespread appreciation for many writers now considered part of the modernist canon, such as Ernest Hemingway, William Faulkner, and F. Scott Fitzgerald. His enthusiasm for the French Bibliothèque de la Pléiade imprint is largely responsible for the Library of America book series, which first appeared ten years after his death.

Winchell, Mark Royden (1948–2008): American writer and professor of literature at Clemson University. He is best known for his literary biographies, including volumes dedicated to Joan Didion (1980), William F. Buckley Jr. (1984), and Leslie Fielder (1985). Journalist and author Joe Scotchie described him as "a traditionalist in literature and an Old Right conservative in politics."

Wirtz, William Willard (1912–2010): US administrator, attorney, and professor of law best known for his time as the US Secretary of Labor under the Kennedy and Johnson administrations from 1962 to 1969.

Wolfson, Harry (1887–1974): American scholar who taught at Harvard University from 1915—the same year he graduated from the institution with his PhD—until his retirement in 1958. As a philosopher and historian, Wolfson focused on Judaic studies.

Worth, Irene (1916–2002): American actress of stage and screen who found success in both American and British theater. During her career, in which she acted with the Old Vic and the Royal Shakespeare Company, she won three Tony Awards, for *Tiny Alice* (1965), *Sweet Bird of Youth* (1976), and *Lost in Yonkers* (1991). Some films she has acted in include *Nicholas and Alexandra* (1971), *Eyewitness* (1981), and *Deathtrap* (1982).

Wright, Richard (1908–1960): Influential American writer who wrote of growing up Black in Mississippi and his life in Chicago and New York. Best known for *Uncle Tom's Children* (a collection of short fiction, 1938), *Native Son* (a novel, 1940), and *Black Boy* (a memoir, 1945). Wrote the text for FSA photographs selected by Edwin Rosskam, *12 Million Black Voices: A Folk History of the Negro in the United States* (1941). The posthumously published *American Hunger* (1977) focuses on his participation with the John Reed Clubs and the Communist Party. After his move to France in 1946 (where he became friends with Jean-Paul Sartre, Albert

Camus, and Simone de Beauvoir), he published an existentialist novel, *The Outsider* (1956). Since his death, a good deal more of his fiction and nonfiction has been published.

Index